ENCYCLOPAEDIA OF INDIAN WOMEN THROUGH THE AGES

ENCYCLOPAEDIA OF INDIAN WOMEN THROUGH THE AGES

Volume—4
Modern India

Simmi Jain

KALPAZ PUBLICATIONS
DELHI–110 052

ENCYCLOPAEDIA OF INDIAN WOMEN THROUGH THE AGES
(Sociology, Women Studies)

Rs. 3600 (Set)
Rs. 900 (each volume)

ISBN: 81-7835-116-1 (Set)
ISBN: 81-7835-175-7 (Vol. 4)

Published in 2011 in India by
Kalpaz Publications
C-30, Satyawati Nagar,
Delhi-110052
E-mail: kalpaz@hotmail.com
Phone : 9212729499

Printed at: G. Print Process, Delhi

Contents

Preface

The status of women in our sub-continent passed through a most intricate and complex socio-economic terrain. The male-dominated society was indeed a glaring phenomenon and had always edged over their social and domestic environments. Being the earning member in the family, he considered himself fairly superior in terms of his status. But women could maintain their identity and emerged as useful partners and bread-earner for her household affairs. Undoubtedly she did not shirk to meet any economic challenge with dignity and respectable disposition. The volumes on *Encyclopaedia of Indian Women Through the Ages* have been diversified into four categories and cover the themes in a fairly comprehensive and analytical way which are as follows.

The volume on Ancient India deals with a detailed description on social status of women in the Vedic period and in the Mahabharata Era. Emphasis has been laid on their marital status, numerous duties of household affairs, basic rights enjoyed by them, sexual life in practice, social status of a widow and the way of life she had to lead, ideology of motherhood, divorce and remarriage, property rights, the sati ritual, the views of Swami Vivekananda, and foreign accounts of marital arrangements.

The second volume lays emphasis on Medieval India. It includes social position of women, female slaves, women in politics, religious education and practices, observance of purdah, and divorce, *mehr* practices, nikah-marriage, valid marriage, irregular marriage, the sense of equality, women in administration, dissolution of marriage, dower, social customs like birth ceremony, naming ceremony, selection of marriage partners, women education including higher education, their academic contribution, particularly of Gulbadan Begum, Hamidah Bano Begum, Zeb-un-Nisa, Jahan Ara and others, fairs and festivals, games, mostly indoor games, playing cards or *Tash* or chess, pigeon flying, kite flying, female costumes including cotton, silken and golden clothes and a detailed study of Khanzada Begum, Ayisha-Sultan Begum, Zainab Sultan Begum, Maham Begum and Bibi Mubarika.

The third volume has deep thrust on women and freedom struggle. The role of eminent women has been a glaring phenomenon in this volume. In fact these women have become a significant part of our history. Commencing from the historic role of Begum Hazrat Mahal, Rani Lakshmi Bai of Jhansi, Rani of Ramgarh, the theme lands us comprehensively into various social Acts, viz., mobilisation of sati, 1829; Widow Remarriage Act, 1856; the role of Consent, 1891 and the prohibition of Child Marriage Act, 1929. The volume has also highlighted the role of foreign women in our freedom struggle, i.e., Sister Nivedita, The Mother, Mira Behn, and Annie Besant. Mrs. Besant was elected Congress President in 1917—during the crucial period of the first global war.

The emergence of Mahatma Gandhi on the political stage of India in 1915 generated a new spirit of sacrifice for the attainment of *swaraj.* Such women were Kasturba Gandhi, Bee Amman, Parvati Devi, Sarojini Naidu, Kamaladevi Chattopadhyaya, Durgabai Deshmukh, Margaret Cousins, Sucheta Kripalani, Hansa Mehta, Mridula Sarabhai, Usha Mehta, Rajkumari Amrit Kaur and several others. They courted arrests in the Gandhian movements along with numerous women satyagrahas. Even after the attainment of Independence, their role in several fields of development including education, medical, defence, politics and administration is quite laudable.

The last volume gives us a comprehensive analysis on historical perspective and legal review. It deals with the changing social status of women, Gandhi and his contribution for the emancipation of women in economic and political sphere, Dalit women in politics and their changing socio-economic status with new awakening, vision of Annie Besant for generating patriotic spirit among women, role of the regiment of Rani Jhansi as a significant part of the Indian National Army, women and family welfare having deep bearing on sincere initiatives shown by women rather than men to plan their families despite their law position and lesser sex ratio. Other significant aspects on women in this chapter deal with their pitiable plight as labourers in a factory, field or road work, life of working women, regional status of women, particularly in Punjab, Haryana, Madhya Pradesh, sensible findings of a survey based research on women in a slum in Mumbai. Last but not the least a chapter has been well-written on Kerala nuns and nurses in terms of their working status and social difficulties. A few significant case studies on the two categories have been well-analysed.

I feel much beholden to several eminent scholars whose writings have been used in these volumes in order to fill up necessary gaps. The consistent academic support and help of several institutions of higher learning including the members of prominent libraries deserve my respectful acknowledgement. But for sincere support from these categories of scholarly and institutional help, these volumes probably would not have seen light of the day.

With this comprehensive academic survey, it could be judged with the remark that these volumes would be certainly welcomed by eminent social scientists, researchers and students in India and abroad.

Simmi Jain

Introduction

It is often said that position of women in any society and community is the true indicator of its cultural evolution. So is true about the society and its culture. There is a lot of discussion on women's question in India. But, in the absence of systematic studies, this discussion often leads to opposite conclusions, and, indeed, it often starts from reverse assumptions about the position of women in society. Some argue that women enjoy a very high status in India and point to the number of distinguished women in high public office. Others maintain the view that the lot of Indian women is very hard, and a representation was made not very long ago to the Backward Classes Commission that women, as a whole, should be regarded as a Backward Class in this country.

Academicians and scholars have differences of opinion about the changes taking place in the position of women in India. Some regard these changes as profound and pervasive; they point to the growing participation of women in public life and to the changes introduced in their legal status. Others maintain that the position of women has changed very little and that Indian society carries on by and large to be a male-dominated society. Though these ambiguities can be resolved in the course of a brief discussion but no proper solution can be found unless we view these questions in their proper sociological perspective.

Before we are able to say anything meaningful about the status of women in a society we must know about the structure of that society. The position of women can change in a significant way only when the structure itself witnesses change.

Let us first of all break Indian society down into its basic structural divisions and examine the place assigned to women in each one of them. The confusion that we find in talks about Indian women often arises from our failure to take sufficiently into account the internal differentiation present in Indian society. The position of women is not the same among Hindus and

Muslims, in the various regions of the country, and, most particularly, among the different social strata.

Moreover, the sociological perspective requires us to pay attention to the position of women not merely as it is supposed to be in principle, but especially as it actually is in practice. Here again, much confusion is caused by both traditionalists and modernists. The former construct an idealised picture of women in traditional India from selected classical texts and, comparing this with her actual position in present times, find the present less satisfactory than the past.

The latter point to the many freedoms granted in principle, to women since independence and compare these with the restrictions from which they actually suffered in the past. The sociological perspective urges caution against such comparisons, and demands that we compare facts against facts, and ideals with ideals. Above all, our perspective also requires us to avoid hasty evaluative judgements on the position of women in the past or present, or in this or that stratum of society. Those who write on the women's question generally come from a specific stratum of society, and are likely to be guided, consciously or unconsciously, by the moral code of that stratum. We must remember that there is nothing final or absolute about this code. We cannot talk logically about the position of women in a particular section of society unless we view it in relation to its own moral code. Any evaluation we may wish to make will have to be made after and not prior to an examination of the values of the people concerned. Study of any important aspect of Indian social life will have to start with a consideration of regional differences. The regions differ from each other both in their geographical features and in their past development.

Corresponding to these factors there are differences between them in material and non-material culture. To take one example, the systems of kinship and marriage are often different in the Dravidian-speaking areas in South India as compared to the Indo-Aryan-speaking areas in North India. To take another, the role of women in agriculture is generally different in the paddy-producing regions in the east and south from their role in the wheat-producing areas in the north.

We all know that the segregation of women is, closely associated with certain religious beliefs and practices. We can, therefore, expect to find important differences in this regard between the different religious groups. In general, segregation is exercised to a greater extent among Muslims than among Hindus; this seems to be more an aspect of the Islamic cultural tradition than of Islamic religious beliefs.

At the other end, women seem to enjoy more freedom among Christians and Parsis than among Hindus. Early marriage for girls, so common in Indian society, has at least some connection with old Hindu values and norms. Early marriage and early motherhood, apart from having important demographic consequences, also hinder the full participation of women in some important fields of social and cultural life. There are significant differences between the different religious groups in the age at marriage for women, and one would expect corresponding differences in their domestic household roles.

It appears that social legislation has not had a very significant effect in raising the age at marriage, giving us a good example of the divergence between law and rituals, which is so common in all human societies. The division into regional and religious groups does not, of course, exhaust the range of cultural pluralism found in India. In the same region and within the same religious group one might find a variety of social customs. Thus, in Kerala, the Nairs and Nambudiris observed very different customs even when they lived as neighbours and were bound by the closest social ties. The Nairs were matrilineal and matrilocal while the Nambudiris were patrilineal and patrilocal. The rights enjoyed by Nair women were in many ways superior to those of their Nambudiri sisters. It is true that women enjoyed higher freedom among the Nairs than among most communities of comparable status in India, it must not be thought that women have necessarily a dominant position in matrilineal societies.

In fact, in all societies, whether patrilineal or matrilineal, women have, in fact, a lower status than men. In matrilineal societies property is transmitted through women, but this only implies that it generally passes from mother's brother to sister's son. In most such cases the woman, instead of being under the control of her husband, is under the brother's or father's control. Neither matriliny nor polyandry is a guarantee of the supremacy of women.

May be, it is a fact that the conspicuous variations in the position of women are the ones we find between the different strata. Indian society is highly stratified, and the marks of stratification are visible in practically every walk of life. Any analysis of the place of women in Indian society will have to take into account the fact that their role in social life in the upper strata is quite different from their role in the lower castes.

Differences of this kind are to be found in every complex society, but the peculiarly rigid character of social stratification in India makes them more conspicuous in this context. Visible feature of stratification in Indian society is its division into a number of castes which are hierarchically graded. Brahmins, Cultivators, Artisans and Harijans were not only assigned different ranks, but there were many differences in their customs which were sanctioned by traditional rules. Among the most significant of these rules were the ones restricting marriage between members of different castes. In addition to the general rule of endogamy which required individuals to marry within their own caste, there also existed the rule of hypergamy according to which, under certain conditions, men of a higher caste could marry women of a lower caste or subcaste. Underlying these rules was the value attached to the purity of women which was the more jealously protected the higher the caste of the woman.

With the dawn of awakening and constitution back up, several castes and communities have attempted a kind of upward social movement which has been described as Sanskritisation. This is a process by which members of lower castes seek to enhance status in society by adopting the customs of the upper castes. This is often associated with important changes in the position of women, particularly in the middle range of the caste hierarchy. The age at marriage tends to be lowered, widow remarriage is given up, the dowry goes up and women are discouraged from going out to work, all this being done in imitation of the old customs of the upper castes.

In this way, at least in rural areas—where the vast majority of our women live—certain kinds of upward social mobility cause a restriction rather than an enlargement of the freedom of women. The institution of caste is a characteristically Hindu phenomenon. Divisions corresponding to castes are found also among other religious categories such as Muslims and Christians in India. In the case of Muslims, the pattern of life among the high-status Ashraf groups is quite different from the life of women from functional castes such as Julaha or Kalal. It would be misleading to talk about *purdah* among Muslim women in general, without taking these differences into account. Similarly, in a state like Kerala, which has a huge Christian population, there are vast differences in the position of women between the Old and the New Christians.

Besides, there are also important economic differences which divide the people of India. Even where the distinctions of caste are weak, those between rich and poor or between workers and non-workers persist. In traditional Indian society the most important economic differences were very closely associated with distinctions of caste. India is still largely an agrarian society, and if we are to well understand the position of women in it we must examine their place in the different agrarian strata. According to most liberal-minded people, the emancipation of women is closely associated with their right to work. But there is also another side to the picture. In agrarian societies, work is more often considered a hardship than as a privilege. If this applies to men, it applies even more to women. It is not true that women in India have always been confined to their homes. In rural India, a great number of them work in the fields as agricultural labourers, and their work is invariably of the most onerous and arduous kind.

As per census figures, women constitute a large though varying proportion of agicultural labourers in the different parts of the country. In general, their proportion is higher in the paddy-producing regions of East and South India than in the wheat-producing areas of the North. In some of the most fertile rice-growing districts of South India women actually outnumber men among the casual agricultural labourers. There are various reasons for this, but it should be noted that wet paddy cultivation is particularly difficult and unpleasant occupation, and it goes without saying that women are always paid less for their work than men.

Not only in social and economic field exist disparities but situation is more or less similar as far their political empowerment is concerned. Despite constitutional provisions and amendments like 73rd and 74th amendments, there is a certain absence of political will to bring women at par with men.

But this is certain that some more need needs to be added to our efforts, may, be, that is sincerity if we are really willing to emancipate them and enhance their status in society and polity.

1

Changing Status

Position of women in Indian society has witnessed a great change from her previous status in ancient, middle and more specifically in post-independence modern period. Before their involvement in the freedom movement, their role was confined to household activities only. Call of national independence activated them in the process of freedom struggle. After independence, shattered socio-political and economic order needed badly women's contribution in development. So, changing requirement of nation has enjoyed contribution from women accordingly.

But when it comes to raising their status, we can hear objectional comments both from leaders of national and regional level as well as the husbands sitting at home. Despite constitutional arrangements, women have been given a share in politics at grassroot level (through 73rd and 74th Amendment Acts) in 1992, 45 years after the Independence. There are still a number of question marks on their participation in national and state politics through elected positions. Are we really serious about women's emancipation or are just matching our voice with the echoing slogans of 'Women's Empowerment.'

Present chapter, presents before us various aspects of transition in women's status as well as double standards of societal attitude towards their 'true empowerment' in fact a lecture presented by the author at Huxley, titled "The Changing Position of Indian Women". The chapter ends with brief description of women in the freedom struggle.

"Anthropologists have long been interested in the study of the position of women in various parts of the world. Such interest has been both 'indirect' and 'direct'—I am aware that this distinction is not a clear-cut one but I think that it is helpful to make it. The 'indirect' interest came from armchair anthropologists who wanted to trace the evolution of marriage, family, and kinship by studying kinship terms and usages, from different countries, and in particular, from what are now referred to as the 'Third World' countries. As is well known, this began in the latter half of the nineteenth century with the efforts of Morgan, McLennan, Maine and Bachofen.

The 'direct' interest came from individuals whose work as administrators, missionaries or anthropologists, brought them into contact with non-Western peoples, and who wrote accounts of the division of labour existing between the sexes, the rules of inheritance and succession, the nature and composition of the household, etc., among the peoples they studied.

Ever since their discipline became established in the universities, anthropologists have regarded the study of the 'position of women' as one of their basic concerns. R.H. Lowie's *Primitive Society,* published in 1920 - which, incidentally, was the first anthropological book I came in contact with - included a chapter on 'The Position of Women' (186-204) which is still worth reading for its caution, scepticism about accepted ideas, and for certain basic distinctions which Lowie considered essential in order to discuss tangibly so broad and elusive, if not fuzzy, a theme. He made a few generalizations and then cited exceptions to them to show how it is necessary to guard against easy generalization. Finally, he emphasized the difficulty of establishing causality when the events under consideration were numerous, and the relationship between them extremely complex.

When I state that anthropologists have been interested in the study of the position of women, I certainly do not mean that it has been confined to them. For it is well known that psychologists, demographers and several others have shared their interest. However, since the end of the Second World War there has been a rapidly increasing concern both with the role and position of women, and with bringing about greater equality between the sexes. Apart from social scientists, feminists have written copiously, and even passionately, on the subject, and of late there seems to be a welcome shift of interest among them from attacking the theory of the biological determinism of women to trying to understand the processes which have resulted in their widespread subjection. Ester Boserup's *Women's*

Role in Economic Development (1970) is a good example of this kind of effort and the book is a valuable contribution to both social anthropology and economics. But while I find Boserup's book stimulating I must confess to a certain sense of discomfort at her tendency for sweeping generalization as, for instance, in her linking dowry in South Asia to the loss of women's agricultural role.[1] At the micro-level, facts are far more complicated in their inter-relationships than Boserup's work would lead one to imagine.

Anthropologists ought to welcome the new upsurge of interest in the study of women: the knowledge and insights produced by other disciplines might stimulate their work in new directions, and in particular, their techniques of fieldwork, might not only promote fruitful co-operation in the field of women's studies but also lead to increased co-operation between the social sciences in other areas as well. An additional gain may be a sharpened awareness of the existence of an androcentric bias in social science research generally. But I think that is naive to expect ethnocentrism (in studying other societies), class or caste-centredness (in studying one's own society), and androcentrism (in studying both one's own and other societies) to disappear as a result of such awareness. What is likely to happen is a keener appreciation of the fact that the observer has his prejudices and preferences, not to mention values, and this may not only improve the quality of the data collected but make him less dogmatic about his conclusions. It may also lead to a realization of the need to have the same social phenomena studied by men and women from different cultures, and from different class and ethnic backgrounds. A clash of multiple views and perspective is not only healthy for the social sciences but also for policy-making.

The subject of my lecture, 'The Changing status vast, and of bewildering complexity. It has many facets, and generalization is pretty nearly impossible because of the existence of a considerable variation between religions, between rural and urban areas, between classes, and finally between different religious, ethnic and caste groups. While in certain contexts the Indian subcontinent is a single cultural region, in many others it is heuristically more rewarding to look upon it as a congeries of micro-regions, differences between which are crucial. For instance, the huge, sprawling Hindi region in the north is backward, if indices such as female literacy and education, male-female ratio, age of marriage of girls, and female participation in economic activity are taken into consideration. If female literacy alone is taken as an Index, it is 53.90 per cent in Kerala in the south-west, while it does not exceed 11 per cent in Uttar Pradesh, Madhya Pradesh, Rajasthan and Bihar. In the country as a whole, only 18.66 per cent of women are literate as against 39.5 per cent for men, while in the rural areas female literacy is only 12.92 per cent.

Apart from differences in female literacy rates between regions, and between rural and urban areas, some institutions which intimately affect the lives of women are confined to certain groups inhabiting particular areas: for instance, polyandry continues to be practised by the Khasas of Jaunsar Bawar, and hypergamy by the Rajputs north of the Vindhyas, by the Khatris and Jats of the Punjab, and finally, by the Patidars and Anavil Brahmins of Gujarat. Matriliny obtains not only among the high caste Nayars and a few other groups in Kerala but also among the tribal Khasis, Garos and Panars in the north-eastern hill areas.

However, inter-regional and inter-group differences are not the only hazard. In a country such as India with a long and recorded history, the existence of a body of literature, sacred and secular, proves obtrusive especially as sanction for present conduct may be derived, directly or indirectly, by reference to ideals and rules which are believed to be expressed in it. This matter becomes all the more puzzling as most Western-educated people actually derive such ideals, norms and rules from their parents or grandparents, or from a priest who himself may be far from well-informed on what the scriptures say on any given matter. (However, when a matter is regarded as critical, a very learned pandit, or the head of a famed monastery may be approached for his opinion). The important point to note, however, is that ideas and beliefs derived at best, second or third hand, from ancient literature influence ideals of conduct and behaviour. Since it is largely members of the Sanskritized high castes who are more influenced by this literature than the others, and since they are both visible and influential in modern India, their perceptions and ideas about how Indians behave and ought to behave, have obtained wide currency. The high castes suffer from a bibliocentric view of society even though very few of them have first-hand knowledge of the sacred literature.

The corpus of literature is, however, a heterogeneous one, and it abounds in inconsistent if not contrary ideas, rules, beliefs and practices. To cite an example: In the 1920s there was a debate between the orthodox and reformist sections of the Brahmins living in Mysore City. The former were of the view that it was sinful to keep a girl unmarried after she had reached puberty but the liberals did not frown on post-puberty marriages. (A distinction must be made here between marriage and consummation, the latter being marked by a separate ceremony, and arranged on an auspicious day after puberty). Strange as it may seem to educated Indians today, it was an emotionally-charged debate: the liberals cited the authority of the Vedas in favour of their view, as against the orthodox faction's reliance on the law-books (Dharmasastras) which were much later than the Vedas, and inferior to them in religious authority.

It is not only that the sacred literature provided sanction for contrary norms and usages, but very rarely was an inconsistency perceivable even in the conceptualization of so basic a relationship as that between husband and wife, and surprisingly, there was little awareness of the existence of such an inconsistency. I shall discuss this point later.

Lowie stresses the need to distinguish between law and fact, between theory and practice, and finally, between formal and informal relations (1920: 186-9). This set of distinctions is basic to my approach to the understanding of the position of women in different sections of Indian society. Until very recently, too much attention has been paid to the legal, theoretical and formal dimensions of women's position, and too little to actual relations between men and women, and their dynamics over a period of time. But concentration on the formal aspects was inevitable in the absence of intimate, first-hand studies of the part played by men and women in local communities, rural and urban. The need for micro-studies is also reinforced from another direction: the data obtained from different macro-surveys such as the census, and the various rounds of the National Sample Survey, conflict with each other, and further, they do not provide a clue to the complex cultural and social processes which are operative at the village level, and to the linkages which exist between them. For instance, how do urbanization and economic and social mobility affect those processes? How have the various programmes of rural change introduced by the government and by voluntary agencies improved the position of women at different economic and social levels? I propose to try and lay bare in this chapter a few of these processes and their linkages. I am aware that no accounts based on field-study exist of these processes, but if they had existed my task would have been much simpler and less hazardous but perhaps also less challenging.

In my discussion I shall be restricting myself to Hindus. Hindus are both numerous enough-453 million at the 1971 Census, and constituting 82.72 per cent of the total population—and complex enough to be the subject of a single lecture.

Eighty per cent of India's population is rural and an equal percentage of the female working force is engaged in agriculture. According to the 1971 census, there were 31 million women workers of whom 25 million were in agriculture, 2 million in the organized sector, and the remaining 4 million in non-agricultural occupations in the unorganized sector (CSWI 1974: 170). These statistics are for the country as a whole and therefore conceal sharp regional disparities.

The above figures have been cited only to stress the essentially rural character of India; a character which, incidentally, is expected to survive into AD 2000. Since it was not practical to discuss rural women in India as a whole, I decided, after much cogitation and with some reluctance, to construct a model of rural society and then consider the role of women in each stratum of it. My model is necessarily an over simplified one, and I have ignored not only the artisan, trading and servicing castes, but variations due to the operation of regional and other factors. I shall first treat the model as synchronic and then as diachronic.

From the point of agricultural activity, I shall distinguish four classes: big landowners who supervise the work of cultivation carried out by servants and labourers but who themselves do not engage in manual work, small landowners who personally cultivate their land but who need the services of labourers during transplantation, weeding and harvesting.

They may also be working as tenants on small patches of land leased out from big landowners; tenants who also hire themselves out to landowners for wages during the busy seasons; and finally, landless labourers who subsist entirely on hiring themselves out as labourers on a daily or seasonal basis.[2] The first and the fourth are distinct categories while there may be different degrees of mix between the second and the third in different villages.

There is a clear and self-understood division of labour between the sexes among agriculturists and this includes both activities inside and outside the household. Each set of activities is seen as supportive of the other, and more significantly, agriculture is a familial activity. In other words, the cultivator must be either married himself, or work as part of his natal family. And where a family owns land, a son is needed to keep the farm cultivated and in the family's possession. The relation between a family and land is a vital one, for economic, political and status considerations, and it is projected into ritual and mystical dimensions. The point which I wish to emphasize here however, is that since agriculture is a familial activity, it underscores the interdependence of the sexes and themeans to such interdependence is marriage. In other words, agriculture implies marriage and a bachelor (or spinster) does not make sense in rural India except when he dons the ochre robes and becomes a sanyasi. A widower (or widow) remarries unless he is too old. I have heard a middle-aged widower tell me that he had to marry as he could not work on his farm without someone cooking for him.

Among all the classes described above, the wife cooks and serves food at least twice a day to all members of the household, and cooking in rural India often involves the processing of the grain grown or bought. This work the woman must do and extramural chores are always an addition. The feeding, disciplining and socialization of your children are also her tasks unless she has a grown daughter who then plays the role of mother to her young brothers and sisters. Among landless labourers, during the transplanting season, which, incidentally, occurs during the heavy monsoon rains, women get up as early as 4 a.m., and cook the food before going out to work in the fields. The evening meal is cooked after they come back after a hard day's work, and the transplantation of rice seedlings is tough works; the women frequently have to stand in six inches or so of water, bending and moving backwards as they transplant the seedlings. This has to be done for eight hours a day, and under pressure, as the bundles of seedlings pulled out from the nurseries need to be transplanted with minimum delay.

Weeding, like transplanting, is exclusively women's work, while harvesting involves a more complicated division of labour between the sexes. During the post-harvest season, landless labourers, both men and women, are employed by contractors on road and canal repair work, and occasionally also hired for special tasks by a rich patron.

The point which I wish to emphasize is that in both intra - and extramural work, whether agricultural or non-agricultural, there are clear and minute rules governing the division of labour between sexes. Inside the house, for instance, oxen are invariably looked after by men or boys while fowls are cared for by women or girls. Either men or women may rear buffaloes or sheep, and the income from the sale of dairy products or sheep goes to the owner in each case.

There is a sense of mine and thine between husband and wife, and only during a real crisis may a husband utilize his wife's money or pawn her jewellery. But he is obliged to return it as soon as conditions return to normal. In a great part of rural society, women stand up for their rights against their men, and public opinion supports them in this.[3]

The idea is widespread that working for wagesis a mark of low status and landowners included in the first category listed earlier, do not work for wages. This is true for both men and women. The women, in particular, find high status inconsistent with even extra-mural movement, with the result that upward mobility leads to their 'immurement'. The men, however, go to their fields but do not do any manual work themselves. They only supervise the work of their servants, labourers and tenants. In pre-independent India, there were a large number of 'absentee landowners' who lived in cities and visited their villages only after harvest to collect their shares.

The objection to working for wages remains even at the second level of the hierarchy but it is circumvented by resorting to labour exchange. Thus, two small landowners work on each other's land during the busy season, and in rural. Mysore, this was referred to as *muyyi*. It was only at the lowest levels of the rural hierarchy that men and women worked for wages, and among landless labourers, that was indeed the sole source of income.

It is well known that caste status varies inversely with participation in manual labour, and that there is an overlap between caste and land status though the degree of overlap varies from place to place.

According to the Census of 1961, 42.9 per cent of women workers from Scheduled Castes were agricultural labourers. In the case of the Scheduled Tribes this figure was 21.33 per cent. Their representation in non-agricultural occupations was negligible. The number of Scheduled Castes women employed as agricultural labourers was over 9 lakhs in Andhra Pradesh, over 6 lakhs in Tamil Nadu and 7 lakhs in Uttar Pradesh (CSWI 1974: 168).

In other words while at the bottom level of the rural hierarchy women do both intra-mural and extra-mural work, the latter being paid for while the former is not, immurement of women characterizes the top level. I do not, however, wish to imply that the wives of big landowners are idle. Far from it. For, generally speaking, it is only among big landowners and the highly Sanskritized castes that joint or extended families occur, and the female heads of such families have considerable work and responsibility. They have to look after the cooking arrangements for a large number of adult men and women including servants, and the special needs of infants, sick and old members. They have to allocate domestic work among the different daughters-in-law and servants look after the guests who usually drop in without notice, and attend to the family's many ritual and kinship obligations. They have to supervise the cleaning and processing of grain, and find time for making the elaborate pickles, curry powders, dried vegetables and *papads*. Additionally, many such women are engaged in some economic activity of their own. They may act as pawnbrokers to their neighbours and relatives, they may sell paddy on the sly, and they may run a *chit* fund (monthly contributions of cash paid to a fund which the needy are allowed to collect at a discount).

Women generally take the initiative in arranging the marriages of their offspring, and they either articulate their networks or put pressure on their husbands to find suitable spouses.

I shall now consider the above model as a diachronic one. But before I do that, I should state that pre-British Indian society did permit a certain amount of mobility. It is undeniably true that the pre-British political system was fluid, particularly at the lower levels, a fact which enabled leaders of the dominant peasant castes and others strategically positioned, to seize power locally during periods of crises at the higher levels. Again, marginal land was available for cultivation until the latter half of the nineteenth century; and finally, membership of Bhakti sects, which contained a strong element of protest against Brahmin supremacy and ritualism, provide opportunities for members of the lower castes to move up. I would now like to add two other sources of mobility, the opportunities for trade and commerce which existed in various parts of the country including Gujarat, Punjab, and south-eastern India and which were taken advantage of by certain trading castes such as Banias, Komati Shettis, and Chettiars; and success in obtaining jobs, however low, in pre-British India was even greater than I had suspected earlier. This is nothing more than a hunch but it is interesting to note that several instances of what appear to be caste names today were originally only honorific titles assumed by certain groups. To cite but two instances, the richer landowning Kunbis transformed themselves into the Patidars of modern Gujarat, while in south-west Karnatak several Chetti groups and others succeeded in passing off for the dominant Coorgs. At least some of the dominant castes of modern India seem to have started their career as tribes, and centuries later, the richer and more powerful sections of them laid claim to being *Kshatriyas. Kshtriya* and *Vaishya,* and to a less extent, even Brahmin, seem to have been positions which were achieved over a period of time by ambitious groups in different parts of India though when the caste system of any small region is viewed *at a single point of time*—and this is what is usually done by synchronic analysts - it is seen as a series of hierarchically arranged hereditary groups which permit of no mobility to any individual or group. Hence the frequent and mistaken description of caste as a closed system of social stratification. The separation of history from sociology and anthropology in India has been disastrous for all the three disciplines.

The establishment and consolidation of British rule brought in greater opportunities of mobility to the people, and while initially, the higher castes benefited from them far more than the others, at a later stage, the dominant peasant castes, minority groups and others, succeeded in obtaining access to political power and education, and entered the professions and the bureaucracy.

Independence brought in vastly-increased mobility opportunities to the Scheduled Castes and Scheduled Tribes, and the other 'weaker sections of the society' as a result of the policy of 'protective discrimination' adopted by both the central and state governments. Improved agricultural practices, of which the 'green revolution' is a part, and higher prices for agricultural produce, have both resulted in higher incomes for the upper layers of rural society and this in turn has generated new types of economic activity. Those sections of rural society which have prospered emulate the life-style of the urban middle classes who are largely recruited from the higher castes.

However, the possession of the secular elements of high status was by itself insufficient—it had to be legitimized, and legitimization was a complex and long drawn-out process. This was where *Sanskritization* was crucial. A mobile *jati*, or the mobile section of a *jati,* changed its occupation and diet, adopted the worship of one or other manifestation of a high Hindu god or his consort, emulated the Brahmanical life-style, and even changed its caste name. A new myth of origin was invested as well.

The need for legitimization of mobility through *Sanskritization* and changed caste status was so compulsive that it was even felt by sectarian movements which were anti-Brahminical in origin, and rejected some elements of Vedic Hinduism. Such movements produced over a period of time mini-caste systems within themselves. To complete the irony, in their new guise, they became more effective agents of Sanskritization than the Brahmins.

To return to my main point: the greatly-increased opportunities for secular mobility available during British rule and in independent India meant also considerable increase in the quantum of Sanskritization. As more and more members of the 'lower' castes obtained access to education, jobs and power, they felt the need to tread the well-worn path to legitimizing their newly-earned status.

Among the Muslims of India, a process which, in some of its effects at any rate, is similar to Sanskritization has been reported by Imtiaz Ahmed (1972: 175-9) and Zarina Bhatty. According to Zarina Bhatty,

> Muslim society in India is sharply divided into two sections: the Ashrafs and non-Ashrafs, of whom the latter constitute the bulk. The Ashrafs are the upper caste Muslims who claim foreign descent, and the non-Ashrafs, the lower caste converts. The non-Ashrafs are either artisans or belong to other occupational castes and have not changed their original customs to any marked degree. They have, on the whole, a more liberal attitude towards their women, particularly in respect of work, and do not observe *purdah*. In matters of divorce and remarriage of widows too, they exhibit much less rigidity of attitude. But it is found that when a non-Ashraf family becomes economically better off, it starts looking up to the manners and morals of the Ashrafs with a view to emulating them, and in doing so puts its women in *purdah*, and withdraws them from participating in the family's economic life. This is a similar process to the one described by M.N. Srinivas as 'Sanskritisation' among the Hindus. Thus the ideal of a good Muslim woman among the non-Ashrafs even today continues to be a woman who observes *purdah*, does not earn a living, enters into a marriage arranged by her parents, lives within the four walls of the house and is submissive to her husband's will or pleasure (1976: 110) (see also Singh 1973).

Converts to Christianity in many parts of India continue to retain their sense of belonging to particular castes long after conversion, and it ought not to be surprising if women from the higher 'castes' are immured in the same manner as their Hindu and Muslim sisters.

I shall now recapitulate the main points I have made. At the highest levels of the land hierarchy, both men and women are withdrawn from manual labour while at the lowest levels, both of them work for a wages particularly in the irrigated areas of the south. The availability of vastly-increased opportunities for secular mobility to the 'lower' castes and classes results in the successful groups trying to legitimize their mobility by resorting to Sanskritization. This alters the life-style of those who have 'arrived', and in particular, it has radical effects on the lives of women. It immures them and changes the character of the husband-wife relationship. Immurement is further compounded in the region north of the Vindhyas, thanks to the institution of the *purdah*. *Purdah* obtains among both high status Hindus and Muslims, with 72.6 per cent of the women in Haryana, 62.18 per cent in Rajasthan, and 60.7 per cent in Delhi (CSWI 1974: 61).

Sanskritization leads to heightened sensitivity to ideas of purity and pollution, and to the performance of elaborate calendrical, and other ritual life-cycle ceremonies. Further, among high caste Hindus, women may be said to be the custodians of the purity of the house and its members, and of ritual. Their greater concern with ritual gives them considerable power as the material and spiritual welfare of the household is believed to depend on the meticulous observance of the purity-pollution rules, and the periodical performance of ritual. Women are important in all domestic ritual, and even when they do not actually participate in it they enable men to perform it by attending to such basic tasks as getting the house, clothes and utensils cleaned and purified, securing the many and diverse ingredients needed for the ritual, and finally, preparing the elaborate food. But there are many other and important rituals in which the husband and wife have to sit together with the priest, while a third type of ritual is almost exclusively feminine. In the last category may be included a part of the wedding ritual where no Sanskrit hymns and *mantras* are chanted, and where banter and abuse are exchanged between the women of the two kin-groups, the bride and groom appearing only as victims. Similarly, puberty ritual, which has now become extinct in urban areas, is the sole concern of women.

A considerable part of ritual has direct reference to the pursuit of secular ends, and to that extent, the performance of ritual only indicates practicality. Thus, the annual propitiation of dead ancestors is not only intended to keep them well-fed and satisfied but is believed to ensure the welfare of the survivors. Similarly *vratas* (optional rituals performed, mostly by women, to gain specific secular and religious ends) are performed,[4] offerings promised to deities, and pilgrimages undertaken to great shrines, to obtain children, good health, long life and prosperity for members of the household, in particular, for the husband, father, or an ailing child. One of the secrets of the vitality of Hindu ritual is the manner is which it meshes in with the pursuit of material ends, and offers solace to secular failures. The popular myth of Hindu spirituality has concealed the fact that Hindu ritual and religion are closely linked to worldly interests.

Rituals have also secular dimensions as distinct from secular goals. They provide women with occasions for socializing with their peers and superiors, and for showing off the family's wealth, clothing and jewellery. During the last few decades in particular, the economic, political and status dimensions of ritual have become increasingly conspicuous, and the number of cars lined up outside a wedding house, and the VIPs who attended the wedding, provide the index to the household's standing in the local community.

Feminine preoccupation with ritual provides them with power over men. Since much of women's ritual is concerned with the welfare of the household and its members, and the husband does not have the time for performing it, he is appreciative of the fact that his wife is looking after an important area of family life. The stresses and strains of modern living which include providing for education and careers for offspring, and arranging suitable matches for them, and anxieties about finance and health, draw both men and women to tradition and religion, particularly in their old age. Proximity to death generally makes both men and women more pious but in those rare cases where men display indifference, or seem to display indifference, their women can be trusted to make them toe the traditional line. I shall consider the consequences of this phenomenon later.

I have stated earlier that there was a basic contradiction in Sanskritic Hinduism in the conceptualization of the conjugal bond viz., one in which the wife is literally the moral and religious half of the husband, and another in which he is her superior. I shall consider the latter first. The husband was not only the wife's master but her deity. In his service was her salvation. He might be a wife-beater, drunkard, gambler and womanizer but her duty serve and obey him. Mythological characters such as Sita and Savitri were held up as ideals of devotion for women of the Sanskritized, high castes.

Such a relationship was strikingly asymmetrical. The wife had to be a virgin before marriage, and chaste subsequently, she was not allowed to divorce her husband whatever the provocation, and if she was widowed, she could not remarry. She had to shed all the symbols of the happy and auspicious condition of her married state on the eleventh day of his death. Her head was shaved, she shed her blouse, and she became an inauspicious person for the rest of her life. But so much has been written about the plight of the Hindu widow that I shall not elaborate on it here except to point out that it was characteristic only of the highest and the most visible castes, and that as far as the bulk of the Hindus were concerned, the widow was entitled to remarry especially if she was young.

While 'virginity' in grooms and chastity in husbands were considered desirable if not necessary, lapses were condoned. A husband could divorce a wife for infidelity, incompatibility, or barrenness. He could even take a second wife though very few took advantage of the provision. (However, monogamy is binding under the Hindu Marriage Act, 1955). A widower was expected to remarry, and in parts of south India, the dead wife's younger sister, if unmarried, was preferred for marriage.

But the existence of a gulf between the nature of the conjugal bond as conceived of a Sanskritic Hinduism and as it actually existed, to which I have referred earlier, does not mean that the ideas expressed in Sanskritic Hinduism were uninfluential. I have heared many orthodox Brahmin women in South India express their desire to die as *sumangalis*, while their husbands were still alive. I have also heard elderly women praise a relative or friend for total devotion to her husband even when the latter was an unworthy person. At the same time, paradoxical as it may seem, as a married couple got older, as a young wife matured into a mother and mother-in-law, the relationship between the husband and wife became increasingly egalitarian. In fact, if anything, the balance was tilted in favour of the wife, but this was concealed more or less effectively by symbols of wifely deference, and expressions of devotion to the lord and master. No important decision was taken, however, without the wife's consent if not permission, and frequently, the push to take a decision came from the wife. Husbands freely gave expression to the constraints imposed on them by their wives. Kinsfolk of the husband recognized the realities and earlier accepted them or limited their points of contact.

While total subordination of the wife to her husband was one aspect of Sanskritic Hinduism, the religious and moral partnership of the conjugal pair was another aspect. The husband was religiously incomplete without his wife, and most important rituals required their joint participation. The wife was referred to as a half-body (*ardhangi*), and she got, as a matter of right, half the religious merit which the husband earned by his piety and devotion. Shiva was represented in one of his forms as *ardhanarishwara*, half-man and half-woman.

Among the less Sanskritized 'low' castes, conjugal relations appear to be more perceptibly egalitarian than among the Sanskritized 'high' castes, and this is true of all the regions, including the Hindi-speaking areas. Among the 'low' castes, widows are permitted to remarry, and a wife is able to divorce her husband under certain circumstances. The elders of the kin on both the sides were brought in when a divorce case had to be adjudicated, and if they failed to bring about a reconciliation, a separation was brought about, and the jewellery, money and gifts given at marriage, returned to each party. Until at least the 1950s most divorces occurring in rural areas were customary ones, unknown to the law courts.

Among the higher castes, a girl was trained to be a wife and daughter-in-law, and success or failure in these roles reflected the credit or discredit of her parents. But even among them, a girl whose marriage ended in disaster, had the right to return to her natal home. According to Mary Chatterjee, marital failures do not seem to be infrequent among the educated women from the higher castes in Benares, and the wives whose marriage broke up returned to their natal families.[5]

High status rural women offer, however, a sharp contrast to urban, educated women, a majority of whom hail from the higher castes. They are found employed as clerks, typists, receptionists, school teachers, nurses, doctors, social workers, academics, and as officials in the government and in the nationalized banks and the Life Insurance Corporation. But the number of women officials is still small compared with men. But one of the significant results of, for instance, success in the IAS is the fact that young women get posted as Collectors at District Headquarters. (As Collectors, they may even have to order firing on riotous mobs). Traditionally, the Collector was regarded as the lord of his district, and it is something of a cognitive revolution for villagers to find that they are being governed by a woman, and a young one at that. The significance of this fact has not been noticed by Indian social scientists.

In the cities, men and women are found working side by side in the same office, bank, firm or school. Men have accepted without protest women as their bosses in government offices, schools, colleges and universities. In a few cities in South India, there are banks which are entirely staffed by women, the only men being either messengers or watchmen. The career woman in India is very visible and it is significant that the society at large has quietly accepted women's assumption of new roles.

In a purely statistical sense, however, educated women are not significant. While 40 per cent of urban women are literate, only 1 per cent of them are either graduate or post-graduate. Of the 9,00,000 educated women in the country, 50 per cent are primary school teachers, 15 per cent secondary school teachers, 15 per cent clerks and typists while the balance comprises doctors, lawyers, college teachers, administrators, artists, etc. But however small the proportion of urban-educated women of the 'status trap' of the latter, and have jobs that give them both regular incomes and social esteem (even from women), demands an explanation. They have made a successful transition from one structural and cognitive frame of reference to another. How did this happen? And the question that naturally arises is whether a period of stay in the 'status trap' is a condition precedent to women's assumption of few and extramural roles.

An essential pre-condition of women's (or for that matter, men's) breaking out of the 'status trap' is migration to urban areas, and the bigger and more cosmopolitan the urban area, the easier the transition. Very small towns, without any industry to support them, and culturally homogeneous, would perhaps present equally hostile environments for women wishing to break out of their domestic walls. Even in the big cities, areas inhabited largely by concentrations of kin-clusters from castes with a reputation for conservatism, are not congenial to women who wish to assume new roles. The interaction between members living in such caste-based wards is intense and departures from tradition generate gossip.

In other words, urbanization is a condition precedent to the adoption of new patterns of behaviour, and this holds good for both men and women. I remember an elder of Rampura telling me, 'When a youth gets a BA it means that he is externed from the village'. In 1948, Rampura could only boast of having produced three graduates but none of them lived in the village. In those days graduates wanted salaried jobs in the government, or entered the professions, for neither of which were there any opportunities in the village. But the situation has changed somewhat over the last twenty years or so: villages lying in irrigated areas or near townships, have each produced several graduates, and land reform legislation has forced owner-cultivators to remain on their land for fear of losing it to their tenants or servants. Also, the fact that agricultural products fetch higher prices has meant prosperity for rural landowners, and the provision of such facilities as schools, hospitals, drinking water and electricity have made villages more livable than before. The improvement of communications combined with high urban rents have contributed to converting villages on the urban fringe into dormitories.

Education is becoming more popular among girls everywhere including villages but the drop-out rate for girls is higher than that for boys. Separate figures are not available for girl drop-outs in rural areas but even the national averages tell a depressing story: according to figures available for 1973-74, only three out of ten enrolled in Class I reached Class V, only one out of 12.5 girls passed the Secondary School Leaving Examination. In 1973-74, there were 9,00,000 girls in colleges,and ironic as it may seem, the proportion of girls to boys was higher in postgraduate classes. However, the ablest among the girls do very well in the examinations, it being usual to find at least a few girls in the first ten places in any university result sheet.

Urban residence is a necessary but not sufficient condition for escape from the 'status trap'. Education is also essential, and in India, female education has not only followed male education but an intimate link exists between female education, marriage and caste.

In this connection, two considerations appear extremely relevant: a girl ought not to be more highly educated than her husband, and she should marry within her *jati*. The level of education which a girl receives is therefore directly related to the general level of male education in that particular *jati*. This is one, but only one, of the reasons for the high drop-out rate among girls.[6] Parents want their daughters to get only so much education as will give them the utmost advantage in the marriage market. Sometimes this means that girls have to be educated enough to have a job as, increasingly, young men from the middle classes prefer to marry such girls. The cost of urban living has made them realize that two incomes are better than one and in the big cities it is not an unfamiliar sight to see a young man drop his pillion-riding wife at her bank or office before he drives to his own. But this occurs generally among the urban middle classes drawn from the higher castes.

The second requirement, that marriage has to occur within the *jati*, continues to be a strict one but needs to be hedged with two qualifications. *Jati* is a slippery entity, and the fact that in the past new *jatis* generally emerged by fissioning themselves off from old *jatis*, makes possible a referential stretch depending on contextual necessity. Thus in one context, a person may refer to the smallest *jati* to which he belongs, comprising the group with which he has the closest interaction including connubial relations, while in a political or economic context he may include that *jati* in a much wider one. Indeed, even for marriages, cognate *jatis* tend to get telescoped to form a single entity. Thus, some South Indian Brahmins nowadays express the view that they would be satisfied if their son (or daughter) married a girl (or boy) from any one of the many South Indian Brahmin *jatis*, and they regard themselves as progressives. It may be safely assumed that in such cases the parents are urban, educated, and belong to the middle classes. Class, education and life-style become increasingly significant within the reinterpreted *jati*.

To come back to women's education: the pressure to get women educated is part of the process of securing good husbands for them. Colleges and universities provide respectable waiting places for girls who wish to get married. As already mentioned, among the urban middle classes belonging to the higher castes, the possession of a basic degree is now regarded as essential for obtaining a 'good' groom. But as a girl gets more and more educated, her connubial circle narrows as there is an implicit rule which is only very rarely broken that the boy ought to be at least as highly educated as she is.[7] Even here, a male doctor prefers to marry a female doctor, a male academic his female counterpart, and a male IAS official, a female IAS official. This section of Indian society is miniscule in size but its life-style is envied and admired by the others.

Indian reformers have shown a concern with female education ever since the mid-nineteenth century (Basu 1976: 39). The reasons for the spread of female education probably varied from one region to another, but according to Pradeep Sinha, a potent factor in the popularity of female education in Calcutta was the urge to prevent high caste widows from being recruited as prostitutes. The proportion of females to males in Calcutta was very low resulting in men resorting to prostitutes from the courtesan castes. As the demand was far greater than the supply, young widows from the high castes, 'helpless victims of family neglect and even torture, were an obvious recruiting ground' (Mazumdar 1976: 49). The awareness of the existence of a profound cultural gap between educated men and their uneducated wives and the need to bridge it in the interests of family solidarity, provided a powerful motive for female education. The reformers argued that 'education would not turn the women away from their traditional familial roles but improve their efficiency as wives and mothers, and strengthen the hold of traditional values on society, since women were far better carriers of these values' (*ibid*).

Concern with improving the miserable plight of the widows, and the desire to bridge the gap between the educated husband and his ignorant wife were shared by reformers in many parts of the country. Girls from the upper castes were preponderant in the schools and colleges, and this continues to be the case even now to a large extent. Among the earliest beneficiaries of the new educational opportunities were widows and women deserted by their husbands.

Since the beginning of this century, an increasing number of men from the higher castes sought English education to obtain jobs in the bureaucracy, and to enter the professions. Such men were in great demand as grooms, and over a period of time, this gave rise to the institution of dowry. Previously, paying sums of cash to obtain brides was prevalent all over South India (excluding Kerala) and Bengal.

Considerations of space prevent me from attempting an analysis of the institution of dowry and I shall rest content with stating that the pressure to pay dowry was compounded by the twin needs of having to get girls married before puberty, and to find grooms within the same *jati*. This triple imposition was, as could be expected, very hard on the parents of girls but its very unreasonableness resulted in some relaxation of the rules. The fact that parents had to accumulate enough cash to pay dowry, and to meet other wedding expenses meant that many girls who had reached puberty remained unmarried. Public opinion, which was at first critical of parents with 'grown daughters', gradually learnt to ignore the fact. Second, subcaste barriers started to fall one by one, the principle of 'horizontal stretch' coming into play, and providing a much larger recruiting ground for grooms while at the same time the illusion was maintained that there was no departure from tradition. Third, since girls could not be kept idle at home till they were married, they were sent to schools and colleges. The fact that they also met a new and growing demand for educated brides helped to spread education among girls.

Marriages involve the spending of unconscionable sums of money by the parents of brides and this is particularly true of the urban middle classes, the traders and the richer peasantry. Dowry adds greatly to their burden, especially as the sums demanded have been steadily increasing; and the gadgets, vessels and furniture demanded as 'gifts', also cost much more than before. (Beginning with the upper levels of the society, dowry has now spread even to so lowly a group as sweepers in Calcutta). The passing of The Prohibition of Dowry Act in 1961 has had no effect whatever in combating this evil. Only a powerful social movement among the educated youth can have any impact on the problem. But all this should not blind one to the fact that dowry has helped to raise the age of marriage for girls and that it has helped to spread female education.

I shall now come to my last point, viz., the contribution which female participation in the freedom struggle has made to its emancipation. That such participation has been crucial can be conceded even by those who regard as an overstatement. Aparna Basu's view that, '... it is doubtful if a century of preaching and social work would have brought about the same change in the position of Indian women as was achieved in the wake of two decades of political struggle in India' (1976: 38-9). In the second civil disobedience movement which Mahatma Gandhi launched in 1930, 'over 80,000 persons were arrested during the salt satyagraha of which more than 17,000 were women'. In addition, there was an association of women student terrorists in Calcutta with one hundred members. According to Aparna Basu, the movement initially attracted women from the urban middle classes but as the nationalist movement gained in strength, industrial workers and 'certain sections of the peasantry' also participated in it.

An interesting and paradoxical factor in women being drawn into the independence movement was the nature of Gandhi's personality which inspired confidence not only in women but in 'their guardians', viz., fathers and husbands. The respect that Gandhi enjoyed among Indians as a saint, and the unique methods of struggle that he forged, persuaded men that they could allow their womenfolk to join his movement.

The gradual transfer of power from the British to Indian hands gave women experience in participating in the democratic process. This included their becoming the representatives of the people, and in holding office. 'The Government of India Act of 1935 extended the franchise to more than six million women, a great improvement on the figure of 3,15,000 under the Act of 1919'. 'In the 1937 elections, eight women were elected from 'general' constituencies and forty-two from 'reserved' constituencies. Six women became ministers when the provincial cabinets were formed'.

It was only natural then that in independent India women participated actively in all aspects of politics, and held political office. Apart from the fact that the country's most important political office has been held by a woman for nearly eleven years, there are two women chief ministers of states, women ministers in almost every state and central government, and finally, there are several women MPs and MLAs. But female participation at the higher levels of the political process seems to be confined to women from families with a political tradition except among the Scheduled Castes and Tribes who enjoy reservation in both state and central legislatures. A proportion of the seats reserved for these two categories has gone to their women.

The relative ease with which Indian women have entered the professions and captured political power is an impressive fact of the modern world, though it is only a tiny urban minority largely hailing from the upper castes which has been the principal beneficiary of the new gains. Quite apart from the fact that Indian men have not opposed feminine emancipation, two little-noticed facts seem to be a part of this process. Educated Indian women are able to hold demanding jobs, and be the housewives and mothers at the same time thanks to the availability of sevants, and to their ability to draw upon their wide kin-networks for help in crises. Thus, a pregnant girl may go to her natal home for her confinement, or if that is difficult, her mother or a married sister might visit her and be with her till she is able to resume her normal life. It may surprise many to know that it is becoming common for Indian wives in the United States, Canada and Britain to get their mothers or sisters to visit them during their confinement.

But the crunch might come when, as is already happening in some cities, servants are not available, and a more remote possibility, when kinship networks become smaller, and kinship obligations decrease in intensity. But what is impressive in the meanwhile is the successful blending of traditionalism and modernity in Indian social life and culture.[8] In fact, several traditional factors such as the desire of girls to be taught by women teachers, and of women patients to be treated by women doctors, have also helped in popularizing female education. Similarly, the horrors of upper caste widowhood and desertion by husbands, have also helped in the spread of education among women. On the other side, educated men and women do maintain links with their tradition, and even self-proclaimed rationalists perform obsequies and *shradhas* for their dead ancestors. Conformity as well as departure from tradition is contextual, and it is hard to see any patterns in either departures or conformities expect to say that wedding, mortuary and *shraddha* rituals are probably regarded as more binding than the others. Even the rationalizations for departures and conformities vary from one individual to another.

After making the point that it is extremely difficult to make general statements about Indian women because of regional, caste, class and other differences, I have tried to show how the upper castes have a bibliocentric view of Indian culture and society, including the place and role of women in it, and how that has acted as a barrier to the observation and interpretation of actual behaviour. This has been compounded by the heterogeneous character of the scriptures, their differential authority, and finally, inconsistencies which are to be found in the scriptures in the conceptualization of certain basic roles and relationships, particularly the conjugal one.

In order to describe the position of women in India, I begar by creating a model of rural society and showed how female role and behaviour varied at different levels of land and caste hierarchy. I then viewed the model as a diachronic one in order to show how even traditionally the caste system permitted a certain amount of mobility, and how opportunities for mobility increased considerably during British rule and subsequently. Since independence, opportunities for mobility have greatly increased for poor and low status Indians, in particular, the Scheduled Castes and Scheduled Tribes. In rural India, movement to the top layer of the rural hierarchy generally led to female 'immurement' among both Hindus, Muslims, and possibly also among Christians. Another consequence of upward mobility among the Hindus was Sanskritization which altered husband-wife relations. Whatever the legal and formal position of women in Hindu society, as a married couple got older, and a wife became a mother-in-law and grandmother, she became a force to reckon with in familial matters. Conjugal relations became egalitarian and this was more or less effectively concealed under well-developed symbols of wifely deference. Finally, migration to the urban areas, female political participation, education, the activities of social reformers, and the inequities of dowry, all enabled women to make a relatively easy transition to new roles and responsibilities. To conclude better positive as well as negative aspects combine to change the role and then status of women. Sometimes, it is all intentionally organised and like a legal provision, a govt. order or a rural employment scheme. But it is also done due to negative developments like death of male head of the family forces women to perform her responsibilities or take up the lead. In either situation, target of female emancipation is not complete still, a lot of conscious efforts need to realise the objective and make sure that the position of women has changed for the better.

References

1. In regions where women do most of the agricultural work, it is the bridegroom who must pay bridewealth, as already mentioned, but where women are less actively engaged in agriculture marriage payments come usually from the bride's family. In South and East Asia the connection between the work of women and the direction of marriage payments is close and unmistakable' (Lowic 1920: 48).
2. I am not discussing here the question of bonded labourers who are to be found in every part of India.
3. A chief is trained to be acquisitive, and this is perhaps much stronger among the richer sections of the peasantry.
4. The Sri Vaishnava Brahmins of South India do not perform *vratas* as they were denounced (inspiritual, worldly) by their founder, Ramanuja, in the twelfth century A.D.
5. Personal communication to the author.
6. A girl may be withdrawn by her parents from school or college if the choice is between her or her brother's education even when she is the better student.
7. It is not unlikely that many of the unemployed women graduates in the arts and sciences, constituting about 96 per cent of the

total women graduates, had discontinued higher studies in order not to decrease their chances of finding a suitable husband in their respective *jatis*.

8. However, this is not to be taken to mean that Indian women do not experience any conflict in traditional and modern roles. What is surprising is that considering the divergent nature of the demands made on them, the conflict is not more acute and widespread. Also, generally speaking, the conflicts are more serious in the first few years of married life.

2

Legal Review

The problem that lies with us today is that we still have in every part of the country a variety of social groups—tribal, peasant and urban—functioning in diverse ecologies. Only broad levels of generalisation are allowed, such as, that the purpose of marriage was the furtherance of caste (*jati*) relations, essentially a social and political concern, and, where it existed, marriage was targetted at the consolidation of property. In the legal texts, however, in the *dharmasastra* and similar literature, the blanket term women is used, irrespective of the social origins or status of any woman. It is important that whereas these texts take great care to classify men with a minutiae of distinctions, women are generally treated as a uniform category. Furthermore the status of women as a whole is surely defined, for they are unambiguously equated with the Sudras.

Even the *Gita* places women, Vaisyas and Sudras in the same category and describes them all as being of sinful birth. As per another text the punishment for killing either a woman or a Sudra is identical. Perhaps the most gruelling of all is the treatment of the widow, which some times borders on the inhumane and this is particularly disconcerting, coming as it does, from the *sastras* of a culture which laid so much stress on respecting and caring for the aged. The subservience of women is clearly summed up in the Manu Dharmasastra where it is stated that a woman should never be independent. As a daughter she is under the surveillance of her father, as a wife of her spouse and as a widow of her son. These attitudes to women reflect both contempt and fear. The latter doubtless derived from the fear of pollution, since women were regarded as impure on many occasions. The association of pollution with women, apart from the popular ritual reasons, would also suggest, at the psychological level, the fear of someone who plays such a central role in procreation. Socio-legal treatises, such as the *dharma-sastras* are not always a description of truth; in fact, more often than not they are indicators of a social ideal-guides and manuals to perfect action, although the underlying assumptions on which the laws are based emanate from real social conditions.

This is particularly so in pre-modern societies where legal rights and obligations are not always very distinctly demarcated. To that extent, these texts cannot be taken too literally. In the same manner, in Islamic law, it is interesting to note that the legal position of women is distinctly better as compared for instance to Hindu law, yet in actual practice their position was nowhere better than of other Indian women.

As we have said in the beginning of the chapter also, caste differentiation among women in these texts occurs in the context of the performance of rituals, where often the ritual varied according to the caste of the performer. The ritual of becoming a *sati,* by the immolation of the wife on her husband's funeral pyre, is discussed at length and Brahmin women are specifically precluded from performing this custom in most of the texts. The custom increased in frequency in the period after the mid-first millennium A.D. and then too was more prevalent among those claiming *kshtriya* status.

Although never clearly said it almost certainly, among other things, had to do with property rights and inheritance. In the legal treatise of this same period, women came to be considered part of a man's property, particularly in those parts of the country where a combination of patrilineal society and private property was by now well-established as part of the elite culture. This is best symbolised in the opinion that a woman could be given as a pledge, the interest being one-seventieth of her value, though how her value was to be computed is nowhere clearly stated.

Denied as she was of the right to inheritance, her own right to property consisted of her *stridhana,* i.e., the wealth which she was given by her family at her marriage, which, although theoretically inviolable, nevertheless gave her hardly any freedom, economic or otherwise. The legal status was not irrevocable in practice, as is suggested by other types of evidence. Nevertheless, it shows the social image. That it was not seriously questioned at the textual level would point to its tacit-acceptance by certain social groups, specifically those most concerned with both property and pollution.

The low legal status of women was common to a number of 'classical' societies, pre-eminently the Roman, where the rationale appears to have derived from the emphasis on the patrilineal structure. As a counterpoint to the legal texts, history provides evidence of alternative perspectives. These are, first of all, the unusual but clear exceptions. Two of the more obvious come to mind: Gargi, a reputed scholar in an age when learning was closed to women due to pollution taboos; and Raziya, who ruled albeit briefly, at a court fiercely male-dominated by militaristic Turkish nobles. That such exceptions were possible would belie a too literal belief in legal status.

Other nuances emerge from more concrete sources. There is the interplay of patrilineal and matrilineal groups which has been active for many centuries until recent years. To identify these as Aryan and non-Aryan respectively is probably simplistic and confusing, since these latter terms cannot be precisely defined. But family and social relationships did follow either of the two dominant forms or an intermingling of the two, and is thus sometimes suggested even by contemporary family structures. This in part accounts for the regional variations in the status (both implied and actual) of women in various regions. Perhaps the most involved facet is that of man and the female diety—the mother-goddess, the goddess of the fertility cult, the deity which remains to this day the most comprehensively worshipped in villages and towns. Through all its different manifestations, whether it be the crude images of the Harappa culture or the consorts of the great angels, both malevolent and benign, or the more esoteric *saktis* of the *tantrics,* the mother goddess is the dominant deity, for she is implicit even in the worship of the *lingam*.

Traditionally in India, the mother-goddess was worshipped in indigenous tribal and peasant societies and in early urban centres. The Rigvedic culture is perhaps the only major culture in which the mother-goddess is conspicuously absent. Being a fertily cult, this can be argued that its dominance is restricted to pre-industrial societies—the decline of the cult of the Virgin Mary in north-western Europe being a case in point. Did the pooja of the mother-goddess strengthen the fear of woman symbolising the power of procreation or was it subconsciously a compensatory gesture? This dualism is also reflected in some rituals where the presence of the woman is essential. The ancient attitude to sex reflects a striking absence of the guilt complex arising from original sin as conceived in the Judaeo-Christian tradition. It was not until the impact of the Christian missionaries and Victorian mores that the concept of the guilt complex took root. The equation of freedom with licentiousness is often used as a brake to giving greater independence to women, where there is an automatic presumption that the moral standards for men and women should be different. The fetish that is made of virginity and pre-marital sexual relations is more often a rationalisation of the desire to keep women inferior than a genuine moral conviction.

In the Hindu tradition sex is sinful only where it is socially illegitimate and the Buddhist tradition although carrying hints of puritanical ethics never really converted the theory of sin into one of a guilt complex. Woman as mother was venerated but woman as an erotic being was not degraded. Far from being seen as sin, the sexual indulgence was symbolic of creative energy. Such an attitude permitted the duality of approach to women. It is noticeable, however, that members of many of the tantric sects held liberal ideas on the status of women.

Although the history of India, there has been a stream of social consciousness urging and encouraging a liberalisation of attitudes to the status of women. The two major heterodox religions, Buddhism and Jainism, both advocated greater freedom for women than did Brahmanism. The Buddha initially objected to instituting an order of nuns but was finally persuaded by his disciple Ananda. The order of nuns in religions Buddhism and Jainism provided an alternative vocation to those women who wished to disassociate themselves from the usual functions of women in society. This practice of thinking was continued in what has come to be called the *Bhakti* movement—in its various forms during different periods. The need of the *Bhakti* movement in the *Bhagavata* tradition was a liberalising perception of religion embedded in the idea of the individual's relationship with a personalised deity. This enfranchisement from both theology and ritual was extended to relationships between men and women.

An early expression of *bhakti* in the teachings of the *Alvars* and Nayanmars not only stressed the personal devotion of the individual to the deity of his liking, expressed in the easily comprehensible hymns composed in the most widely used language of the region (rather than in the more erudite Sanskrit) and divested of much complicated ritual, but also stressed the right of women of *bhakti*, to their joining in congregational worship and to a generally freer life for them. This is also reflected in the early teachings of the Lingayatas, in the preaching of the 'saints' of Maharashtra, to certain degree in the teaching of Chaitanya in eastern India and to a considerable degree in the verses of the northern *bhakti* teachers, particularly Kabir and Nanak. Without surprise, it was the bhakti teaching which produced the women 'saints' - Andal, Mirabai and Lalla. The support for the heterodox religions and also the *bhakti* movement came in the initial stages from similar groups of people; largely the urban traders, merchants and artisans and up to a point the more well-to-do peasantry. Royal patronage went on to be occasional, though the ladies of the court were often staunch patrons of Buddhism and Jainism.

The rulers tended to support these sects once they had become better established since, largely for political reasons, they had to be more judicious in their patronage to religious sects. The social composition of these sects was doubtless a further cause in their support of a liberal attitude to the status of women. The leading impetus, in recent years, in bringing about a change in the attitude to women has come from the national movement for independence, a movement which had its inception in the nineteenth century and whose social impacts continues to linger with us. Originally an essentially middle-class movement with its roots in various urban centres in the country, it was converted into a mass movement greatly through the efforts of Mahatma Gandhi.

In order to build a mass movement, the slogan of freedom had to be extended to a number of 'depressed' groups—untouchables, farmers and workers and women. The participation of women in the national movement became a necessary part of the programme. This participation was also needed to mobilise entire families which gave more strength to the movement. The appeal to women *per se* was a major plank in Gandhi's policy and derived, perhaps marginally and subconsciously, from the earlier Jaina and *Bhakti* ethic.

Involvement in the politics of the national movement was an act of patriotism and political life became a respectable vocation for a woman. This may in part account for the more success of women politicans in ex-colonial countries as compared to the more industrialised countries of north-western Europe and the USA. It may also account for the downfall of women politicians in the post-independence period in India. Tied into the concept of nationalism was the debate on culture and society and the pendulum swung in middle of what were regarded as the two poles of Tradition and Modernity: a debate which seems to have been intensified with independence. The 'burning questions' in this context during the initial days were the age of consent to marriage, widow remarriage, property rights and education. Some advocated a return to tradition as the only sources of salvaging Indian society, but the definition of tradition remains extremely elusive. Others wanted either a social reform or a socially radical change of Indian society, which in a sense is as utopian as the first proposition. Moreover demand for political reform also opened the pandora's box of social reform. Possibly, we have seen the culmination of the debate in the passage of the Hindu Code Bill in 1956, which in theory at least, provides both security and freedom to the Hindu woman, and may to that extent become the prototype of further changes in the civil code applicable to all Indian women folk, irrespective of their religion.

Laws Related to Women

The law relating to women in India requires drastic alterations. Though there has been considerable legislation in regard to women during the post-constitution era, in reality the position of women today is not very different from the pre-constitution days. The parity clause in the Constitution has made little or no impact on the social and economic life of women in India. A woman continues to be a dependent—economically, socially and even psychologically. Her status is still that of a daughter, wife or mother and she seldom feels an individual in her own right. Legislation enacted during the last two decades is out of reach for most women because, by and large, they have neither the mental conscious awareness nor the financial resources to take advantage of these beneficent provisions.

Who will not accept that even though the Constitution recognises the fact that women have been subjugated for long by being denied basic rights and has provided for the enactment of special laws to improve their position no solid steps have been taken by the Indian legislature in this direction so far. It may be noted in this context that in admission to state-owned and state-aided educational institutions delivering technical and other vocational education and in practically all appointments under the state, reservation has been provided for in favour of Scheduled Castes, Scheduled Tribes and other backward classes (OBCs) by means of legislative and executive measures but the claims of women have been singularly overlooked. Hindu law, as it existed, when the Indian Constitution came into force, imposed various disabilities on women.

Let us talk of this one a woman had only limited interest in the property she held. This meant that she could not use the full rights which a male owner could; for instance, she could not alienate property except for certain enumerated reasons called legal necessities. She could not be a coparcener and ensure partition of the joint family estate. She was not legally competent to make an adoption—her consent was not required in an adoption made by her husband—and a widow could adopt only with the authority and instructions given by her deceased husband. A testamentary appointment made by her husband could defeat a widow's right as guardian of minor children. She could not have a guardian by testament. An illegitimate daughter had no claim against the putative father even to maintenance, whereas among the Shudras, an illegitimate son was admitted to a part in the putative father's property. These disabilities were sought to be removed by the enactment in 1955-56 of laws relating to issues like marriage and divorce, succession, adoption, minority and guardianship.

(a) Marital Makes and Breaks. Undoubtedly, many of these laws require improvement. For example, one that calls for immediate attention is the law relating to divorce. Law recognises sacramental marriage, marriage before the Registrar of Marriages and any other kind of marriage recognised by customary law. When it comes to divorce, this law is not so simple. The Hindus are granted divorce on certain limited grounds which are generally hard to prove, but, importantly divorce by mutual consent is not one of the grounds mentioned. Likewise, the Christians have to allege and prove adultery in order to establish a matrimonial crime before divorce can be granted under the Indian Divorce Act.

The Parsis have to get the approval of ten assessors chosen from their community who pronounce on the divorce proceedings. Muslim men obtain a divorce by the mere utterance of certain words in succession whereas women have to establish certain enumerated grounds. Strangely, in none of above said laws (except in the Special Marriage Act, 1954) is there any mention of divorce by mutual consent. Consenting spouses, generally, resort to change of religion and create a basis for divorce. It is imperative that this deplorable state of the law be rectified and provision be made for divorce by mutual consent.

If mutuality be the ground of marriage, law should enable the parties to separate when the mutuality ceases. It may be noted that under Section 29(2) of the Hindu Marriage Act, any right recognised by those customary law or conferred by any special enactment is specifically saved and preserved. By this provision, the Nair Regulations which provide for the execution of a registered means of divorce get preserved and divorce can be granted without the intervention of the court by the mere execution of a registered document.

Further, under the laws applicable to the Bunts of South Kanara, divorce can be had by the unilateral act of one party filing a petition in the marriage court. As said earlier, all these are good laws even today by virtue of Section 29(2) of the Hindu Marriage Act. In this state of the law where some sections of the population are entitled to larger rights, is it not fit and proper that the legislature amend and codify the law and make it equally applicable to all?

It is submitted in this context that when the Hindu Marriage Act of 1955 providing for divorce for the first time came to be enacted, the makers of the Act forgot that the Indian law of divorce has always been a liberal one and it was not necessary to import Anglo-Saxon notions of rigidity into it.

(b) Mother without Marital Status. As has been seen in some Western countries, with the emergence of women as socially and economically independent beings, there is a demand for recognising an unmarried mother and her infant as a family unit. In recent seminars held in various regions of the world, this problem was kept in sharp focus. A draft resolution was put before in the twenty-fourth session of the UN Commission on the Status of Women.

This resolution recommended that maternal affiliation be recognised as a consequence of the factum of birth, and further, that the unmarried mother be given full rights and privileges granted by the law to a parent. In most of the socialist countries, the right of the unmarried mother is recognised and protected under the Constitution itself. Sooner or later the Indian legislature also had to attend to the problem of the unmarried mother.

And now it gives equal right and protection to unmarried mother and their children. There are, for instance, victims of rape or other unfortunate circumstances or of hostile aggression as in Bangladesh and the problem of rehabilitating these victims becomes a hard social reality. Many of them are driven to a life of prostitution because society refuses to accept them. If legislative protection is given to the rights of the unmarried mother, she can be protected from this eventuality and ensured a respectable place in society. The difficulty of the unmarried mother is understood when we look at a few sections of the Indian Penal Code. Section 309 of the I.P.C. provides that any attempt to commit suicide is punishable with simple imprisonment for a duration which may extend to one year or with fine or with both. In order to liberalise abortion laws and thereby reduce the rigour of the Indian Penal Code which makes any termination of pregnancy a punishable offence, the Medical Termination of Pregnancy Act was brought in.

But this Act does not improve the position because it provides for termination of pregnancy only on limited medical grounds. To illustrate, the Act permits termination of pregnancy by a registered medical practitioner in case it is of a duration of twelve weeks provided, however, that the said registered practitioner is of the opinion, in good faith, that the continuance of pregnancy would involve threat to the life of the pregnant woman or "grave injury" to her mental or physical health or where there is a "substantial risk" of the child being born with physical or mental deformations "so as to be seriously handicapped". The Act requires two registered medical practitioners to opine similary in good faith before a pregnancy of a duration longer than twelve weeks can be aborted.

But above said requirement is very difficult to fulfil because many registered medical practitioners would hesitate to issue the requisite certificate for fear that it may be debated in courts that the practitioner concerned had not formed the required opinion or that the said opinion, when formed was not *bonafide*. Again, the concept of "grave injury" to the mental or physical health of the pregnant woman is such a nebulous idea that a registered practitioner may well hesitate to take the responsibility of sustaining the opinion in a court of law.

Worse still, while the pregnant woman is still busy looking a medical practitioner who would be willing to certify that her pregnancy is terminable, she may cross the twelve-week period, inviting the necessity of producing two such certificates. It is recommended that this requirement should be dropped. The Act should provide that if a couple is desirous that the next child should not be born for causes economic or otherwise, they should have the right to approach the first available medical practitioner and to have the pregnancy terminated. One more good reason for doing away with the medical certificate under the Act would be the fact that registered medical practitioners are not easily available in rural areas where the Act is most required. Also such a requirement may lead to abuse in the hands of those who may be so inclined. Another serious weakness of the Act is that it does not consider the implications of poverty. For instance, rape or failure of contraceptive are permissible reasons, because they cause injury to the mental health of the victim.

But malnutrition, which plagues a number of Indian women and which gets exaggerated with frequent child-bearing is not a good enough reason. Nor is the straightforward economic reason of not being able to afford one more mouth to feed. The most important case of omission is that of the unmarried mother about whom there is not a whisper in the Act. It goes without saying that it is in this kind a case that the consequences of child-birth are most serious.

Looking at the object of the Act, it is hard to understand how an unmarried woman is not entitled to the same safety as a married woman. The distinction made does not seem to have any rational nexus to the object sought to be achieved and one wonders if such an enactment cannot be held to violate the constitutional guarantee of equality given through under article 14 of the Constitution. In a similar situation, the US Supreme Court struck down a similar classification on the ground that it was against the equal protection clause of the Constitution (Eisenstadt Vs. Baird, 1972). Even abandonment of a child is punishable under Section 317 of the Indian Penal Code which states that any intentional abandonment of a child is punishable with imprisonment of either description for seven years or with fine or with both.

(c) Problem of Children Born without Marriage. In this state of the law, the Indian Parliament took its step towards solving the problem of illegitimate children when it enacted in Section 20 clause 2 of the Hindu Adoptions and Maintenance Act,1956, that: "A legitimate or illegitimate child may claim maintenance from his or her father or mother so long as the child is a minor."

With it was brought uniformity among Hindus in this branch of the law. The old law recognised the rights of illegitimate sons only among *Shudras* and there was no law for the maintenance of illegitimate daughters. They could, anyway, claim maintenance from the putative father under Section 488 of the Criminal Procedure Code. In such a proceeding, the maximum amount that can be a reward by way of maintenance is Rs. 500 and therefore, this section provides only very limited relief. Another revolutionary step has been taken by the Indian Parliament in bringing in the Adoption of Children Bill, 1972, which provides for parents of illegitimate children to adopt their own child. Section 4 as it stands today, allows the mother or father of an illegitimate child alone or commonly to adopt such a child whether or not they have completed the age of 21 years or are older than the child by 21 years. As per the Hindu Adoptions and Maintenance Act, 1956, it was an essential requirement that the difference in age between the adopting parent and the adopted child be at least 21 years in the event of a man wanting to adopt a female child, and vice versa, hence the second clause was necessary.

(d) Uniform Civil Code (UCC). Bill known as the Adoption of Children Bill, has further been made applicable to all citizens, irrespective of their being Hindus, Muslims, Parsis or Christians. This step is a tremendous stride in the promulgation of uniform civil code which is a crying need of the day. A common code of personal laws applicable to all alike will be easy of understanding and implementation. It may be worthwhile for the state or the government to appoint a high-powered commitee to study all personal laws and suggest steps towards the enactment of a common civil code for all in whole country.

(e) Muslim Personal Law. Among Hindus, women have been dealt with at length because it is they who suffered disabilities primarily and it is their personal law that has undergone legislative changes. They, incidentally, are from the majority community in India. But as far as Muslim women are concerned, they have a right of inheritance and this law remains unchanged even today.

Under Muslim law, however, the right of divorce is easily available to males but the same is not given to women with the same degree of ease even though marriage is characterised as a contract and not a sacrament. The legislatures at the centre and the states in India have made practically no improvements in the personal laws of the Muslims so far. The Christian, Parsi and Jewish women are governed by the Indian Succession Act as they do not have any personal laws like the Hindus and Muslims.

Under this laws, women can succeed to property and suffer no disabilities regarding property rights. They, like all other women in India, need reform for the law relating to divorce. Notwithstanding these laws, what measures are necessary to make women frée and equal in the real sense of the word? The government should make special laws enabling women to have compulsory free education. This is imperative because the education of girls is usually subordinated to that of boys on account of tradition.

It may be noticed that this provision would be permissible under Article 15(3) of the Constitution, which enables the legislature to make special provisions for the advancement of women. Women should be given preference in matters of appointment on the ground that they are socially and economically backward in the same way that the Scheduled Castes and Scheduled Tribes are given preference. In each appointment under the state at least ten per cent of the posts should be reserved for women for at least an initial period of 25 years. Equal wages for equal work should be provided in all employment—whether it is under the state or otherwise. Also free legal aid and advice should be made available to women on a priority basis. Without such aid, their rights already granted would remain unasserted due to ignorance and lack of funds. Several illustrations can be made to show the importance of this service.

Let us take an example, an Indian woman whose husband had sued her for divorce from Nevada (USA) failed to reply to the bill of summons within the time prescribed because she could not afford counsel to fight the case. The result was that divorce was granted with no provision for maintenance of herself and her minor son. In this case, the husband had misrepresented to the law court that there were no dependents and the court proceeded on that basis, there having been no opposition from the wife. During another case, the brothers of a woman from Punjab had sold the property inherited from their father, after fraudulently getting her thumb impression. Years later she felt that she had rights of inheritance under the Hindu Succession Act, but had not been given her share. Ignorance of the legal provisions had stopped her from asserting her rights.

(f) Setting up of Family Courts. These family courts is yet another aspect which will have to be taken in hand immediately by the legislature. In some Western countries there are special courts for adjudication of matrimonial matters. It is recommended that such courts with exclusive matrimonial jurisdiction be established immediately. These courts will render justice speedier and also ensure privacy which is necessary in such issues.

Thus, once all the legislative reforms mentioned above are effected and women are able to emerge as socially and economically independent beings, reform will have to be undertaken to amend and codify the law of marriage and divorce to enable both the parties to marry at will and to separate at will; to establish family courts to enable speedy and effective justice in matrimonial matters; to enact uniform laws of maintenance to enable the poorer of the partners to be maintained; and to provide for the woman to be the natural guardian of her child. Today the law recognises the father as the natural guardian since the mother is economically dependent and is in no position to look after the child on her own. Once economic independence comes, this position will have to change.

3

Some Facts and Figures

Constitution of India guarantees equality of men and women and prohibits any discrimination on grounds of age, sex, marital status, domicile, etc. But the hard fact is that women have ever been treated inferior to men and this has caused a great gap in the status of the two (men and women). In order to remove these differences, Article 15(4) of the Constitution makes arrangements for special provisions by the State to enhance position of women. The most remarkable among these are 73rd and 74th Constitution Amendments Acts passed in 1992 which makes compulsory 33 per cent representation of women to bodies of local self governance both in rural and urban areas. This is a significant step towards political empowerment of women.

In the coming pages of the chapter, we will see figures about various aspects of women/girl children ranging from their sex ratio to their economic and political participation and about various crimes committed against them. These cover both negative as well as positive aspects of discrimination the former ones dominating over the latter.

The chapter has been divided in two Sections I and II. Section I talks of special provisions/arrangements for women at formal level and Section II presents statistics of various aspects related to women.

I

ARRANGEMENTS

Provisions under the Constitution

The supreme law of the land, i.e., The Constitution of India not only grants equality to women but also empowers the State to adopt measures of positive discrimination in favour of women for neutralizing the cumulative socio-economic, education and political disadvantages suffered by them. Fundamental Rights, among others, ensures equality before the law, equal protection of law, prohibits discrimination against any citizen on grounds of religion, race, caste, sex or place of birth, and guarantees equality of opportunity to all citizens in matter concerning employment. Articles 14, 15, 15(3), 16, 39(a), 39(b), 39(c) and 42 of the Constitution are of specific importance in this regard.

Legislative Arrangements

Significance social legislation's relating to women are:

(a) The Maternity Benefit Act, 1961;
(b) The Medical Termination of Pregnancy Act, 1971;
(c) The Dowry Prohibition Act, 1961;
(d) The Immoral Traffic (Prevention) Act, 1986;
(e) The Indecent Representation of Women (Prohibition) Act, 1986;
(f) The Commission of Sati (Prevention) Act, 1987.

Special Provisions for Women

(a) Establishment of National Commission for Women (NCW). During the month of January 1992, the Government set-up this statutory body with a specific mandate to study and monitor all matter relating to the constitutional and legal safeguards provided for women review the present legislation to suggest amendments wherever necessary, etc.

(b) Reservation for Women in Rural and Urban Local Self-Government. In the year 1992, the 72nd and 73rd Constitution Amendment Acts passed by the national Parliament ensure one-third of the total seats for women in all elected position in local bodies whether in Panchayat or in Municipal Bodies.

(c) Special National Plan of Action for the Girl Child (1991-2000 AD). The National Plan of Action is to ensure survival, protection and developmnt of the girl child with the ultimate objective of building up a better future for the female child.

II

SAME STATISTICAL FACTS ABOUT WOMEN/GIRL CHILDREN

Table 3.1
Male and Female Population and Sex Ratio

Year	*Population (in millions)*			*Sex Ratio*
	Female	*Male*	*Total*	*(males per 100 female)*
1901	117.4	120.8	238.4	103
1911	123.7	128.4	252.1	104
1921	122.8	128.5	251.3	105
1931	135.8	142.9	279.0	105
1941	154.7	163.7	318.7	106
1951	175.6	185.5	361.1	106
1961	212.9	226.3	439.2	106
1971	264.1	284.1	548.2	108
1981	329.9	353.4	683.3	107
1991	407.1	439.2	846.3	108

Source: Registrar General, India, General Population Table 1981, Census of India 1991, Paper 2 of 1992.

Note: 1981 figure also include projected population of Assam and 1991 figures include that of Jammu and Kashmir too.

Table 3.2 (a)
Sex Ratio at the Time of Birth, India*

Duration	*Sex Ratio Male/100 Females*
1981-83	109
1982-84	110
1983-85	110
1984-86	110
1985-87	110
1986-88	110
1987-89	110
1988-90	110
1989-91	110
1990-92	111
1991-93	112

Source: Registrar General, India, New Delhi.

Note: Figures are based on the data from Sample Registration System.

* Jammu and Kashmir not included.

Chart 3.1

Growth in Population (in million) by Sex: India 1901-1991

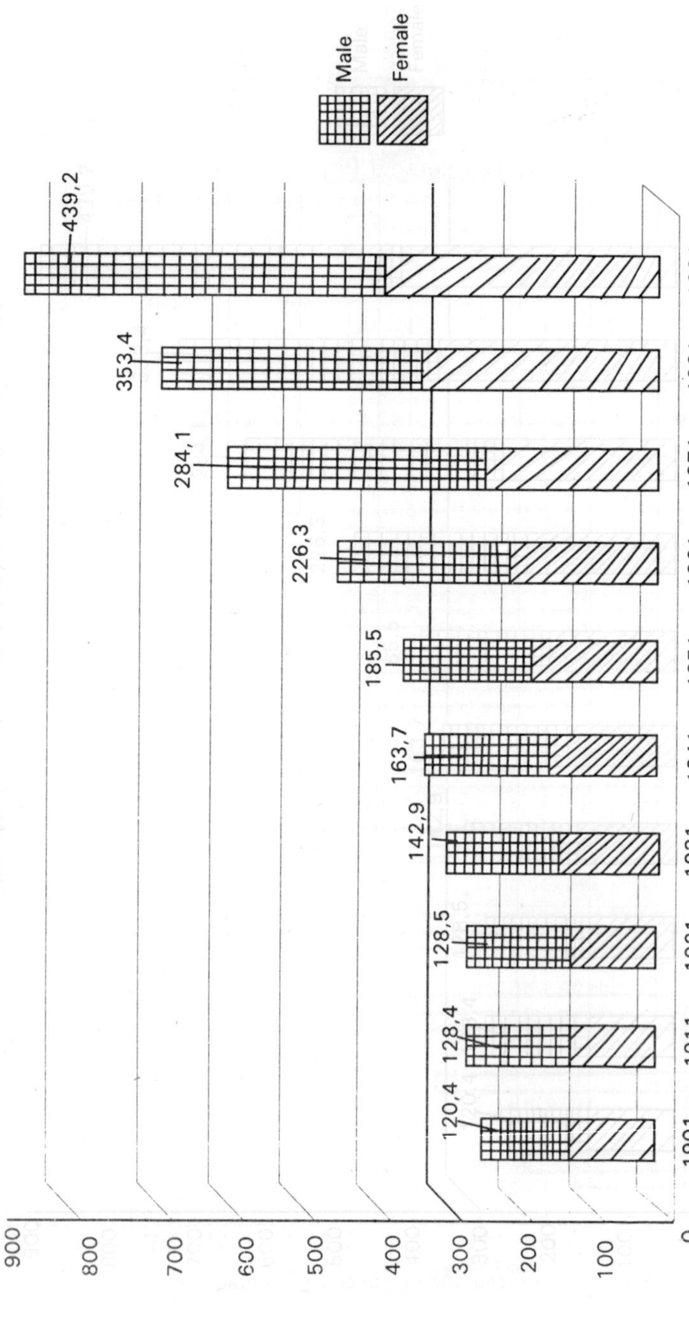

Chart 3.2
Population of Males Per Hundred Females

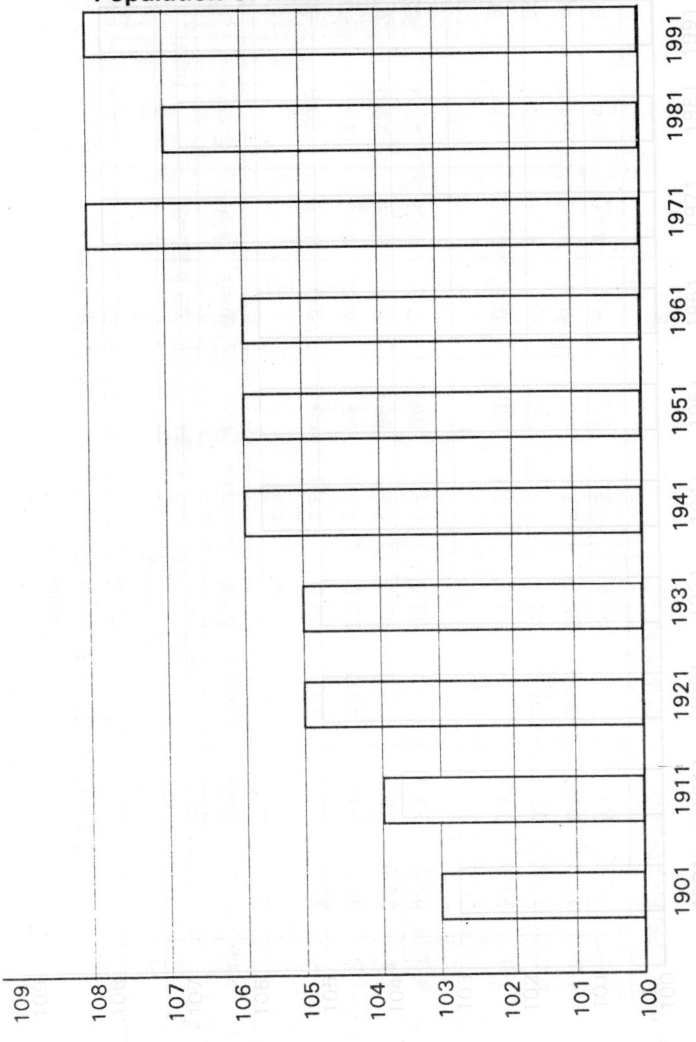

Table 3.2 (b)
Sex Ratio for the Age-Grcup 0-4 Years

Years	*Sex Ratio (Males/100 Females)*
1951	102
1961	101
1971	102
1981	102
1991	105

Source: Registrar General, India, New Delhi.

Note : Figures are based on the statistics from the Population Censuses, Social and Cultural Tables of respective Censuses.

Table 3.3
Rate of Population Growth

Duration	*Average Annual Exponential Growth Rate Per cent*		
	Female	*Male*	*Total*
1901-1911	0.52	0.61	0.56
1911-1921	– 0.07	0.01	– 0.03
1921-1931	1.01	1.06	1.04
1931-1941	1.30	1.36	1.33
1941-1951	1.27	1.25	1.25
1951-1961	1.93	1.99	1.96
1961-1971	2.15	2.27	2.21
1971-1981 @	2.22	2.18	2.20
1981-1991 +	2.10	2.17	2.14

Source: Registrar General, India, New Delhi.

@ : The 1981 Census could not be done in Assam. The Population figures for 1981 for Assam worked out by interpolation have been included.

\+ : The 1991 Census was not done in Jammu & Kashmir. The Population figure include projected population of Jammu & Kashmir having been projected by the Standing Committee of Experts on population projections (Oct 1989).

Table 3.4
Age-distribution of population (in per cent)

Age Group	1970		1980		1990		1992*		1993*		1994*	
(years)	Female	Male	Female	Male	Female	Male	Female	Male	Female	Male	Female	Male
0-4	15.2	15.7	13.2	13.3	13.2	13.3	13.0	13.2	12.8	12.9	11.9	12.0
5-9	14.3	14.2	12.6	12.7	11.7	11.7	11.8	11.9	12.0	12.2	12.8	12.9
10-14	12.1	12.5	12.0	12.2	11.6	12.1	11.0	11.2	11.0	11.3	11.4	11.8
15-19	8.7	9.2	11.1	11.3	10.2	11.0	10.2	10.9	10.2	10.9	9.5	10.2
20-24	8.1	7.5	9.3	9.5	9.6	9.4	9.9	9.7	9.7	9.6	9.5	9.0
25-29	7.6	7.2	7.2	7.4	8.1	7.9	8.1	8.1	8.3	8.1	8.7	8.3
30-34	7.1	6.6	6.3	6.0	7.0	7.0	7.1	7.0	7.0	6.9	7.2	6.9
35-39	6.0	6.1	5.8	5.5	5.9	5.8	6.1	6.0	6.2	6.2	6.3	6.5
40-44	5.2	5.5	5.4	5.2	5.0	5.0	5.0	5.0	5.0	5.0	4.9	5.1
45-49	4.0	4.4	4.5	4.5	4.4	4.3	4.5	4.4	4.5	4.4	4.4	4.4
50-54	3.7	3.9	3.8	3.9	3.7	3.7	3.7	3.7	3.6	3.6	3.5	3.6
55-59	2.4	2.5	2.8	2.9	3.0	3.1	3.1	3.1	3.1	3.0	3.0	2.8
60-64	2.5	2.4	2.4	2.3	2.3	2.1	2.3	2.2	2.4	2.3	2.6	2.5
65-69	1.3	1.3	1.6	1.5	2.0	1.8	1.9	1.7	1.9	1.7	1.9	1.7
70 +	1.8	1.6	2.0	1.8	2.2	1.8	2.3	1.9	2.4	2.1	2.5	2.3
All Ages	100.0	100.0	100.0	100.0	100.0	100.0	100.0	100.0	100.0	100.0	100.0	100.0

Source: Registrar General, India, Sample Registration System

* : Jammu & Kashmir not included.

Table 3.5
Marital Status with Population (per cent), India, 1994*

Age-Group (Years)	*Never Married*			*Married*		
	Female	*Male*	*Total*	*Female*	*Male*	*Total*
< 10	24.7	25.0	24.8	0.0	0.0	0.0
10-14	11.3	11.8	11.6	0.1	0.0	0.1
15-19	6.8	9.5	8.2	2.7	0.7	1.6
20-24	2.0	5.6	3.8	7.4	3.4	5.3
25-29	0.5	2.1	1.3	8.0	6.1	7.0
30-34	0.1	0.5	0.3	6.8	6.3	6.5
35-39	0.1	0.2	0.1	5.9	6.2	6.0
40-44	0.0	0.1	0.1	4.4	4.9	4.7
45-49	0.0	0.1	0.0	3.7	4.1	3.9
50-54	0.0	0.0	0.0	2.7	3.3	3.0
55-59	0.0	0.0	0.0	2.1	2.5	2.3
60-64	0.0	0.0	0.0	1.4	2.2	1.8
65-69	0.0	0.0	0.0	0.8	1.4	1.1
70 +	0.0	0.0	0.0	0.6	1.6	1.2
All Ages	45.6	54.9	5.4	46.6	42.7	44.6

Source : Registrar General, India, Sample Registration System.

* : Jammu & Kashmir not included.

Table 3.6
Age Based Rate of Fertility/Thousand

Age Group (Duration)	*1970*	*1980*	*1990*	*1992**	*1993**	*1994**
15-19	104.8	88.2	83.1	74.4	69.6	68.1
20-24	256.3	246.1	237.0	235.2	234.4	244.6
25-29	269.7	227.6	198.5	189.6	189.7	188.9
30-34	207.9	163.1	121.6	113.0	114.3	119.1
35-39	130.5	97.1	72.5	66.0	61.1	56.8
40-44	65.0	44.8	31.2	30.9	28.5	25.4
45-49	26.5	20.2	12.9	11.4	10.1	4.4

Source : Registrar General, India, Sample Registration System (Various Years)

* : Jammu and Kashmir are not included.

Table 3.7
India's Total Fertility Rate (TFR) and General Fertility Rate (GFR)

Period	*TFR*			*GFR*		
	Rural	*Urban*	*Total*	*Rural*	*Urban*	*Total*
1970	5.6	4.1	5.3	173.4	133.2	165.8
1980	4.7	3.4	4.4	144.9	111.4	137.9
1990	4.1	2.8	3.8	132.6	96.1	123.9
1992*	3.9	2.6	3.6	127.6	89.1	118.6
1993*	3.8	2.8	3.5	125.2	93.5	116.6
1994*	3.8	2.7	3.5	128.6	89.7	118.3

Source : Registrar General, India, Sample Registration System (different years)

* : Jammu and Kashmir are not included.

Table 3.8
Age Based Mortality Rate—India

Age Group	1970		1980		1990		1992*		1993*		1994*	
Years	Female	Male	Female	Male	Female	Male	Female	Male	Female	Male	Female	Male
0-4	55.1	51.7	43.5	4.1	27.9	24.8	28.2	24.9	24.8	22.7	24.2	23.6
5-9	5.0	4.6	4.0	3.3	2.8	2.3	3.3	2.4	2.5	2.0	2.3	1.9
10-14	2.4	2.0	1.7	1.7	1.4	1.4	1.6	1.3	1.6	1.2	1.3	1.2
15-19	3.7	2.5	2.9	2.0	2.5	1.7	2.6	1.9	2.2	1.6	2.0	1.6
20-24	4.6	2.9	3.8	2.3	3.1	2.4	3.3	2.3	3.0	2.1	3.0	2.1
25-29	4.9	3.3	4.0	2.2	2.8	2.5	3.0	2.4	3.0	2.3	2.8	2.7
30-34	5.2	4.0	3.6	3.4	2.9	3.1	3.2	3.2	2.7	2.9	3.1	3.2
35-39	5.7	4.7	4.6	4.7	3.2	3.9	3.6	3.9	2.8	4.0	3.4	3.7
40-44	5.9	8.0	5.5	7.2	4.4	5.7	4.5	5.6	3.9	5.1	4.0	5.5
45-49	8.0	11.9	7.3	9.6	6.3	9.0	5.6	9.3	5.3	8.0	5.7	8.5
50-54	12.9	17.9	10.4	14.6	9.0	13.2	9.7	13.1	9.0	13.2	8.9	12.9
55-59	16.5	25.5	16.7	21.5	14.4	20.9	15.4	20.1	14.4	20.6	12.3	19.6
60-64	31.4	42.7	27.3	35.0	23.0	28.9	24.6	32.4	24.2	30.7	22.6	31.2
65-69	41.5	8.0	41.2	59.0	37.8	47.3	40.4	47.4	34.6	46.2	31.5	45.1
70 +	104.0	117.1	85.3	98.5	79.4	91.4	87.7	95.7	81.1	94.5	81.3	94.2
All ages	15.6	15.8	12.4	12.4	9.6	9.7	10.2	10.0	9.1	9.5	8.9	9.6

Source: Registrar General, India, Sample Registration System (Various Years).

* : Jammu and Kashmir are not included.

Table 3.9
Mean Age at the Time of Marriage—India

Year	*Female*	*Male*
1951	15.4	19.9
1961	16.1	22.3
1971	17.1	22.7
1981	17.9	23.3
1992*	19.5	X
1993*	19.6	X
1994*	19.4	X

Source : Registrar General, India, Population of India : ESCAP Country Monograph No. 10 and female age at marriage Census of India Occasional paper No. 7 of 1988.

Note : Figures for 1951, 1961, 1971 and 1981 are singulate mean age at marriage based on data of population census. 1992 and 1993 figures are the mean age at effective marriage based derived from Sample Registration System.

* : Jammu and Kashmir not included.

X : Not available.

Table 3.10
Female Headed Families and Their Average Size

Year	*Rural/ Urban*	*Families (in millions)*	*Female Headed families (in millions)*	*Per cent Female Headed Families*	*Average Size of Female Headed Families*
1984	Rural	100.53	9.70	9.65	3.49
	Urban	33.99	2.95	8.68	3.72
1988	Rural	108.36	11.22	10.36	3.30
	Urban	34.28	3.40	9.92	3.50
1994	Rural	119.53	11.64	9.74	3.20
	Urban	43.45	4.59	10.57	3.20

Source: National Sample Survey Organisation, Report No. 351, 1989 and Survekashna, Special Number, September, 1990.

Note : Figure for 1984, 1988 and 1994 are based on 39th round (January-June, 1984), 43rd round (July 1987-June 1988) and 50th round (July 93-June 94) respectively.

Table 3.11
Distribution (Per cent) of Migrants in Various Migration Streams

Sex	*Period*	*Rural to urban*	*Rural to urban*	*Urban to rural*	*Urban to rural*	*Total Migrants*
	Rural					
Female	1961	81.3	9.7	5.8	3.2	100.0
	1971	77.7	10.5	6.7	5.1	100.0
	1981	73.3	12.5	8.7	5.5	100.0
	1991	72.2	13.5	8.8	5.5	100.0
Male	1961	56.7	25.7	13.0	4.6	100.0
	1971	53.5	26.0	14.0	6.5	100.0
	1981	45.6	30.0	17.4	7.0	100.0
	1991	43.4	31.6	17.8	7.2	100.0

Source: Registrar General, India, New Delhi.

Note (a) : Table excludes persons who were born outside India.

(b) : 1981 data exclude Assam State where 1981 Census could not be conducted.

(c) : 1961, 1971 and 1981 figures are based on place of birth and excludes the unclassifiable data.

Table 3.12
Distribution (Per cent) of Migrants by Reasons, 1981

Reasons for Migration	*Female*	*Male*
Employment	1.9	31.0
Education	0.9	5.3
Family shifted	14.5	30.2
Marriage	72.4	3.1
Others	10.3	30.4

Source: (i) Registrar General, India, Census of India 1981, Series - 1, India, part V—A & B.

(ii) Migration Tables.

Table 3.13
Infants, Mortality Rate

Period	*Female*	*Male*	*Total*
1985	98	96	97
1986	97	96	96
1987	96	95	95
1988	93	95	94
1989	90	92	91
1990	81	78	80
1991*	80	81	80
1992*	80	79	79
1993*	75	73	74
1994*	73	75	74

Source : Registrar General, India, Sample Registration System (Various Years).
* : Jammu and Kashmir not included.

Table 3.14
Expectation of Life at the Time of Birth (Years)—India

Duration	*Female*	*Male*	*Total*
1901-11	23.3	22.6	22.9
1911-21	20.9	19.4	20.1
1921-31	26.6	26.9	26.8
1931-41	31.4	32.1	31.8
1941-51	31.7	32.4	32.1
1951-61	40.6	41.9	41.3
1961-71	44.7	46.4	45.6
1970-75	49.0	50.5	49.7
1976-80	52.1	52.5	52.3
1981-85	55.7	55.4	55.4
1986-90	58.1	57.7	57.7
1987-91*	58.6	58.1	58.3
1988-92*	59.0	58.6	58.7
1989-93*	59.7	59.0	59.4

Source : Registrar General, India, Census Actuarial Report and SRS based reduced Life Tables 1986-90 (Occasional Paper No. 1 of 1994).

Notes : Statistics for 1901-11 to 1961-71 are based on Census Actuarial Reports and for 1970-75 onwards on the basis of estimates from Sample Registration System.

* : Jammu and Kashmir are not included.

Chart 3.3
Infant Mortality Rate by Sex : India, 1985-1994

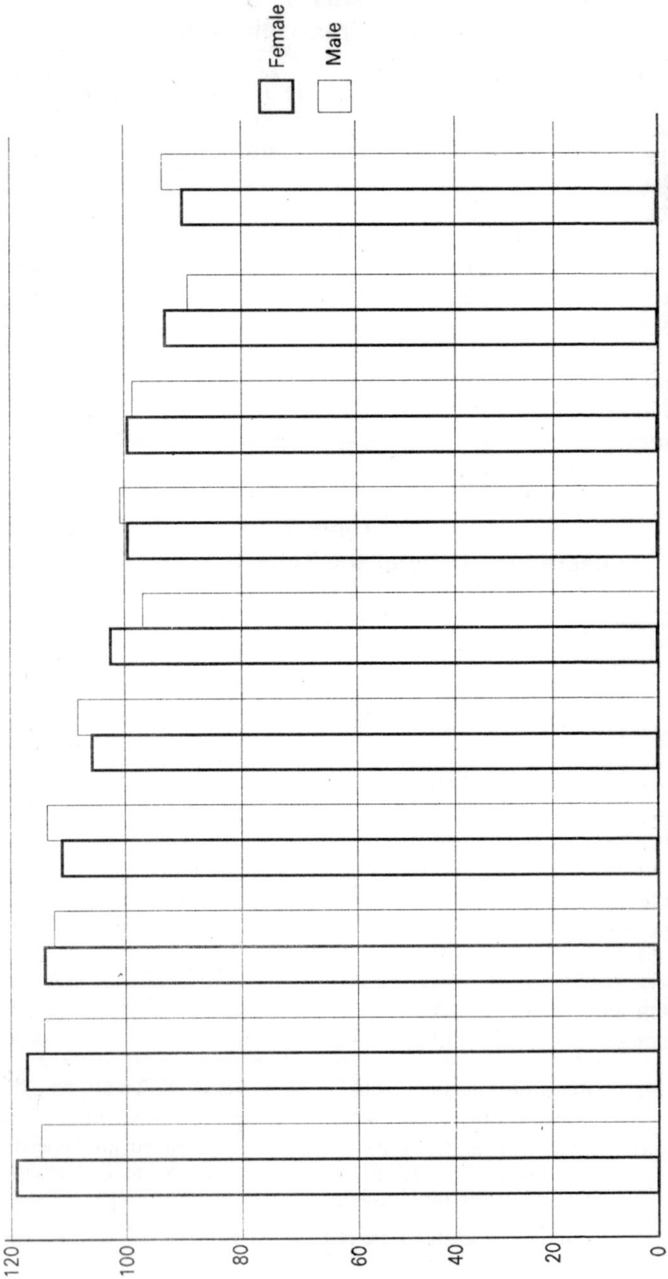

Chart 3.4
Expectation of Life at Birth

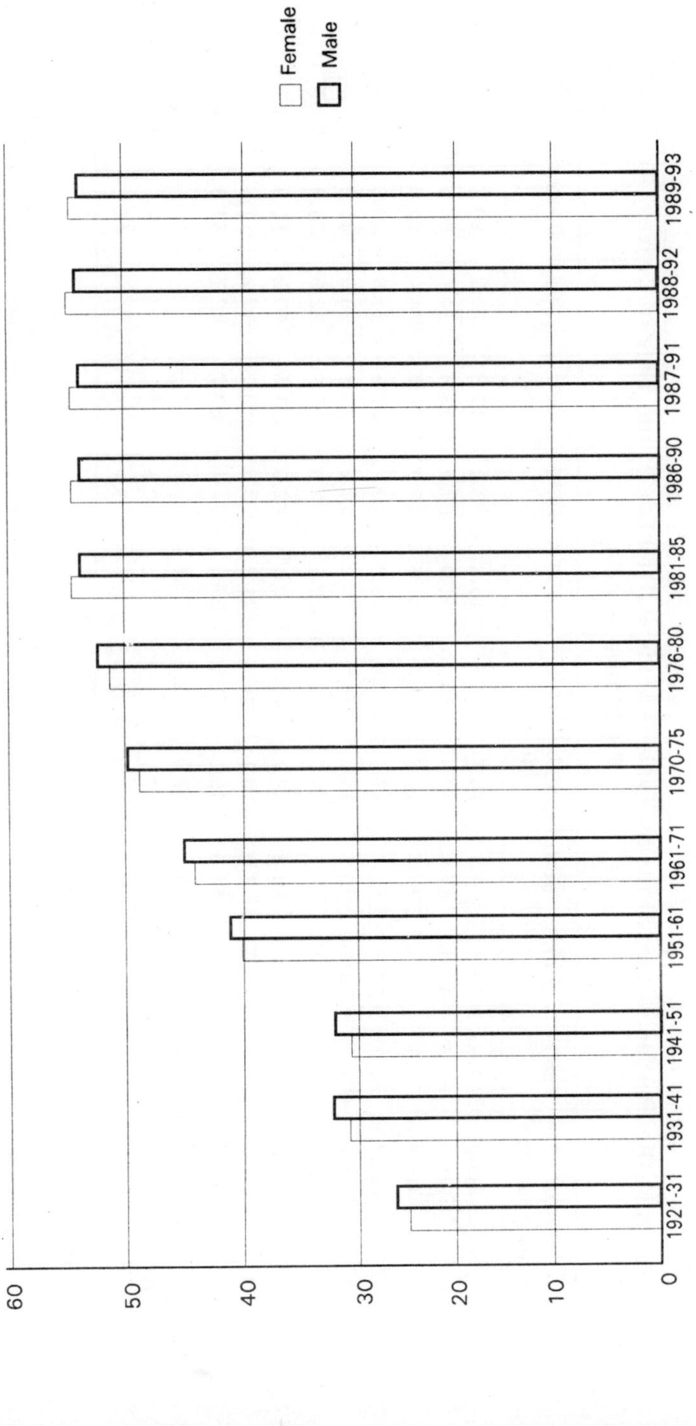

Table 3.15

Per cent Distribution of Live Births by Type of Medical Attention at the Time of Delivery Received by the Mother—India

Year / Type of Facilities		1980	1985	1986	1987	1988	1989	1990	1991+	1992+	1993+	1994+
	Rural	11.0	13.3	14.3	14.7	14.9	15.2	16.2	17.6	18.0	20.2	16.9
I	Urban	37.7	47.4	47.8	48.7	49.7	51.0	52.8	53.8	54.8	56.5	54.7
	Total	17.4	19.9	20.7	21.2	21.5	21.8	22.9	24.3	24.4	24.5	22.3
	Rural	13.2	17.2	17.7	17.8	18.6	19.3	20.2	20.8	21.8	23.3	26.7
T	Urban	27.3	24.9	25.0	25.5	24.5	25.7	26.1	26.9	28.0	31.6	33.8
	Total	16.7	18.7	19.1	19.3	19.7	20.5	21.3	21.9	22.9	24.3	27.7
	Rural	55.4	50.0	48.3	49.7	63.6	62.1	62.0	61.5	60.2	56.5	56.4
U	Urban	26.5	19.5	18.6	18.1	24.1	21.8	20.6	19.2	17.2	11.8	11.5
	Total	48.4	44.1	42.6	43.6	56.2	54.6	54.4	53.7	52.7	51.3	50.0
	Rural	20.4	19.5	19.7	17.8	2.9	3.4	1.5	*	*	*	*
O	Urban	8.5	8.2	8.6	7.7	1.7	1.5	0.6	*	*	*	*
	Total	17.5	17.3	17.6	15.9	2.6	3.1	1.4	*	*	*	*

Source: Registrar General, India, Sample Registration System (Different Years)

I : Agencies like hospitals, maternity/nursing homes, health centres, etc.

T : Delivery conducted in the home by doctor, trained dai, trained midwife, qualified nurse, etc.

U : Delivery conducted in the home by untraind village dai or other unqualified professional functionary

O : Delivery conducted in the home by women relative and others excluding the above

* : Included in category U.

Table 3.16

Percentage Distribution of Deaths Due to Reasons Related to Child-Birth and Pregnancy Recorded in the Survey of Causes of Deaths

Reasons	*Number*			*Per cent*		
	1989	*1992*	*1993*	*1989*	*1992*	*1993*
Abortion	22	37	45	10.9	13.7	11.7
Toxaemia	16	34	49	7.9	12.6	12.8
Anaemia	41	53	78	20.3	19.6	20.3
Bleeding of Pregnancy and Puerperium	48	68	87	23.8	25.2	22.6
Malposition of child leading to death of mother	22	23	21	10.9	8.5	5.5
Puerperial Sepsis	12	31	48	5.9	11.5	12.5
Not Classifiable	41	24	56	20.3	8.9	14.6
Total	202	270	384	100.0	100.0	100.0

Source : Registrar General, India, Survey of Causes of Deaths 1989 and 1992.

Table 3.17

Routine Average Intake of Energy and Proteins Against Recommended Intake by Age/Sex Groups, 1996

Age in Years	*Sex*	*Activity*	*Energy (Kcals/day)*		*Proteins (g/day)*	
			Intake	*RDI*	*Intake*	*RDI*
1-3	Boys and Girls		779	1240	21	22
4-6	Boys and Girls		1165	1690	31	30
7-9	Boys and Girls		1401	1950	37	41
10-12	Boys		1654	2190	44	54
	Girls		1564	1970	41	57
13-15	Boys		1991	2450	50	70
	Girls		1892	2060	49	65
16-18	Boys		2378	2640	61	78
	Girls		2066	2060	51	63
> 18	Male	Sedentary	2292	2425	59	60
		Moderate	2515	2875	65	60
> 18	Females (NPNL)	Sedentary	1954	1875	50	50
		Moderate	2137	2225	53	50

Source : From NNMB-NCEAR linked surveys conducted during 1993-94 in rural areas of Kerala, Tamil Nadu, Karnataka, Andhra Pradesh, Maharashtra, Madhya Pradesh, Gujarat and Orissa.

RDI : Suggested Intakes.

Table 3.18
Family Planning Adopters by Methods

(Figures in thousands)

Period	*Sterilisation*		*I.U.D. Inser-tions*	*Equivalent C.C. users*	*Equivalent oral pill users**	*Total Acceptors*
	Vasec-tomy	*Tube-ctomy*				
1970-71	879	451	476	1963	-	3769
1975-76	1438	1230	607	3495	32	6804
1980-81	439	1614	628	3718	91	6490
1985-86	639	4262	3274	9387	1358	18920
1986-87	810	4234	3935	9825	1829	20632
1987-88	754	4186	4356	11342	2064	22702
1988-89	617	4061	4851	12422	2416	24368
1989-90	342	3847	4942	14159	2793	26082
1990-91	255	3871	5370	14735	3125	27356
1991-92	174	3916	4386	13875	3366	25717
1992-93	150	4136	4740	15004	3001	27031
1993-94	150	4347	6017	17283	4302	32099
1994-95	144	4436	6702	17707	4873	33862

Source: Department of Family Welfare, Ministry of Health and Family Welfare

* : Programme was started in November, 1974

IUD : Intra-Uterine Device

CC : Conventional Contraceptives

Note: 1. The equivalent CC users is reached by dividing the offtake of condoms, diaphragms, jelly/cream, tubes and foam tablets by 72,2,7 (3 in the case of Deflin cream of increased capacity and efficacy, i.e., 100 gms with a dosage of 2.5 ml from the year 1987-88) and 72 respectively needed on an average by a couple in a year to give full protection.

2. Equivalent Oral Pill users is reached by dividing the offtake of Oral Pills Packet by 13 which is required on an average by a couple in a year to give total protection.

Table 3.19
Number of Couples (in per cent) Effectively Protected by Different Family Planning Methods

Period	*Protected Couples ('000)*	*Percentage of Couples Protected by*				
		Sterilisation	*IUD*	*Oral Pill*	*CC*	*All methods*
1970-71	94489	8.0	1.4	—	1.0	10.4
1975-76	105239	14.2	1.1	—	1.7	17.0
1980-81	116033	20.1	1.0	0.1	1.6	22.8
1985-86	129432	26.5	3.7	1.1	3.6	34.9
1986-87	132572	27.9	4.5	1.4	3.7	37.5
1987-88	135710	29.0	5.2	1.5	4.2	39.9
1988-89	138850	29.8	5.9	1.7	4.5	41.9
1989-90	141990	30.1	6.3	1.9	5.0	43.3
1990-91	145140	30.3	6.7	2.1	5.1	44.1
1991-92	148430	30.3	6.3	2.2	4.7	43.6
1992-93	151720	30.3	6.3	2.0	4.9	43.5
1993-94	155020	30.3	6.8	2.7	5.6	45.4
1994-95	158310	30.2	7.2	5.4	3.0	45.8

Source: Based on figures of Department of Family Welfare, Ministry of Health and Family Welfare.

IUD : Intra Uterine Devices.

CC : Conventional Contraceptives.

Table 3.20
Participation Rate in Work Force (in Per cent) by Sex

Period	*Rural*		*Urban*	
	Female	*Male*	*Female*	*Male*
1972-73	31.8	54.5	13.4	50.1
1977-78	33.1	55.2	15.6	50.8
1983	34.0	54.7	15.1	51.2
1987-88	32.3	53.9	15.2	50.6
1993-94	32.8	55.3	15.5	52.1

Source: National Sample Survey Organisation, New Delhi.

Note : Data for all the years are based on usual status approach and includes principal status and subsidiary status workers of all ages.

Chart 3.5

Protection under Family Planning in India

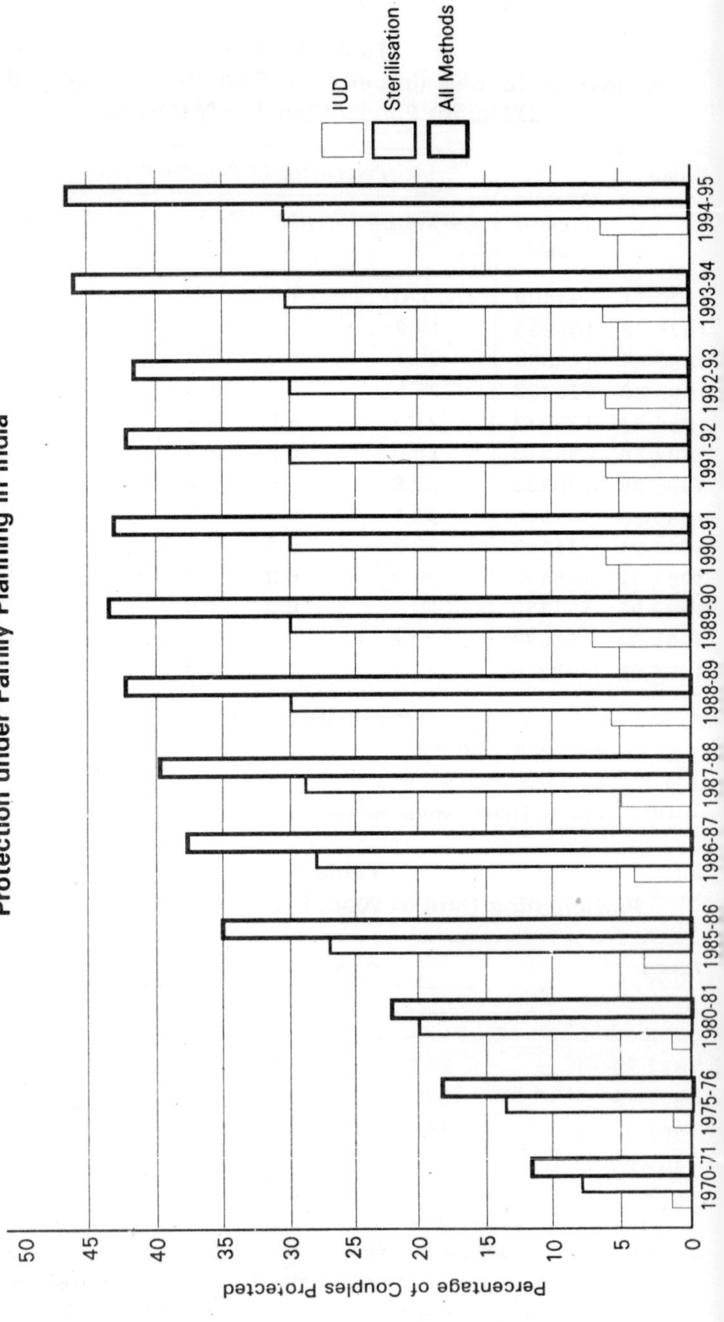

Table 3.21
Participation Rates Labour Force (in per cent) by Age

Duration	Age-Group											
	5-14		15-29		30-44		45-59		60 & above		Total	
	Female	Male	Female	Male	Female	Male	Female	Male	Female	Male	Female	Male
					Rural							
1977-78	9.1	13.1	39.7	86.1	49.2	99.0	41.6	95.9	16.0	64.6	30.5	63.7
1983	9.0	11.6	37.2	82.8	46.0	98.6	40.8	95.2	15.6	64.2	29.1	62.6
1987-88	6.3	7.4	36.9	79.7	47.6	98.7	42.2	95.7	16.3	64.9	29.2	61.4
1993-94	5.5	5.9	32.2	77.7	42.7	98.8	40.1	96.4	17.3	68.3	27.2	63.0
					Urban							
1977-78	3.8	5.8	21.9	73.6	27.2	98.9	24.1	93.6	10.5	50.5	17.1	60.1
1983	3.0	5.6	17.2	72.9	23.9	98.6	23.0	92.8	11.6	48.8	14.8	60.3
1987-88	2.4	4.2	17.2	69.7	23.9	98.7	22.4	93.1	9.3	46.6	14.6	59.6
1993-94	1.9	3.3	16.5	67.4	23.6	98.4	23.2	93.4	9.2	43.0	14.8	60.1

Source : National Samples Survey Organisation, New Delhi.

Note : The statistics relate to the usual principal status.

Table 3.22
Rates* of Unemployment (Per cent) by Age

Period	Age-Group									
	15-29		30-44		45-59		60 & above		Total	
	Female	Male	Female	Male	Female	Male	Female	Male	Female	Male
					Rural					
1977-78	8.5	4.9	4.1	0.6	3.0	0.4	2.0	0.3	5.5	2.2
1983	2.8	4.7	0.5	0.5	0.4	0.2	0.6	0.2	1.4	2.1
1987-88	5.4	6.2	2.4	0.9	1.9	0.5	1.8	0.5	3.5	2.8
1993-94	3.2	4.8	0.5	0.4	0.1	0.1	0.2	0.0	1.4	2.0
					Urban					
1977-78	31.4	14.0	10.4	1.3	4.8	1.0	2.2	1.5	17.8	6.5
1983	15.5	12.2	2.1	1.4	0.7	0.7	9.1	0.6	6.9	5.9
1987-88	18.8	13.6	3.5	1.2	1.1	0.7	1.1	1.1	8.5	6.1
1993-94	19.4	10.8	2.7	1.1	0.4	0.3	0.4	0.3	8.3	4.5

Source: National Sample Survey Organisation, New Delhi.

* : The percentage of unemployed in total labour force

Note: 1. The figures of various rounds relate to the usual principal status

2. Total includes data for ages 5-14 years also

0.0 : Negligible.

Table 3.23
Distribution of Main Workers Except Cultivators and Agricultural Labourers According to Various Occupational Categories, 1981

Code	*Occupational category*	*Percent Distribution*		*Per cent share of Different occupations in female employment*
		Female	*Male*	
0–1	Professional, Technical and concerned workers	20.5	79.5	15.6
2	Administrative and managerial employees	2.3	97.7	0.6
3	Clerical and other concerned workers	6.4	93.6	5.1
4	Sales workers	6.7	93.3	7.3
5	Service workers	17.9	82.1	8.8
6	Farmers, Fisherman, Hunters, Loggers and other related workers	17.0	83.0	13.0
7-8-9	Production and other related workers, Transport equipment operators and Labourers	12.8	87.2	46.5
	Miscellaneous	12.5	87.5	3.1

Source: Registrar General, India, New Delhi.

Table 3.24
Division of Main Workers by Industrial Groups

Industrial Group		*Per cent of workers*			
		1981		*1991*	
		Female	*Male*	*Female*	*Male*
I	Cultivators	33.09	43.71	34.22	39.63
II	Farming Labourers	46.34	19.57	44.93	21.05
III	Livestock, forestry, fishing, Hunting and plantations Orchards and related activities	1.83	2.37	1.60	1.99
IV	Mining and quarrying	0.35	0.63	0.34	0.70
	PRIMARY	81.61	66.28	81.09	63.38
V(a)	Manufacturing, processing, Servicing and repairs in household sector	4.57	3.18	3.53	2.09
V(b)	Manufacturing, processing, Servicing and repairs in other than households sector	3.60	8.91	3.88	8.89
VI	Constructions	0.87	1.87	0.66	2.32
	SECONDARY	9.04	13.96	8.07	13.30
VII	Trade and Commerce	2.04	7.41	2.26	8.98
VIII	Transport, storage and Communication	0.37	3.36	0.32	3.54
IX	Other services	6.94	8.99	8.26	10.80
	TERTIARY	9.35	19.76	10.84	23.32
	All	100.00	100.00	100.00	100.00

Source: Registrar General, India, Census of India 1991, Final Population Totals Paper 2 of 1992.

Chart 3.6
Sectoral Categorisation of Workers by Sex: India 1991

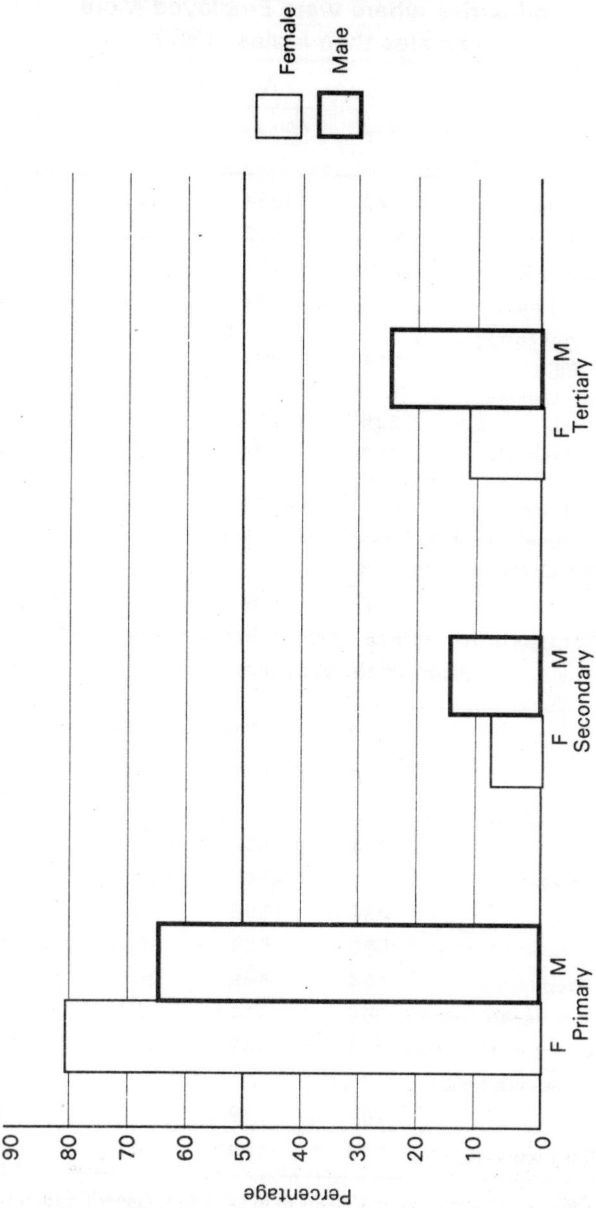

Table 3.25
Industries where were Employed More Females than Males, 1981

Industrial sector	*NIC Group*	*Number of workers in Hundreds*		
		Female	*Male*	*Per cent female*
Bidi Manufacture	226	8934	7127	56
Cotton Textiles, n.e.c.	239	1920	1669	53
Cotton Spinning (Charkha)	233	872	519	63
Manufacture of matches	317	764	418	65
Cashewnut Processing Tobacco stemming,	214	267	76	78
redrying, etc. Canning, preserving and	225	224	167	57
Processing of fish etc	203	128	109	54

Source: Registrar General, India, Census of India, General Economic Tables
NIC : National Industrial Classification, 1968
n.e.c : Not Elsewhere Classfied.

Table 3.26
Occupations where Female Workers were More than Male Workers, 1981

Industrial sector	*NCO Group*	*Number of workers in Hundreds*		
		Female	*Male*	*Female (per cent)*
Bidi Makers	784	8862	6754	57
Domestic servants	531	4050	4024	50
Nurses	084	1556	116	93
Ayahs, Nurses and Maids	530	524	67	89
Teachers, Preprimary	154	449	203	69
Midwives and health visitor's	085	414	82	83
Food Preservers and canners	773	247	1477	14
Tobacco Preservers Maids and related	781	219	101	68
Housekeeping workers n.e.c.	539	159	81	66

Source: Registrar General, India, Census of India, 1981, General Economic Tables.
Note : The statistics for 1981 exclude Assam.
NCO : National Classification of Occupations, 1968.

Table 3.27
Educational Levels of Labour Force

Educational competence	*1983* Female	*1983* Male	*1987-88* Female	*1987-88* Male	*1993-94* Female	*1993-94* Male
			Rural			
Illiterate	86.2	52.1	82.3	48.3	79.0	43.7
Literate Upto primary	10.2	29.2	12.0	29.6	13.7	29.0
Middle	2.1	10.8	3.2	11.6	3.9	13.5
Secondary	1.2	6.4	2.0	8.4	2.7	10.9
Graduate and Above	0.3	1.5	0.4	2.1	0.7	2.8
			Urban			
Illiterate	56.5	21.7	51.8	19.6	44.5	17.9
Literate Upto primary	17.5	30.1	19.0	30.5	17.7	25.4
Middle	6.3	18.1	7.3	16.4	8.1	17.5
Secondary	11.6	19.9	12.3	21.8	15.1	24.5
Graduate and Above	8.0	10.1	9.6	11.7	14.6	14.6

Source: National Sample Survey Organisation, New Delhi.

Note : Data relate to usual status of individuals and are for popularion aged 15 years and above.

Table 3.28
Participation of Women in Employment Generated under Poverty Alleviation Programmes in Rural Parts

Duration	*Total Number of Families assisted under self-employment programmes (IRDP + TRYSEM)* million families*	*Percent Share of Women*	*Total Number of Man days generated under wage programmes (NREP + RLEGPT JRY + EAS)** (million man days)*	*Percent Share Women*
(1)	*(2)*	*(3)*	*(4)*	*(5)*
1985-86	3.2	11.52	564.0	9.67
1986-87	3.9	16.61	701.5	15.47
1987-88	4.4	20.77	674.9	18.05
1988-89	4.0	24.53	691.5	20.75
1989-90	3.6	27.00	864.4	22.04
1990-91	3.1	32.29	873.8	24.64

(Contd.)

(Contd.)

(1)	*(2)*	*(3)*	*(4)*	*(5)*
1991-92	2.8	35.20	809.2	24.01
1992-93	2.3	35.22	782.1	24.69
1993-94	2.8	35.47	1075.3	22.82
1994-95	2.5	35.42	1225.7	22.25
1995-96	2.3	34.16	1239.4	29.67
1996-97	1.7	31.39	730.1	30.52

Source : Department of Rural Employment and Poverty Alleviation, Ministry of Rural Areas and Employment, New Delhi

*IRDP : Integrated Rural Development Programme

TRYSEM: Training of Rural Youth for Self Employment

**NREP : National Rural Employment Programme (during 1985-89)

RLEGP : Rural Landless Employment Guarantee Programme (during 1985-89)

JRY : Jawahar Rozgar Yojana (since 1989-90)

EAS : Employment Assurance Scheme (since 1993-94).

Table 3.29
Improvement in Literacy

Period	*Per cent of Literates to total Population*		
	Female	*Male*	*Total*
1951 +	8.86	27.16	18.33
1961	15.34	40.40	28.31
1971	21.97	45.95	34.45
1981#	29.75	56.37	43.56
1991 +	39.29	64.13	52.21

Source: Registrar General, Census of India 1991, Paper 1 of 1991, Provisional Population Tables and Paper 2 of 1992, Final Population Table

\# : Assam not included

\+ : Jammu and Kashmir not included

Note : Literacy rate for 1951, 1961 and 1971 relate to population aged 5 years and above while rate for 1981 and 1991 relate to the population aged 7 years and above.

Table 3.30
Age and Sex-based Literacy Levels (Per cent)

Age group (Years)	1961			1971			1981			1991*		
	Female	Male	Total	Female	Male	Total	Female	Male	Total	Female	Male	Total
5-9	14.4	25.0	19.8	18.9	27.2	23.1	25.6	34.7	30.2	51.0	62.6	56.9
10-14	28.4	54.4	42.3	38.2	59.8	49.6	44.8	66.8	56.4	59.7	77.0	68.8
15-19	23.8	52.0	38.4	37.7	63.3	51.3	43.3	66.1	55.4	54.9	75.3	65.8
20-24	18.2	49.8	33.6	28.7	60.7	44.7	37.1	66.6	52.0	43.8	71.6	57.8
25-34	13.9	42.5	28.5	19.3	50.1	34.8	28.9	60.7	45.1	36.6	64.7	50.8
35 and above	7.7	35.3	22.2	10.7	38.0	25.2	14.5	44.7	30.3	22.0	52.6	30.1
All ages	13.0	34.5	24.0	18.7	39.5	29.5	24.8	46.9	36.2	39.3	64.1	52.2
5 and above	15.3	40.4	28.3	22.0	45.9	34.5	28.5	53.5	41.4	39.1	64.0	52.0
10 and above	15.5	43.6	30.1	22.6	49.9	36.8	29.0	57.0	43.6	37.8	64.1	51.5
15 and above	13.2	41.5	27.8	19.4	47.7	34.1	25.7	54.9	40.8	33.7	61.6	48.2

Source: Registrar General, India, Census of India (Various Years).

Note : For 1981, Statistics exclude Assam state where 1981 Census could not be conducted

* : Based on population 7 years and above. Age-Group 5 and above also excludes age not stated. 1990-91 data also excluded Jammu and Kashmir since the census was not held in that State.

Table 3.31
Division of Population on the Basis of Education (Per cent)

Educational Qualifications	*1971*		*1981*	
	Female	*Male*	*Female*	*Male*
Illiterate	81.3	60.6	75.2	53.1
Literate without educational level	6.8	12.2	8.6	14.4
Primary	7.1	13.7	8.1	13.6
Middle	3.0	7.5	4.2	8.4
Matriculate/Secondary	1.5	4.9	2.3	5.9
Higher Secondary/ Intermediate/Pre-University	—	—	0.8	2.2
Non-technical diploma or certificate not equal to degree	—	0.1	—	—
Technical diploma or certificate not equal to degree	—	0.1	0.1	0.3
Graduate and above	0.3	0.9	0.7	2.1
All Levels	100.0	100.0	100.0	100.0

Source: Registrar General, India, Census of India, Social and Cultural Tables (1971 and 1981)

Note : The data for 1981 exclude Assam where the census could not be conducted.

Table 3.32
Gross Enrolment as Percentage to the Population of the Concerned Age/Sex

Period	*Age (6-10 yrs)*			*Age (11-13 yrs)*		
	Female	*Male*	*Total*	*Female*	*Male*	*Total*
1950-51	24.8	60.6	43.1	4.6	20.6	12.9
1955-56	31.0	68.2	50.0	6.6	24.6	15.9
1960-61	41.4	82.6	62.4	11.3	33.2	22.5
1965-66	56.5	96.3	76.7	17.0	44.2	30.8
1970-71	59.1	92.6	76.4	20.8	46.5	34.2

(Contd.)

1975-76	62.0	95.7	79.3	23.8	47.0	35.6
1980-81	64.1	95.8	80.5	28.6	54.3	41.9
1982-83	69.7	103.0	86.8	31.8	58.3	45.5
1983-84	72.6	106.9	90.2	33.2	60.6	47.3
1984-85	76.0	110.3	93.6	34.9	61.3	48.1
1985-86	79.2	111.1	95.6	35.3	61.8	49.0
1986-87	79.2	111.8	96.0	39.0	66.5	53.1
1987-88	81.6	113.1	97.9	40.6	68.9	55.1
1989-90	81.3	109.7	95.9	42.2	72.0	57.4
1990-91	85.6	115.3	101.0	46.1	73.4	60.1
1991-92P	88.1	116.6	102.7	47.4	74.2	60.2
1992-93P	92.7	118.1	105.7	53.8	80.5	67.5
1993-94P	92.9	115.3	104.5	55.2	79.3	67.7
1994-95P	92.6	114.8	104.0	55.0	79.0	67.2
1995-96P	93.3	114.5	104.3	55.0	79.5	67.6

Source: Department of Education Ministry of Human Resource Development, Education in India, Vol. I.

P : Provisional.

Table 3.33

Number of Female Students 100 Male Students Enrolled in Schools and Colleges

Period	*Primary (I-V) Standard*	*Middle (VI-VIII) Standard*	*Secondary (IX-X) Standard*	*Colleges and Universities for General education*
1950-51	39	18	16	11
1955-56	44	25	21	14
1960-61	48	32	23	21
1965-66	57	37	30	25
1970-71	60	41	35	27
1975-76	62	46	39	39
1979-80	62	48	41	42
1980-81	63	49	44	42
1981-82	63	49	43	46
1982-83	64	51	41	46
1983-84	64	51	43	46
1984-85	65	52	44	49
1985-86	67	54	44	51

(Contd.)

1986-87	69	54	46	51
1987-88P	69	55	47	46 @
1988-89P	70	55	50	46 @
1989-90	70	56	50	48 @
1990-91	71	58	50	50 @
1991-92	72	62	52	48 @
1992-93P	74	63	53	50 @
1993-94P	75	65	55	50 @
1994-95P	75	64	55	..
1995-96P	76	64	57	..

Source: Department of Education, Ministry of Human Resource Development, New Delhi

P : Provisional

@ : Does not include professional, technical and special courses.

Table 3.34
Number of Females per 100 Males in University Education in Leading Disciplines

Discipline Period	*Arts*	*Science*	*Commerce*	*Engineering Tech.*	*Medicines*
1950-51	15.4	–	0.5	0.3	18.5
1955-56	19.5	–	0.7	0.2	18.9
1960-61	22.3	–	2.8	0.4	25.8
1965-66	36.9	–	4.9	2.2	29.4
1970-71	50.2	21.2	12.8	1.1	26.5
1975-76	55.8	27.3	16.8	1.8	22.9
1979-80	61.1	38.3	15.2	3.7	28.3
1980-81	59.7	38.9	18.5	4.6	29.2
1981-82	64.1	41.4	21.2	5.1	32.3
1982-83	63.4	42.2	22.9	5.3	34.8
1983-84	62.6	42.1	24.3	5.7	37.3
1984-85	66.8	45.8	25.9	7.5	39.7
1985-86	66.7	47.9	28.1	8.1	41.6
1986-87	65.6	47.5	29.2	8.4	43.4
1987-88P	64.5	44.3	27.9	8.6+	48.4+
1988-89P	63.9	47.1	28.5	8.6+	48.6+
1989-90P	63.3	56.8	30.0	11.9+	52.6+

(Contd.)

(Contd.)

1990-91P	65.5	58.3	31.6	12.2+	52.1+
1991-92P	65.3	45.7	33.8	9.5+	53.3+
1992-93P	64.7	48.0	35.9	11.9	52.4
1993-94P	64.7	49.1	36.5	12.5	57.5
1994-95P	66.7	49.8	39.5	15.1	51.2
1995-96P	71.8	54.9	41.6	16.6	52.7

Source: Department of Education, Ministry of Human Resource Development, New Delhi.

+ : Only for graduation level, not post graduate

P : Provisional

Note : Arts and Science figures have been combined for the years 1955-56, 1960-61 and 1965-66.

Table 3.35
Drop-out Rate (Per cent) at Various Stages of School Education

Year	*Primary (I-V Standards)*		*Elementary (I-VIII Standards)*		*Secondary (I-X Standards)*	
	Girls	*Boys*	*Girls*	*Boys*	*Girls*	*Boys*
1960-61	70.93	61.74	*	*	*	*
1965-66	70.49	63.17	*	*	*	*
1970-71	70.92	64.48	83.40	74.60	*	*
1975-76	66.18	60.21	82.80	74.30	*	*
1980-81	62.50	56.20	79.40	68.00	86.60	79.80
1981-82	57.30	51.10	77.70	68.50	86.81	79.44
1982-83	56.30	49.40	74.96	66.04	86.24	78.21
1983-84	53.96	47.83	75.27	66.10	84.79	76.41
1988-89	49.69	46.74	68.31	59.38	79.46	72.68
1989-90	50.35	46.50	68.75	61.00	77.72	70.99
1990-91	45.97	40.10	65.13	59.12	76.96	67.50
1991-92	44.30	40.30	62.40	56.10	76.30	69.60
1992-93P	43.02	40.07	60.06	53.99	74.69	68.15
1993-94P	39.05	36.07	56.78	49.95	74.54	68.41

(Contd.)

(Contd.)

1994-95P	37.79	35.18	56.53	50.02	73.78	67.15
1995-96P	41.31	37.92	61.70	54.99	74.07	66.36

Source: Department of Education, Ministry of Human Resource Development, Education in India, (Different Years).

Note : Total dropout during a course (stage) has been taken as per cent of intake in the first year of the course (stage), Primary, Middle and Secondary stages consist of standards I-V, I-VIII, I-X.

P : Provisional

* : Not Available.

Table 3.36
Number of Female Teachers Per 100 Male Teachers at Various Levels of Education

Duration	*Primary School*	*Middle School*	*High/Higher Secondary School*	*College and University Levels*
1950-51	20	18	19	9
1955-56	20	19	23	12
1960-61	21	32	27	14
1965-66	24	30	30	16
1970-71	27	38	33	18
1975-76	29	40	36	20
1979-80	33	42	38	24
1980-81	33	42	38	24
1981-82	34	44	40	25
1982-83	34	44	40	25
1983-84	35	45	41	26
1984-85	35	46	42	29
1985-86	37	46	43	28
1986-87	38	47	44	28
1987-88	40	48	44	—
1988-89	40	49	45	—
1989-90	41	49	45	—
1990-91	41	50	46	—
1991-92	43	51	48	—
1992-93P	41	47	49	—
1993-94P	42	52	50	—

(Contd.)

(Contd.)

1994-95P	45	53	51	–
1995-96P	46	54	52	–

Source: Department of Education, Ministry of Human Resources Development, New Delhi.

P : Provisional.

Table 3.37
Representation of Women in the Central Council of Ministers

Year	Number of Ministers			Number of Women Ministers		
	Cabinet Minister	MOS	Deputy Minister	Cabinet Minister	MOS	Deputy Minister
1985*	15	25	0	1	3	0
1990@	17	17	5	0	1	1
1995$	12	37	3	1	4	1
1996$$	18	21	0	0	1	0
1997**	20	24	0	0	5	0

Source: Lok Sabha Secretariat, New Delhi

MOS : Minister of State

* : as on 4th February

$: as on 31st January

** : as on 10-6-97

@ : as on 31st August

$$: as on 5th August

Table 3.38
Number of Voters and Percentage Voting in Various General Elections

General Election (National)	Year	Total number of Voters (million)			Percentage of Voters participating in the election		
		Female	Male	Total	Female	Male	Total
First	1952	–	–	173.2	–	–	61.2*
Second	1957	–	–	193.7	–	–	62.2*
Third	1962	102.4	113.9	216.4	46.6	62.0	55.0
Fourth	1967	119.4	129.6	249.0	55.5	66.7	61.3
Fifth	1971	–	–	274.1	–	–	55.3
Sixth	1977	154.2	167.0	321.2	54.9	65.6	60.5

(Contd.)

Seventh	1980	170.3	185.2	355.6	51.2	62.2	56.9
Eighth	1984	192.3	208.0	400.3	59.2	68.4	64.0
Nineth	1989	236.9	262.0	498.9	57.3	66.1	61.9
Tenth	1991	234.5	261.8	498.4	51.4	61.6	56.7
Eleventh	1996	282.8	309.8	592.6	53.4	62.1	57.9

Source: Election Commission of India, New Delhi.

* : Calculated on the basis of valid votes polled.

Note: 1. Sex-wise break up of voters is not available for the first, second and fifth General Elections.

2. Data relates to Lok Sabha elections.

— : Not available

Table 3.39
Number of Persons Contesting and Elected in Different General Elections

General Election	Year	Number of Seats Available for Election	Total Number of Contestants	Average Number of Contestants per seat	Female			Male		
					Total number contesting	Elected	Percentage Winning	Total Number Contesting	Elected	Percentage Winning
First	1952	489	1874	3.8	—	—	—	—	—	—
Second	1957	494	1518	3.1	45	27	60.0	1473	467	31.7
Third	1962	494	1985	4.0	70	35	50.0	1915	459	24.0
Fourth	1967	520	2369	4.6	67	30	44.8	2302	490	21.3
Fifth	1971	520	2784	5.4	86	21	24.4	2698	499	18.5
Sixth	1977	542	2439	4.5	70	19	27.1	2369	523	22.1
Seventh	1980	542	4620	8.5	142	28	19.7	4478	514	11.5
Eighth	1984	542	5574	10.3	164	42	25.6	5406	500	9.2
Ninth	1989	529	6160	11.3	198	27	13.6	5962	502	8.4
Tenth	1991	521	8699	16.7	325	37	11.4	8374	484	5.8
Eleventh	1996	543	13952	25.7	599	40	6.7	13353	503	3.8

Source: Election Commission of India, New Delhi

Note: 1. Total no. of contestants include the number of candidates elected unanimously , if any.

2. Data relates to Lok Sabha Elections

— : Not available.

Table 3.40

Number of Women in Panchayati Raj Institutions (PRIs) (after 73rd Constitutional Amendments)

States/UT's	*Members*						*Chairpersons*		
	GP		*PS*		*ZP*		*GP*	*PS*	*ZP*
	Total	*Women*	*Total*	*Women*	*Total*	*Women*			
Andhra Pradesh	396000	78000	14643	5054	1093	363	15065	366	6
Arunachal Pradesh	5733	86	1205	39	77	—	—	—	—
Haryana	48201	17928	2418	807	—	101	1994	38	5
Himachal Pradesh	18258	6013	1661	558	252	84	970	23	4
Karnataka	78476	34073	3334	1343	919	335	1877	59	7
Madhya Pradesh	443429	150181	9097	3109	946	319	11953	123	9
Punjab	90565	23832	2441	326	274	89	158	47	5
Rajasthan	112897	33566	5257	1740	997	331	3064	80	10
Sikkim	827	27	—	—	148	1	1	—	—
Tripura	5421	1805	196	67	70	24	184	6	1
Uttar Pradesh	804000	234420	55750	18620	2230	756	19535	301	22
West Bengal	61398	21742	9516	3202	664	227	153	10	—
A & N islands	667	229	67	25	30	10	—	—	—
Daman & Diu	63	25	—	—	15	5	6	—	—

Source: Department of Rural Employment and Poverty Alleviation Ministry of Rural Areas and Employment, New Delhi.

Note : Information in respect of remaining states/UT's has not been received

GP—Gram Panchayat PS—Panchayat Samiti ZP—Zila Parishad.

Table 3.41

Female Employment in Central Government, State Government and Local Bodies (in millions)

Year (as on 31st March)	CENTRAL GOVERNMENT			STATE GOVERNMENT			LOCAL BODIES			TOTAL		
	Female	Total	Female (per cent)	Female	Total	Female (per cent)	Female	Total	Female (per cent)	Female	Total	Female (per cent)
1981	0.14	3.19	4.3	0.65	5.67	11.4	0.41	2.04	20.4	1.20	10.91	11.0
1982	0.15	3.25	4.6	0.69	5.85	11.7	0.42	2.03	20.6	1.25	11.13	11.2
1983	0.16	3.27	4.8	0.73	6.01	12.1	0.47	2.11	22.1	1.35	11.41	11.8
1984	0.16	3.31	5.0	0.77	6.25	12.5	0.48	2.13	22.6	1.41	11.60	12.2
1985	0.17	3.33	5.2	0.81	6.28	12.9	0.50	2.16	23.0	1.48	11.77	12.6
1986	0.18	3.35	5.3	0.86	6.47	13.2	0.52	2.19	23.6	1.55	12.01	12.9
1987	0.19	3.35	5.6	0.90	6.67	13.5	0.52	2.21	23.6	1.61	12.23	13.2
1988	0.20	3.38	5.9	0.95	6.78	14.1	0.53	2.21	23.8	1.68	12.37	13.6
1989	0.20	3.39	5.9	1.00	6.89	14.5	0.54	2.24	24.1	1.74	12.51	13.6
1990	0.21	3.40	6.2	1.03	6.98	14.8	0.55	2.26	24.3	1.79	12.64	14.2
1991@	–	3.41	–	–	7.11	–	–	2.31	–	–	12.83	–
1992@	–	3.42	–	–	7.19	–	–	2.20	–	–	12.81	–
1993@	–	3.38	–	–	7.29	–	–	2.16	–	–	12.83	–
1994@	–	3.39	–	–	7.34	–	–	2.20	–	–	12.93	–
1995@	0.23	3.39	6.8	1.23	7.35	16.7	0.55	2.19	25.1	2.01	12.94	15.5
1996@	0.24	3.36	7.1	1.26	7.41	17.0	0.57	2.19	26.0	2.07	12.96	16.0

Source : Directorate General of Employment and Training, Ministry of Labour, New Delhi.

Note : Data are based on Employment Market Information (EMI) Programme

@ : Statistics for years 1991 to 1995 are provisional based on Quarterly Employment Review and separate figures for females are not available.

Not available

Table 3.42

Permanent Central Government Employees by Gazetted and Non-Gazetted Positions

(in hundred thousands)

Category	1983				1989				1990				1991			
	Female	Male	Total	Percent Female	Female	Male	Total	Percent Female	Female	Male	Total	Percent Female	Female	Male	Total	Percent Female
Gazetted	0.03	0.96	0.99	3.0	0.08	1.23	1.31	6.10	0.10	1.25	1.35	7.47	0.10	1.26	1.36	7.60
	(2.4)	(2.8)	(2.8)		(3.2)	(3.5)	(3.5)		(3.6)	(3.6)	(3.6)		(3.6)	(3.6)	(3.6)	
Non-Gazetted	1.33	33.09	36.39	3.9	2.39	33.78	36.17	6.60	2.73	33.66	36.39	7.51	2.79	33.98	36.77	7.58
	(97.6)	(97.2)	(97.2)		(96.8)	(96.5)	(96.5)		(96.4)	(96.4)	(96.4)		(96.4)	(96.4)	(96.4)	
Total	1.36	34.05	35.41	3.9	2.47	35.01	37.48	6.60	2.83	34.91	37.74	7.51	2.89	35.24	38.13	7.58
	(100)	(100)	(100)		(100)	(100)	(100)		(100)	(100)	(100)		(100)	(100)	(100)	

Source: Directorate General of Employment and Training, Ministry of Labour, New Delhi.

Note:1. Totals may not tally because of rounding.

2. Figures are based on census of central government employees.
3. Figures in brackets are per cent.
4. Due to difference in scope and coverage of EMI Programmed and Census of Central Government Employees, the figures given in table 40 and 41 are not comparable.

Table 3.43
Various Types of Crimes Committed Against Women

Crime type	*Incidence of Crimes*						*Per cent share of Crimes in 1995*
	1990	*1991*	*1992*	*1993*	*1994*	*1995*	
Rape	10068	10410	11708	12218	13208	13754	12.92
Kidnapping and Abduction	11699	12300	12077	11837	12998	14063	13.21
Dowry Deaths	4836	5157	4962	5817	4935	5092	4.78
Torture	13450	15949	19750	22064	25946	31127	29.24
Molestation	20194	20611	20385	20985	24117	28475	26.75
Eve-Teasing	8620	10283	10751	12009	10496	4756	4.47
Inside Trafficking of Girls	–	–	–	–	167	191	0.18
Sati Prevention Act	–	–	–	–	2	1	0.00
Immoral Traffic (Prevention) Act	–	–	–	–	7547	8447	7.94
Indecent Representation of Women	–	–	–	–	389	539	0.51
Total	68867	74710	79633	84930	99805	106445	100.00

Source: National Crime Records Bureau, Ministry of Home Affairs, Crime in India (Publication)
Rape : Crime in India
All other Crimes : Monthly Crime Statistics. Figures are provisional.

Chart 3.7
Percentage Share of Different Crimes Against Women During the Year 1995

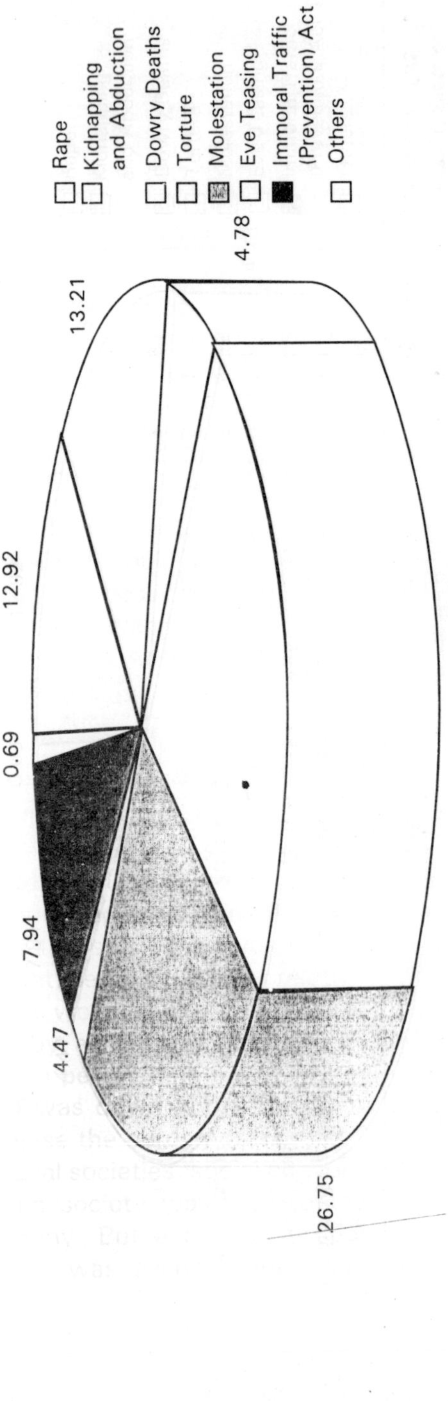

Table 3.44
Victims of Atrocity/Rape by Age Groups

Year	*Below 10 years*	*10-16 years*	*16-30 years*	*30 years and above*
1988	233	1869	5832	1165
1989	369	1965	5646	1772
1990	394	2105	6028	1541
1991	1099	2630	5377	1319
1992	532	2581	7000	1621
1993	634	2759	7038	1792
1994	734	3244	7442	1798
1995	747	3320	7752	1955

Source : National Crime Records Bureau, Ministry of Home Affairs, Crime in India.

Table 3.45
Rate of Suicide

Year	*Rate (Incidence of Suicides per Hundred Thousand Population)*		
	Female	*Male*	*Total*
1971	6.5	9.2	7.9
1972	6.2	9.2	7.8
1973	5.6	8.4	7.1
1974	6.4	9.1	7.9
1975	5.8	8.3	7.2
1976	5.9	7.5	6.8
1977	5.4	7.2	6.3
1978	5.2	7.2	6.3
1979	4.8	6.7	5.9
1980	5.4	6.9	6.3
1981	4.9	6.7	5.8
1982	5.4	7.3	6.3
1983	5.6	7.3	6.4
1984	6.0	7.7	6.8
1985	6.2	7.9	7.1
1986	6.3	8.0	7.1

1987	6.5	8.6	7.5
1988	6.9	9.3	8.1
1989	7.3	9.6	8.5
1990	7.6	10.2	8.9
1991	7.9	10.5	9.2
1992	7.8	10.5	9.2
1993	8.1	10.8	9.5
1994	8.4	11.3	9.9
1995	8.2	11.0	9.7

Source : National Crime Records Bureau, Ministry of Home Affairs, 'Accidental Deaths and Suicides in India' Publication.

Table 3.46
Juvenile Delinquency

Year	*Delinquents (IPC + LSL) (in thousand)*			*Percentage of girls to total*	*Rate of Incidence of Crime* per hundred thousand population*
	Girls	*Boys*	*Total*		
1971	5.4	98.0	103.4	5.3	4.9
1972	7.2	121.0	128.2	5.6	5.6
1973	5.6	122.2	127.8	4.3	6.4
1974	8.5	132.1	140.6	6.1	6.9
1975	9.3	132.6	141.9	6.6	6.6
1976	9.4	124.6	134.0	7.0	6.0
1977	10.4	138.5	148.9	7.0	7.0
1978	9.7	151.2	160.9	6.0	6.9
1979	9.7	160.3	170.0	5.7	7.1
1980	9.5	178.1	187.6	5.0	8.3
1981	8.7	181.9	190.6	4.6	8.9
1982	10.7	157.6	168.3	6.3	8.4
1983	11.1	160.5	171.6	6.5	7.7
1984	12.5	149.8	162.3	7.7	5.8
1985	11.4	157.1	168.5	6.8	6.6
1986	10.1	160.0	170.1	6.0	7.3
1987	13.6	166.4	180.0	7.5	6.7
1988	5.1	33.1	38.2	13.4	3.1

1989	11.6	24.8	36.4	31.9	2.3
1990	5.5	25.3	30.8	18.0	1.8
1991	6.4	23.2	29.6	21.6	1.5
1992	3.9	17.4	21.3	18.2	1.3
1993	3.7	16.4	20.1	18.3	1.1
1994	3.4	13.9	17.3	19.5	1.0
1995	4.3	14.5	18.8	22.6	1.1

Source : National Crime Records Bureau, Ministry of Home Affairs, Crime in India (Publication).

Note : 1 IPC—Indian Penal Code.

2. LSL—Local and Special Laws
3. Figures for 1988 are not at all comparable to earlier years due to change in the definition of Juveniles. Till 1988, boys and girls below 21 years were taken juvenile whereas after 1988 boys below 16 years and girls below 18 years were treated as juvenile.

*: Crimes registered under the Indian Penal Code (IPC).

Chart 3.8
Cases of Suicidal Deaths

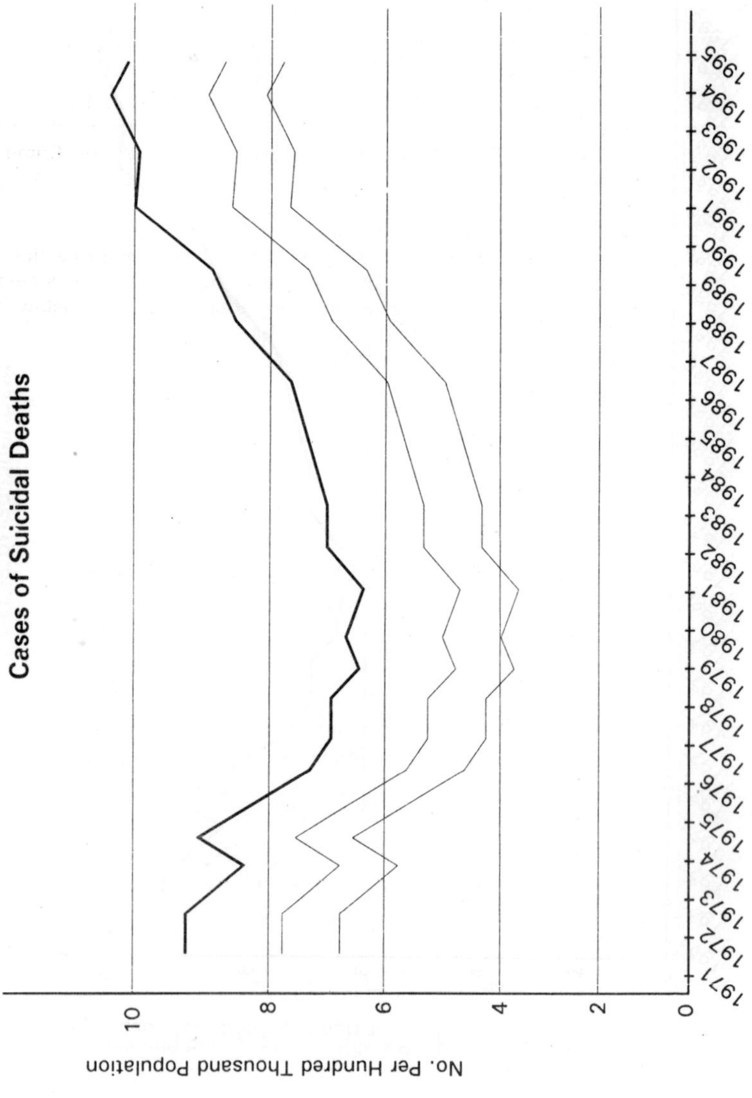

Chart 3.9
Juveniles Apprehended (in Thousands) by Sex, 1988-95

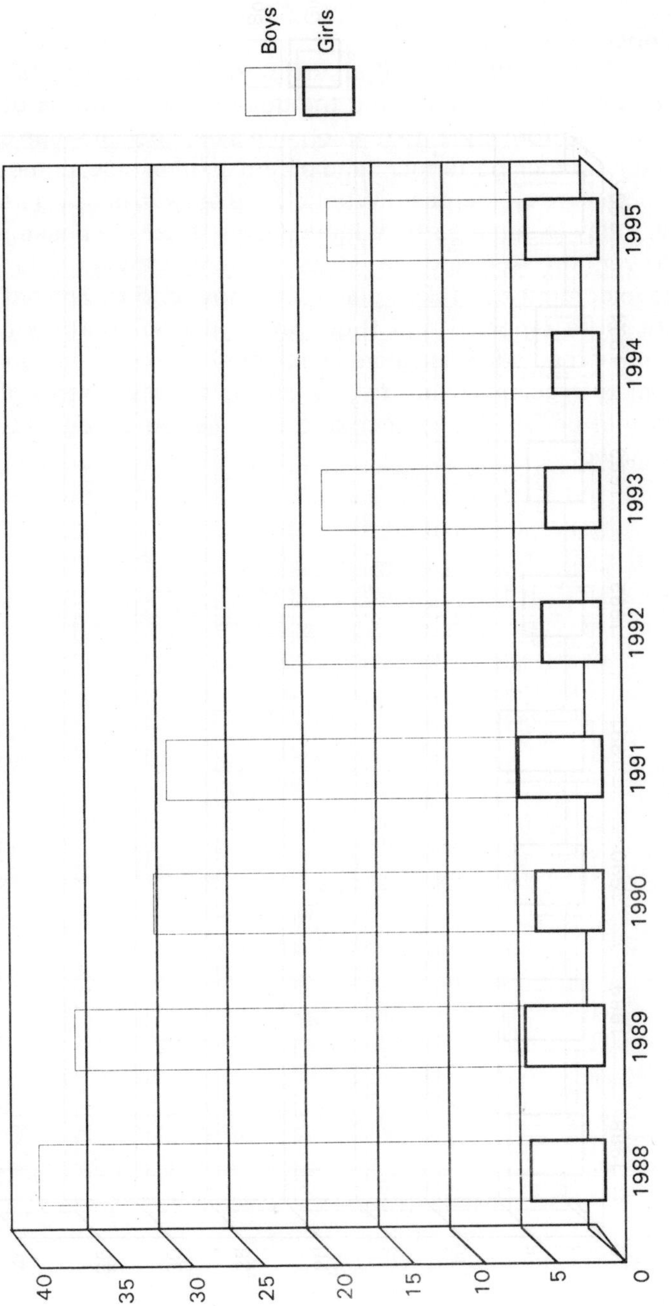

Conclusion

Thus, we find that despite various efforts by the constitution, the state and the governments, status of women is still far from equal to men on one side, special steps are being taken for their betterment and on the another side, crimes against women are on increase. What else, even *sati* is being performed till today in some parts of India decade after the passage of Sati Prevention Act and its strict implementation. One positive development has taken place, i.e., now crimes against women are more reported and thus get organised treatment. At the same time, administrative machinery in particular and whole society in general needs to be senitised about problems of women so that constitutional mendate of male-female equality can be attained.

4

Gandhi and Politico-Socio-Economic Regeneration

Whenever there is a mention of emancipation of Indian women, unforgettable contribution of a great social reformer is bound to be discussed. Yes! Mahatma Gandhi. Today, any socially sensitive person would admit that had Gandhi not come on the front, position of Indian women would not have been elevated to the extent it is at present. Therefore, in this book also, which is about women in India, we could not help including Gandhi's works particularly towards women.

This chapter is based on the findings of a survey conducted with various levels of respondents about contribution of Gandhi towards improvement of various aspects of women's lives and removal of evil pertaining to them. Among the respondents are included living members of Gandhi's family, Ashram inmates, women have been associated with Gandhi in his lifetime through freedom struggle or otherwise, constructive workers, non-Gandhians who turned Gandhians at later stage, women social workers, critics of Mahatma Gandhi, some foreigners and many others. These respondents are from varied fields so as to prove authenticity and reliability of the responses.

Prior to Gandhi

It has been rightly said by someone that position of women in society is a measuring rod and a true index of its civilisation and cultural attainments. The Indian woman with her long lineage has left her mark on different periods of our history. To talk or write about her is somewhat tough as her position has differed from period to period and varied in different parts of the country at the same time. It is assumed, from the numerous finds from Mohenjodaro that a form of matriarchate prevailed; the love of mother-worship, female figures richly adorned, a bronze of a dancing-girl, ornaments and toilet jars, all point to a society where women were in the forefront. Jainism allowed men to be come *munis* and equally they allowed women to become Aryika, they granting them equal respect as available to males. Buddhist bhikhshunis were also a respected lot.

But in one way she was a beneficiary; marriage was a contract and not a sacrament; thus there were no child marriages or enforced widowhood; the widow could marry if she so desired. Monogamy was the general rule although consistent with the age, kings and nobles kept more than one wife. Both the religions held celibacy superior unlike Hinduism which regarded marriage as a "social and religious duty and necessity."[1] Under patriarchal Hindu society, the birth of girl was always unwelcome in the Vedic period. But a talented and scholarly daughter was preferred to an ordinary son. She was even regarded as the pride of the family. Altekar writes.

"The reasons why daughters were relatively less unpopular in ancient India during the early centuries are not difficult to understand. They could be initiated in vedic studies and were entitled to offer sacrifices to gods; the son was not absolutely necessary for this purpose. The marriage of the daughter was not a difficult problem; it was often solved by the daughter herself. The dread of a possible widowhood did not very much weigh upon the mind of parents; for ... remarriage was allowed by society and was fairly common.[2]

We can say that in another respect her position in society couldnot be worse. She was like a chattel to be gifted away by the husband. Several hymns bear testimony to this undignified custom. The man's proprietary right in his wife was recognised; but at times it met with social disapprobation. However, "in cultured circles, the wife was regarded as the co-owner of the family property along with her husband, as the term *dampati* would show."[3]

As per Hindu ideas which traditionally prevailed a girl, a young women or a matron must do nothing for her own pleasure, even in her own dwelling place. It is clearly stated on the Hindu texts that in childhood, she is subordinate to her father, in youth on her husband, in widowhood on her sons; if she has no sons, she must depend upon the kinsmen of her deceased husband; if he left no kinsmen, she must be dependent upon the kinsmen of her father; if she has nothing such kinsmen, she must be dependent on the *Reya*. A woman must never seek to be independent; she must never wish to separate herself from her father, her husband, her sons, for by this kind of separation, she exposes both her father's family and her husband's family which is a sin according to the Hindu view of life.[4] Another consequence was the growing seclusion of women. Early Hindu texts refer to the participation of women in the civic, social and religious life of the community.

Very slowly at first, but inexorably, women came to be segregated, the age of marriage went on dropping, first to prepuberty and then below ten years, till in the 18th and 19th centuries it dipped down to infants in arms. Child marriage was the order of the day. One of its natural results was the child widow. As the prejudice against widow remarriage, permitted and recognised in Vedic times, intensified, it began to affect child widows too. Some young widows decided to immolate themselves on the funeral pyre of their husbands rather than go through life as widows. *Sati* came to acquire a greater social content when Rajput women preferred to die with their warrior husbands instead to be captured by the conquerors. It came to be considered the highest and noblest form of self-sacrifice.

Through the ages, force was used perhaps on a large number of *Satis*; few, perhaps very few, embraced the flames that devoured the husbands. In 1829 *Sati* was abolished by law, yet in distant villages, it was voluntarily practised surreptitiously on rare occasions. As a social custom it had died out, but in recent times it has been revived in certain parts of the country and efforts are being made to seek justification for it.

One more modern custom was unkown to ancient India, the dowry, although it is recorded that fond and affluent fathers gave their daughters, at the time of their marriage, gifts of jewels and domestic animals; but they mostly given after the marriage. It was only in the second half of the last century that the dowry not only assumed scandalous proportions but became a bargaining counter in the arrangement of wedding occassion. As far as the social indignities suffered by widows are concerned, in no other country and among no other people has it been so appalling as among the Hindus. Tonsure, *ghunghat* in the household, prohibition of remarriage, all contributed to her misery, "Her head is shaved and all her rights and privileges as a woman are lost. She eats little, sleeps little, rises very in the morning, and gives herself up to melancholy thoughts the whole day. She is exposed to the severest privations incident upon her state ..." So bemoaned a pupil of Elphinstone Institute, Bombay in 1841.[5] Bengal, Maharashtra, and Bombay blazed the trail in improving the lot of the widows.

In this situation, social reformers were touched to the quick by the plight of women. Raja Ram Mohan Roy's services in this regard are unmatched. He was unsparing in his exposure of the evils from which women suffered. No apology is required for quoting at length his opinion on their deprivations:

"...a woman who is looked up to the sole mistress by the rest of a family one day, on the next, becomes dependent on her sons, and subject to the slights of her daughters-in-law ... Cruel sons often wound the feelings of their dependent mothers, deciding in favour of their own wives ... step-mother, who often are numerous on account of polygamy being allowed in these countries, are still more shamefully neglected in general."

Again:—"It is not from religious prejudices and early impressions only, that Hindu widows burn themselves on the pyres of their deceased husbands, but also from their witnessing the distress in which widows of the same rank in life are involved, and the insults and slights to which they are daily subjected, that they become in great measure regardless of their existence after the death of their husbands, and this indifference accompanied with the hope of future reward held out to them, leads them to the horrible act of suicide. These restraints on female inheritance encourage, in a great degree, polygamy, a frequent source of the greatest misery in native families, a grand object of Hindus being to secure a provision for their male offspring, the law, which relieves them from the necessity of giving an equal portion to their wives, removes a principal restraint on the indulge of their inclinations in respect to the number they marry ... The evil consequences arising from such polygamy, the public may easily guess.."

It was also said that "To these women there are left only three modes of conduct to pursue after the death of their husbands. 1st to live a miserable life as entire slaves to others, without indulging any hope of support from another husband. 2ndly to walk in the paths of unrighteousness for their maintenance and independence, 3rdly. To die on the funeral pyre of their husbands, loaded with applause and honour of their neighbours.[6]

It was with the efforts of Raja Ram Mohan Roy, Iswar chandra Vidyasagar, Keshab Chandra Sen, Byramji Malabari, G. Subramanian, D.K. Karve and a host of others that the betterment of the widow and her lot in society started improving. Rabindranath Tagore in his various novels and short stories painted the light and shade of Indian womanhood.

Pandita Ramabai was one of the early pioneers among women to work untiringly for their uplift and to redress their complaints. To us, today, this preoccupation of sensitive minds of the last century with the issue of widow remarriage may appear a bit overdrawn and overstretched. It was not so. Not just unfficial effort but legislation was necessary. Under pressure from social reformers, the Government of India Act I of 1856 legalised the remarriage of Hindu widows, Child Marriage Act III of 1872 banned child marriage and fixed the minimum age of marriage at 14 for the girl and 18 for the boy, permitted widow remarriage, and inter-caste marriage and penalised polygamy among the Brahmo Samaj.

It was question of time before these benefits were to accrue to Hindus in general. The Age of Consent Bill, 1891, raised the age of consent from 10 to 12 for all. The reform movements of the last century, thus concentrated on mitigating the hardships and handicaps of women and then on elevating their position. The Brahmo Samaj of Ram Mohan Roy, the Prarthana Samaj of Ranade, the Arya Samaj of Swami Dayanand Saraswati, all aimed at ameliorating the lot of women and shedding the dross that Hinduism had gathered over the ages. Lala Lajpat Rai, himself a leading Arya Samajist, has pithily narrated up the factors that initiated the change in social attitude:

"English education and Western ideas played an important part in bringing about this change, but an equally great, if not even greater part has been played by an appeal to ancient Hindu ideals of womanhood and to the teachings of the ancient Hindu religion in the matter of the relation of the sexes. A study of the ancient Hindu literature made it abundantly clear that the present deplorable condition of Indian womanhood was due to a fall from their old ideals and that it was only a phase, though a much regretted phase of the general downfall".[7]

Despite all this, the impact on society was not all that was desired. Even when we come to the twentieth century the dead-weight of tradition and custom lay heavily on society. In cities, the grip was relaxed but in the villages the change was non-existent. Official inertia on the request of non-interference in religious and social affairs, added to the discomfort of the reformers. The census of 1921 put the figure of child and girl widows as under:

Widows of age upto 5	11,892
Widows of age from 5 to 10	85,037
Widows of age from 10 to 15	2,32,147

Shocking by, this figure was higher than in the previous two decades. This was so in spite of eighty years of efforts by three generations of social reformers. That even in an era of comparative enlightenment more then three lakhs of our girl children were condemned as widows and social outcastes shows how deep the roots of social injustice lay.

Reformation movement spread in different parts of India as far apart as Bengal, Gujarat and Maharashtra. The pioneers and leaders set themselves up as practical examples by marrying widows: the outstanding among them were the only son of Ishwar Chandra Vidyasagar, a renowned great social reformer and fighter in the cause of women's rights, particularly of widows and child widows. Bipin Chandra Pal, the extremist leader; Rabindranath Tagore's son and many others in Bengal; Madhavdas Ranchoddas and a few more in Gujarat; Dhondo Keshav Karve and others in Maharashtra. Gurudev Tagore, aware of the "sensitive human heart throbbing with pain and desire" even in the widow, contributed substantially towards exposing the hypocrisy of a section of selfish people preaching "the high ideals of prepetual widowhood". His novels, poems, plays, put him in the category of the greatest and finest of our social reformers. D.G. Karve's sister-in-law, Parvatibai Athavale, herself a widow and under Karve's benign influence, gave some thought to 'the duty of widows and how they should live from the religious point of view". She became interested in the issue of the shaving of the widow's head:

"... I thought of this shaving off of hair as a religious rite, and that it was my religious duty to continue that practice. Even when I began to teach in the Widows' Home at Hingane (founded by Professor Karve) and saw a widow give up her marks of widowhood, I thought she had committed a great sin. But as I thought further, I began to see that the compulsory shaving of a widow's head was not right. If thought, however, that a voluntary shaving off of her hair, as an initiatory rite into the order of those who give up their worldly life, was a rightful religious act. I also began gradually to realise that unless widows themselves protested against the compulsory shaving off of their hair the question would not be settled".[8]

Also, she has well described the social reaction to her young and widowed sister Baya, then 22 years of age, marrying Karve:

"Baya was remarried at Poona. The Press informed the public that the marriage had taken place with the approval of the bride's father and elder brother. As soon as the news of the remarriage reached the village of Devrukh our home experienced excommunication. We were boycotted even by the barber and washerman. But our father was not all troubled by being put out of caste..."

"The boycott lasted for a year, and we had to suffer a great deal od inconvenience. Finally our father gave a hundred rupees for the repair of the three temples in the village, fell at the feet of the citizens, and thus regaining their good will, the boycott was lifted.[9]

Is not it surprising that if the father was doughty enough, the mother "belonged entirely to the old way of thinking. She had not approved of Baya's remarriage. Moreover she had this fear that one of her widowed daughters having remarried, the others might follow her example".[10] This would otherway mean stain on the family. Rather than that it would be better for the daughter to go on a pilgrimage with the parents and die of cholera, if need be. Hardly a perceptive attitude, this. Women have always been their own worst enemies. If Parvati Athavale has graphically described the plight of widows, her contemporary Ramabai Ranade, the second wife of Mahadeo Govind Ranade, has, from personal experience, related the harsh treatment meted by the mother-in-law and the sister-in-law to the young bride. Her situation was worse as she followed the instructions of her reformer husband and educated herself and learnt to take part in public life, specially concerned with women's betterment. Few narrations can be more pathetic than the following.

"... I used to go downstairs to start on time, and taking my courage in both hands would say. I'll come back soon', and rush out without waiting for Wansa's (sister-in-law's) assent. As I walked to the building where the *Sabha* (founded by Pandita Ramabai) met, my mind would be absorbed and sad as I anticipated all the trouble that would be waiting for me when I return in the evening. But all of this was forgotten the moment I joined the other women ....

"When I returned home later, losing all the joy and courage I had found at the *Sabha*, I would stand at the entrance of the house paralysed with terror, because, in the evening. Taisasvbai, Himself's step-mother, and Wansa always sat on the verandah and they used to see me first. At that time of day all the menfolk were away, and these two felt utterly free to say what they would. In Himself's hearing, they would merely issue strict injunctions to me, `You have been to the *Sabha* and come back. Don't think that you can merely change your garment and then help with the cooking and serving the food. Don't even touch the chutney or curry. It is not fitting that ladies who attend *Sabhas* should do such humble tasks! Go on upstairs and sit in your husband's apartment in idleness. Then you will look well'. This was the sort of comment I had to listen to morning, noon and night, besides the other relatives in the family, there were five or six women who were family connections. They craved favour by aiding and abetting, the older either publicly of privately, in persecuting me. All I could do when it went too far while I was down with them, was to let a few tears fall silently to ease the burden of my heart.[11]

As in all patriarchal societies, social conventions detracted from the law. Muslim society was akin to the Hindu in the acceptance of polygyny. But a new institution came to be introduced—*Purdah*. It was alien before although some di advocate the veil for royal ladies as a matter of added prestige. But it came into vogue in the ruling and aristocratic Hindu families consequent of Muslim dominion. "It was accepted by Hindu society partly in imitation of the manners of the conquerors, and partly as an additional protection for the women folk".[12] But the working and peasant women could not and did not accept the purdah. Till the beginning of the twentieth century, among the Hindus it was restricted to the rich families; others were free to visit temples, participate in family and social jobs and listen to religious discourses.

The Muslim woman, nonetheless, regardless of class or wealth had to be in *purdah*. It was only recently that the wealthy among them have discarded it, the middle and the poorer classes still adhere to this outmoded, even immoral custom; what is more regrettable is that there is no concerted move or effort to do away with it. Another unsavoury custom that continued in to the nineteenth century from the third century onward was that of the *devdasis*.

It tended to lower the moral and religious atmosphere of the temples, but nothing that the social or religious reformers could do suppress the practice. Marriage considered as a sacrament, polygyny without divorce stress of faithfulness on the part of the wife (though not on the part of the husband) all made their individual and joint contribution to lowering the position of woman in society. This handicap was sufferedby a large majority. At the lower rungs of the social pyramid, however what may be termed divorce prevailed.

This Hindu Law of marriage was unjust to woman; and the hold of tradition was constricting. Society would neither think nor talk of doing away with polygyny, nor release the unwanted, discarded wife or the child widow from the dutches of matrimony. Social reformers of the early twentieth century began to advocate divorce, but they were not as persistent or as single-minded as their predecessors were with the subject of widow-remarriage. In another sphere of essential activity, too, woman was a great sufferer—*education*. When even men were not educated and illiteracy was widespread, women could hardly be expected to go to school. Gopal Krishna Gokhale was untiring in his efforts to educate women, one of the purposes of the Servants of India Society which he founded in Poona in year

1905 was "assisting educational movements, especially those for the education of women".

"Combination of enforced ignorance and overdone religion not only makes them willing victims of customs unjust and hurtful in the highest degree but also makes them the most formidable and the most effective opponents of all attempts at change or innovation ... It is obvious that under the circumstances a wide diffusion of education with all its solvent influences among the women of India,is the only means of emancipating their minds from this degrading thraldom of ideas inherited through a long past ..."[13]

Sh. D.G. Karve, with a munificient donation by Sir Vithaldas Thackersey, established the first and the only university for women for a very long time. It was just like a heaven of refuge to the hardpressed and home-bound women. Slowly at first, but with greater pace later, the Shreemati Nathibai Damodar Thackersey University started on its long voyage to help render yeomen services to the cause of the emancipation and betterment of women.

In a predominantly illiterate country women's literacy was one of the most neglected subjects. After all the possible stress on women's education for about half-a-century, the total number of girls enrolled in primary schools was 1,19,647 or 6 girls for every 100 boy enrolled in 1881-82. As years passed, the position improved slightly and was 10 girls for every 100 boys by the second decade of the outgone century. In 1921 while 13.0 per cent men could read and write, only 1.8 per cent of women could do so; this meant that less than one woman in fifty was literate. This was the situation after almost 70 years of efforts at women's education by Christian missionaries and social reformers both men and women

This reveals the magnitude of the task facing society. Lack of education and training is reflected in the lack of employment opportunities. At the root of the social and economic pyramid women worked as agricultural labourers or were engaged in unskilled labour, in factories, mills and workshops. Yet their contribution to the labour force was negligible. Discrimination was there in the payment of even the meagre wages. If men were paid 3-4 annas a day, women were paid about half that amount. Neither quantum of work nor efficiency was considered in fixing wages. The outcame is inevitable that:

"This unjust system is part of the tradition handed down under masculine dominance. Masculine standard is the accepted one and according to that measure wages are fixed. That a woman worker spends proportionately as much energy and labour and is entitled to the same wages is lost sight of".[14] This type of discrimination was rampant whether in the field, factory or plantation. Some of the causes were that women were uneducated, ignorant and unorganised. Even in famine relief works this disparity prevailed. Kamaladevi Chattopadhyaya clearly summarised women's status: "In all domestic service, too, women are at a disadvantage in the matter of wages. And nowhere can they expect redress and get the principle of equal wages established unless this male-dominated society is changed to one founded on equal opportunities and equal rights".

Also it was said that "This is the dark and sorry tale of nearly 90 per cent of the women in India. The bourgeois leaders of the feminist movement would do well to remember that what these weary hunger-stricken women cry for is not the right to work but the 'right to the gains of their labour'. The legal rights of inheritance touch them not. They inherit but sorrow and pain from generation to generation. They are the producers of the wealth but they remain beggars".[15]

Undoubtedly, the joint family, despite other advantages as the cradle of the young, the training ground of the adults and the refuge of the old and the sick, certainly had a negative effect on the young wife. It was a hard grind for her with little or no appreciation. This in turn influenced her position both in the house and in society. As the nineteenth century encouraged industrialisation, men left their village homes to aggregate in fresh townships and cities.

This led to further deterioration in the family standing of the young wife who had none to defend her. It is a truism that economic independence and social status go together. This is so with regard to the status of women. Wherever she is economically in an inferior position her lot is one of subordination in a man-dominated society. Economic independence elevates her. Among the underprivileged sections women is definitely a co-worker and co-sharer, and hence, a co-equal. Among the wealthy and leisured class her status gets somewhat depressed.

In spite of the legend of *Dharma* staking his wife Draupadi in the gambling room, woman was not a chattel to be bartered away at the pleasure of man.

The Vedic age recognised that the husband and wife were joint owners of the household and its property; rather the husband had to row at the time of his marriage that "he would never transgress the rights and interests of his wife in economic matters."

This was too idyllic a state to last and in practice the wife secured minor rights and privileges. She had the ownership of movable goods like jewellery or apparel; but where landed property was concerned, joint ownership was only a legal fiction. Yet Altekar opines that the "... history of *Stridhana* is undoubtedly a proud and glorious chapter in the history of Hindu civilisation. It discloses a constant and continuous tendency in Hindu society to increase the scope of *Stridhana*, usually at the expense of men's rights. Women were also invested with the right of its independent disposal; even the husband could not touch it save under special circumstances".[16]

What about the woman's share in the father's property? The first to get her right recognised was the daughter who had no brothers.The daughter with brothers found the going rather heavy. Through history the general view was that women should have a share in the husband's property rather than in the father's. It took a long time to recognise the widow's right and even then it was a limited right; she could not dispose of the property inherited by her except probably for religious purposes. Law apart, in practice, woman continued to be among the disinherited of the earth.

Ultimately, social reformers gave some thought to it and worked for giving her some legitimate share in the husband's income or wealth as well. Something like *Stridhana* of old should by law be made bound for the wife and widow; she must have a claim on the husband's property. Under the Dayabhaga law, which prevailed only in Bengal, the widow had some rights over the inheritance even when the husband expired a member of a joint family. Not so under the Mitakshara law which operated in the rest of the country. Since, on marriage, a woman fully belongs to the husband's family she definitely must be given her rightful place in wealth and inheritance. Over and above economic inequality and social indignities heaped on them, women also suffered from legal disparities. India recognised and continues to recognise, the personal law of different religious groups that live here and though criminal law is uniform for all, civil law is not. And here discrepancies, divergencies and inequities exist. When we speak of efforts at social reform or at improving the lot of women the concentration is on the Hindu women almost to the exclusion of the others.

This does not mean that only the Hindu woman was oppressed; that the others were free and considered men's equals. The status in society of the Muslim woman was not so very high either. True, child marriage was not known, not again was widow remarriage, banned. Marriage was a contract, not a sacrament. This was normally between adults but marriage of minors was valid if the elders gave their consent. The contract was beneficial to the woman as it gave her some economic benefits. She received the dower as a right. This was of two kinds: the amount settled at the time of marriage and that to be given to her when divorced.

The Hindu woman suffered as divorce was not recognised; the Muslim woman suffered as divorce was much too easy for the husband to cast away his wife. *Talaq* put the woman in an unhappy situation — the husband had merely to repeat the word three times and he was free; the woman became homeless and an outcast most of the time among the poorer sections of society. Divorce was also available by natural consent without the intervention of the law or the wife could move the court for granting divorce. To this extent her position was some better than that of the Hindu women. But while the Hindu woman could take an active part in religious ceremonies and visit the temples, the Muslim woman's social participation in religion was prohibited. Congregational prayers were offered only by men. This again was a deprivation they suffered. In another respect, also the Muslim woman was discriminated against. While the finer minds among the Hindu reformers, both men and women, could not reconcile themselves to the practice of polygamy and sought to reform the law and social practice. Muslim reformers did not give any thought to it. It was taken as a very normal, natural, social and also religious institution. In another respect, however, she was a beneficiary. She was successor to the family estate in her own right. The Muslim law of inheritance and succession is generous to her. As a daughter, sister or wife, her claim to property has been unchallenged. The husband cannot swallow his wife's property except with her consent: she, if she so desired, could alienate it.

Despite these provisions, the average women's life was not what law meant it to be. Social oppression prevailed, women were illiterate so they hardly knew their rights; they were only made aware of their obligations and family duties.

So what the law offered was filched by society. But, in the other respect she was really inhibited. She came to be cribbed and cabined within the *purdah*. It soon became an institution whose rigidity was total. Now woman could leave her home unless her whole self was covered by the *burqa*. This led to segregation and lowering of her status. Very much as Hindu social reformers of the nineteenth and early twentieth century were exercised over child marriage and imposed widowhood, Muslim social reformers were primarily concerned with the *purdah* system.

Badruddin Tayabjee was the foremost among them. Try as he did, he did not and could not succeed. The constricting bond was not released. Attention was also diverted to education; but the Muslims took a longer time to sending their young girls to schools for an obvious reasons. In larger cities they could start schools only for girls: but in the smaller towns and laterin the larger districts there were co-education schools run by the District Local Boards.Muslim parents were chary of sending their daughters to co-education schools. And the ratio was even less than 2 girls for every 100 Muslim boys at schools. In the country's average they hardly mattered. Whatever advantages law and religion permitted came to be corroded by the social net and social inhibitions.

It was after Mahatma Gandhi came to India after his long sojourn in South Africa, that ground for women's emancipation was prepared. Sensitive to imposed indignity, conscious of the worth of men and women, he dovetailed or wove women's needs into the fabric of the fight for freedom; and women could not have desired for a better champion.

Women's Upliftment in Society

We get to read often that an integrated man in an integrated society' was Gandhi's cherished ideal. It was, therefore, his constant effort to help every maladjusted section of the society to adjust with the whole so that the society can function well and harmoniously. In Gandhi's time, there were present both political and social maladjustments. As seen in the earlier chapter, many eminent reformers and social and political institutions tried to remove these maladjustments but unfortunately, they failed to push in the Indian society.

Realising that social and political reforms are inter-connected and that social evils impeded the country's march towards swaraj, Gandhi stressed the importance of raising the status of two very significant suppressed sections of the society, viz., the Harijans and women só much so that C.F. Andrews was prompted to observe that among all the different interests which occupied Mahatma Gandhi's attention in India, only a few can be compared with his earnest support to the women's movement.[17] We can well see from Table that the interviewees too when asked to indicate their order of preference about Gandhi's important contributions to India's national life, considered the raising of the status of Harijans and women as one of the leading contributions made by him in the social field.

Table 4.1

Gandhi's contributions	*First Preference*	*Second Preference*	*Third Preference*
Non-violent style of struggle	49	21	14
Moralising politics	28	22	12
Raising the status of Harijans and women	23	50	40
Inculcating the Swadeshi spirit	13	14	16
Village reconstruction	6	11	15
Basic education	3	4	11
Encouragement of National language	1	—	6

Some more contributions mentioned were promotion of communal harmony, equal regard for all religions and creating of a sense of dignity and self-respect among the people. It is noteworthy that though popularising the non-violent way of struggle and moralising politics were rated high in the list of contributions, raising the status of women and Harijans occupied the third place in the first preference list and first place in the second and the third preferene lists, this proving that though not a spectacular achievement like conducting non-violent political campaigns, emancipation of women was a significant achievement of Gandhi according to the respondent. Some viewed that it is to the lasting credit of Gandhi that he raised the status of women and made people understand what an important contribution they made in upholding and continuing our cultural rituals. Two respondents who did not accept Gandhi's programme fully maintained that Gandhi's work for the emancipation of women cannot be separated from his work for the political emancipation of the country and the upliftment of all suppressed sections of the society.

Messiah of Non-violence

Because of his faith in the divinity of all human beings irrespective of caste or creed or status or sex, Gandhi believed that men and women are fundamentally the same. He, however, was very much aware of the fact that man has dominated woman and done great injustice to her nearly since the beginning of time and that woman has developed an inferiority complex because of this. Though a large majority of the respondents attributed Gandhi's belief in eqality of men and women to his belief in the divinity of all human beings, there were others who held that it was because he regarded women as apostles of non-violence that he advocated conferring an equal status on them. Some of the interviewees were of the opinion that his belief in equality had its origin in his desire to fight all injustice and his inherent compassion for the suppressed sections of the society.

As many as 41 mentioned all the four reasons. Among some of the other reasons given were his belief that woman is the cultural backbone of the society and that certain basic qualities like tolerance, benevolence, purity, adjustibility, integrity and spiritual strength owned by them entitled them to equality.

Among the main contributions made by Gandhi towards the emancipation of women were mentioned his efforts at making them participate in the freedom struggle and work shoulder to shoulder with men shedding all fear, helping them to be economically independent as also professionally qualified and entrusting them with responsibilities in various fields of constructive work.

His plea for imparting education to women as also removing the *purdah* system, encouraging widow remarriage and his campaign for the removal of child-marriage, unequal marriage (age-wise) and the dowry-system were referred to. So too, was helping women to realise that they are equal partners with men in the task of achieving social regeneration and making them conscious of their spiritual strength.

While answering to a question regarding the period of his life when Gandhi became conscious of the problems facing women, 12 interviewees stated that his wife Kasturba's dignified behaviour and refusal to leave his house when, asserting his dominance as a husband, he asked her to do so made him understand both the pitiable plight of women as also the quiet strength possessed by them. It is true that he trained Kasturba to rise to his ideal, but even while adjusting his wife to him, she retained her own individuality and afforded him an opportunity to get a glimpse of women's latent capacity.

The fact that after launching Satyagraha in South Africa, when he was arrested, it was his steno-typist, Sony Schellesin, who held full charge of the movement, strengthened his belief in women's ability to take up the leadership mainly because her incorruptibility was beyond doubt and her capacity was acclaimed by all concerned. He had come in contact with a number of women at the Phoenix Ashram also. This gave him an insight into the working of their minds. Eight of the interviewees maintained that Gandhi was aware of the problems of women right from his childhood. His feeling of his mother's piety and singleness of purpose as also the lessons his nurse, Rambha, gave him in fearlessness were instrumental in making him look upon women as apostles of moral strength. This impression was further strengthened by women voluntarily coming forward to participate in Satyagraha against the unjust laws of the Government in South Africa.

Among respondents, women were of the opinion that Gandhi's stay in England made him aware of the glaring contrast between the freedom enjoyed by women in England and their utter subjugation to men in India. Also, the suffragette movement there, they felt, must not only have made a lasting impression on him but also encouraged him to work for the emancipation of Indian women. Three interviewees were of the view that it was at Champaran in 1917 that Gandhi felt that the condition of women was so bad that some drastic remedies had to be adopted to improve it. A few others felt that it was the magnificent response of the Indian women to his call for non-violent resistance for the British government that made him realise both their handicaps and their inherent strength. Though opinions differed regarding the most effective means adopted by Gandhi for emancipating women a large majority of the respondents, 60, held that his own attitude towards Kasturba and other women inmates of his Ashram proved to be greatly potent instrument for this work. Next in order were spread of education among women and constructive workers.

Participation in the Salt Satyagraha of 1929 and picketting of liquor-shops and jail-going also were said to be the two unique ways of bringing women out of the four walls of their houses and making them aware of their capacity to struggle against injustice. The *Charkha* which was utilised by Gandhi for making women win for themselves was stated as an effective weapon by 33 respondents. It may be noted that a majority of the active participants in the freedom struggle gave greater emphasis to active participation in the freedom movement and jail-going; whereas constructive workers emphasised the importance of *charkha* and social workers stressed the role of education in changing the status of women.

Some of the other means mentioned were Gandhi's discourses at the time of prayer meetings and articles in *Harijan* and *Young India* and making women aware of their ability by entrusting them specific responsibilities both in mass struggles and constructive work. Perhaps, he believed that women in India had fine traditions of sacrifice and self-effacement behind them and that if properly guided, they may be able to show the way to the whole world. With a view to helping women to achieve freedom, Gandhi carried on an incessant struggle to root out social evils like child marriage, the dowry system, sanctions on widow remarriage, prostitution, and the *purdah* system prevailing in some parts of the country. His humanitarian spirit revolted against the many wrongs meted out to women in the name of law, tradition and religion and he did not hesitate to repudiate the sanctity attached to ancient texts wherein disparaging references were made to women.

About the saying attributed to Manu that 'there can be no freedom for women', Gandhi refused to take it as sacrosanct and drew attention to the fact that woman was also referred to as Ardhangini or the better-half of man or as *sahadharmini* an equal share holder in the performance of one's *Dharma*. He was firmly of the opinion that texts which are contrary to known and accepted morality should be rejected.

Marital Aspects

We all know that Gandhi regarded marriage as a sacrament imposing discipline upon the two partners and not as a mere licence for physical union. An ideal marriage, according to him, is one which leads to spiritual union with physical union.Spiritual development, service, interest of the social order and love were the four conditions laid down by him for marriage.

Since love finds the last place among these conditions, love by itself was not considered by him to be a just or sufficient reason for marriage. Marriage for the satisfaction of carnal desires only was no marriage but *vyabhichara,* i.e., concupiscence, for him. He was firmly of the view that woman was not the servant of her husband but his comrade and companion, an equal partner in his joys and sorrows and that the obligations of the two towards the world are reciprocal. His ideal of a wife was Sita who, instead of cursing Rama for making her bear all sorts of privations, unequivocally declared that one thing which she ardently desired was that she may get Rama as her husband even in her next birth and never be separated with him.

However, the obligation preached by him was not one-sided. If he wanted wives to act as Sitas, he also wanted the husbands to be loving and considerate like Rama. Realising that Hindu culture has erred on the part of excessive subordination of the wife to the husband, he does not hesitate to state that when the husband becomes oppressive, "the wife has a perfect right to take per own course and meekly brave the consequences when she knows herself to be right and when her resistance is for a nobler purpose.[18] He wanted both the partners to be honest, upright and dutiful. Gandhi was in favour of reform in the marriage ceremony.

He, therefore, appealed to all sections of the society especially the richer sections to simplify the marriage ceremony and reduce the spending to the barest minimum. Considering marriageto be a social necessity, he favoured monogamous marriages. Being a great advocate of unity and harmony he put forward a plea for inter-communal marriages as also marriages among caste Hindus and untouchables. To quote him: "The society will not cease to be sacred on that count and children born out of such parentage, if they turn out to be good, would form active agents for the removal of such social evils as untouchability".[19]

As per findings, forty respondents (9 critics, 8 foreigners, 7 social workers, 6 constructive workers, 5 ashram inmates, 4 participants in the freedom struggle and one family member of Gandhi) maintained that efforts for the abolition of child-marriage and unequal marriage was one of Gandhi's important contributions to the emancipation of women. Thirty-seven (14 participants in the freedom struggle, 5 each from the groups of foreigners, and critics of Gandhi, 2 women social workers, 4 constructive workers, 3 women associated with Gandhi, 3 ashram inmates and one non-Gandhian turned Gandhian) felt that his plea for the abolition of dowry can be rated as an important contribution to the cause of women. In the opinion of 35 interviewees (including 7 freedom fighters and 7 critics, 5 foreigners, and 5 ashram inmates, 3 social workers, 3 constructive workers, alongwith 2 ashram inmates, 2 women associated with Gandhi and one member belonging to Gandhi's family) his advocacy of widow-remarriage went a long way in emancipating women from age-old traditions, while 36 (8 critics, 7participants in the freedom struggle, 6 constructive workers, 5 foreigners, 4 social workers, 3 ashram inmates and 3 women associated with Gandhi and one member of his family) were of the view that the efforts put in by him for the abolition of the *purdah* helped women a great deal in liberating themselves.

Abolition of Child Marriage

Mahatma Gandhi lent whole hearted support to the efforts of earlier reformers to put an end to the evil custom of child marriage. He believed that both the boy and the girl should be developed physically and mentally at the time of marriage and that they should have a voice in the choice of their life partner. Repudiating the claim that child marriage had a religious sanction, he not only called it uncivilised but a crime against God to call the union of children a married state because it undermines morals and leads to physical degeneration.

Young widows and young mothers dying in child birth are some of the evil consequences following from child marriage. In 1931, the rate of maternal mortality in India was 24.5 per thousand as compared to 4.5 in England. Over and above harming the mother, such marriages also harmed the child and hence the race. Gandhi looked with contempt those men who married young girls at a late age, with a view to have male progeny. This, in his opinion, was merely an excuse put forward by lustful men who looked upon marriage as a mere license to perpetrate all sorts of atrocities on young girls in their teens. Advising a man of 70 from Gujarat who was planning to marry for the fifth time on the plea that he had no son, he wrote. "It is better that you cease to entertain the desire for having a son. Desire to have a son is not always good. In a country where generally, the birth and death rates are properly balanced, it is more desirable to curb the desire for having a son rather than entertain it. In today's slave India where everyone is fearstricken and has lost the capacity to protect oneself, one's kith and kin and one's property, I believe it to be a sin to produce children".[20]

The alternatives suggested by him for eradicating these evils were cultivating public opinion and spreading of the consciousness of their rights among women as also legislation. He fully supported the Child Marriage Restraint Bill of Harbilas-Sarda in spite of bold opposition to it from the orthodox sections of the society. He also advocated opening of special institutions like *Mahilashramas* for young girls who fell victims to the evil designs of such greedy men or were sold by their parents for the sake of a paltry sum of money.

He favoured not only the rescuing of such girls but was prepared to arrange new matches for them because marriage under duress was no marriage but in fact rape according to him. Even if the criminal law allowed such marriages, Gandhi saw no objection in breaking these laws as he attached greater importance to the higher law - the law of one's conscience than to state imposed laws. His advice to all social reformers and especially to women social reformers was to go ahead in their mission of mercy with faith in themselves and their cause disregarding the supreme laws of the land.

Evil of Dowry

System of dowry, according to Gandhi, was a cruel custom which turned young girls meant to be queens of homes into mere chattels to be bought and sold. Though confined mainly to the middle classes, it had to be opposed because of its far-reaching psychological impact on young girls. Since the dowry system was closely connected with the caste-system, Gandhi recommended abolition of caste as one of the steps by which the system could be eradicated. Curtailing wasteful expenditure on the marriage ceremony and making it a simple and dignified affair was another remedy suggested.

He also made strong appeals to young men and women, especially educated men and women, to take active steps to do away with this evil."Any young man", he wrote, who makes dowry a condition of marriage discredits his education country and dishonours womanhood".[21]

His suggestion to the young girls was to prefer to remain spinsters rather than to get married to boys who demand dowry. To develop the right type of mentality to fight this evil, he stressed the role of education. Pleading for a revolutionary improvement for this purpose, he wrote, "whatever can be done to abate the evil must be done; it is clear to me that this evil and many others which can be named, can be tackled, if there is education which responds to the changing conditions of the country ... of what value is their education, if it does not enable them to dare defy a custom which is wholly indefensible and repugnant to one's moral sense?[22]

Along with mature methods like change in education, Gandhi also stressed the need of taking recourse to radical measures like organising youth movements and offering Satyagraha against those perpetrating the system. Such measures can be introduced by youth associations aiming at a reformation of the society instead of indulging in self-eulogising activities. Some conditions laid down for a successful Satyagraha are that the person offering it must be pure, true, and disciplined and entertain no grudge against the evil doer; though hating the evil, he must have faith in himself and his cause and must adopt silent but effective methods like cultivating moral strength and educating public opinion rather than take recourse to demonstrative action. Showing how both silent work and progressive measures can be adopted simultaneously, Gandhi said "Strong public opinion should be created in condemnation of the degrading practice of dowry and young men who soil their fingers with such ill-gotten gold should be excommunicated from society. Once public opinion is prepared, legislation may put the final seal over it. [23]

Introduction of Widow-Remarriage

In consistency with his view that marriage is a sacrament and not a contract, Gandhi admired those widows who remained faithful to their husbands and if possible, carried on the husband's unfinished work and served society like Ramabai Ranade or C.R. Das's widow, Smt. Basanti Devi. Like the Harijan, a widow also is looked down upon by Hindu society.

Protesting against the prevalent belief that a widow denotes ill-luck and that a widow crossing one's path is an ill-omen, Gandhi announced "I do not consider it inauspicious to see a widow. I consider it to be my good fortune to see a widow in the early hours of the day. Her blessings are a great boon for me. Seeing her, I forget all my difficulties. Man is an insignificant creature compared to a widow. It is impossible to imitate the widow so far as her patience is concerned. What value can a man's temporary renunciation have before the ancient heritage possessed by the widow? Service is the main goal of a widow's life".[24]

In this whole person, this attitude of his, however, should not be construed to mean that he was opposed to widow-remarriage. His view can be best expressed in his own words. "Voluntary widowhood consciously adopted by a woman who has felt the affection of the partner, adds grace and dignity to life, sanctifies the home and uplifts widowhood imposed by religion or custom whereas forced widowhood is an unbearable yoke and defiles the home by secret vice and degrades religion."[25] While he regarded voluntary widowhood as the glory of Hindu religion, the existence of young widows was construed as a blot on the Hindu society. Four main rules formulated by him for safeguarding both the widow and the Hindu society are:

"(a) No father should get his daughter married before she reaches the age of fifteen,

(b) in case of girls under 15 who have already become widows, their fathers should make arrangements to get them well-married,

(c) if a girl of 15 becomes a widow within one year of her marriage, her parents should encourage her to get married again.

(d) every family should treat a widow with utmost respect and the parents and parents-in-law should give her facilities to expand her knowledge".[26]

Above said rules, according to him, were not drastic enough to eradicate the evil. Therefore, the real remedy lay in seeing that like the widow, the widower also does not get remarried. So long as this cannot be ensured, observance of the above-mentioned four rules may help in easing the situation to some extent. The ultimate remedy suggested by Gandhi, viz., considering the widow and a widower on par so far as remarriage is concerned shows his genuine concern for equality and fair play. His advice to the guardians of girl child widows was to get the child widows well-married. He preferred not to call it remarriage because he refused to believe that they were really married even though the orthodox sections of the society including *pandits* cited texts to prove that the first marriage of the girls was righteous and sacrosanct, thus proving that he cared more for being true to his own conscience than accepting old text and traditions.

Of course, with regard to those women who became widowed at a mature age, his opinion was slightly different; not that he considered remarriage a sin in their case but his preference was certainly for such widows leading a celibate life. He would perhaps have endorsed the sentiments of the poet who wrote "Widowhood and a life devoted to the sacred memory of the deceased partner is purer than the pleasures of married life".[27]

Purdah System

The system of *purdah* prevailing in some parts of the country was strongly resented by Gandhi. He was of the opinion that the system was doing incalculable harm to the country. He failed to understand why men should arrogate to themselves the right to regulate female purity when women do not claim any such right with regard to men's chastity. The prevalence of *purdah* pained him deeply but what made him sadder still was that even educated families did not have the courage to reject the custom. He made an appeal to the public in general and women in particular to tear down the *purdah* with one mighty effort. His attempt was to make them understand that chastity was no hot-house growth and that it should grow from within and not be superimposed. It was his firm belief that it is not *purdah* but purity which works as a shield and gives protection to the woman against a man with malicious intentions.

Prostitution and the Custom of *Devdasi*

Among all the evils for which man has made himself responsible, none is so degrading, shocking or brutal as his abuse of the better-half of humanity, the female sex. Gandhi protested against prostitution which he called moral leprosy but not against the prostitutes who were to be pitied and helped to regain their virtue rather than hated and condemned to lead a life of sin. Holding men who visited the pestilential haunts inhabited by the prostitutes equally responsible like women for perpetuating this evil he wrote: "Prostitute is commonly supposed to apply to women of lewd character. But the men who indulge in vice are just as much, if not more, prostitutes than the women who in many instances have to sell their bodies for the sake of earning a livelihood".[28]

Regarding *Devdasi*, the custom of dedicating young girls to temples theoretically in the service of the deity but practically for immoral purposes was openly denounced by Gandhi. Even though the system had the support of Hindu law, his advice to the Hindus was to purge the society of this "pest" at any cost.

His whole soul rebelled against it. He considered it to be a double crime to indulge in immoral traffic and again that too in the name of God. He was perhaps the first crusader against this evil practice. So far as remedies for this evil are concerned, Gandhi suggested a two-pronged attack-propaganda amongst women who shed their honour for livelihood and among men to behave better towards these unfortunate women. He also favoured legislative measures and appealed for active support to Muthulaxmi Reddi her efforts to get a law passed to stop the system of *Devdasi*. Legislation, however, should be accompanied by strong public opinion in favour of abolishing the system and cultivation of the capacity to discriminate between virtue and vice among the people.

Divorce and Population Control

Keeping in view the ancient texts, Gandhi believed that the aim of marriage far from being the fulfilment of fleeting passions was the preservation and furtherance of *Dharma*. It was looked upon more as a duty and disciplined state of life than a duration meant for enjoyment and sexual indulgence. His advice to both the partners was to observe discipline and carry on the household duty with mutual regard and utmost consideration for each other. If one of the spouses breaks the discipline, he grants the right to break the bond to the aggrieved partner but makes it very clear that the breach, being moral, precludes divorce, i.e., the partner is allowed to separate but only for serving a larger end and not for entering into a fresh marital union. It may, however, be noted that in extreme cases like cruelty and constant harassment, he permitted divorce.[29] Though Gandhi did not quite accept the thesis of Indiabeing overpopulated, he did favour controlling the population mainly because India was a slave country and he did not want India to multiply slaves and weaklings. This was considered by him to be a type of violence. He, therefore, advocated birth-contrtol. It was, however, not birth-control through contraceptives which he equalled with race suicide but by self-restraint and leading a celebate or semi-celibate life by restricting physical union only for the purpose of procreation by the married pairs. "It is my deepest conviction," writes he, "that if this method of artificial means gains popularity all over the world, it will lead to more degradation of mankind.[30] He wanted both the partners to understand that abstention from satisfaction of sexual desire ends not in disease but in health and vigour. He knew this was difficult but was convinced that it was not impossible only if both the partners had the will to practice it. "The conquest of lust," in his word "is the highest endeavour of a man's or woman's existence whereas physical union for the sake of carnal satisfaction is reversion to animality which had to be avoided by both."[31]

Quoting his own instance, he observed that he really came to enjoy his married life only after he ceased to look upon Kasturba sexually. He was definitely of the opinion that like truth and non-violence, abstinence from sex too is not meant only for the chosen few but can be practised by all. So far as sterilisation is concerned, through Gandhi opposed the imposition of the sterilisation law on the people, he was ready to accept it in case of men suffering from chronic diseases provided they were agreeable to it but not in case of women who were advised by him to learn the art of resistance against man the aggressor.

In 1936, Margaret Singer, the great crusader for the birth control movement had an interview with Gandhi. She raised the question of irritations and disputes that would arise out of thwarted desires by following Gandhi's advice. She cited several instances of nervous and mental break-down as a result of the practice of self-control. Of course, he cited examples from his own life to disprove this point but it did not carry conviction with Singer. It was argued by some protagonists of birth control that the 'safe-period' method, according to which physical union occurs only during that period which is considered to be safe, i.e., a period in which there is no possibility of conception taking place would be acceptable to Gandhi because it does not depend on any artificial means of birth control. As will be seen from Table 4.2, 94 out of 151 interviewees said that they approved of the family planning programme followed by the government as against 39, who disapproved of it. Thirteen said they approved of it partly whereas there was no response from 5 persons.

Table 4.2

	Yes	No	Not	Partly Relied	Total
Family members	1	—	1	—	2
Ahram inmates	7	6	1	3	17
Women associated with Gandhi					
Active Participants	14	6	—	2	22
Constructive workers	12	5	1	—	18
Non-Gandhian turned Gandhian	1	1	—	—	2
Women social workers	15	3	1	1	20
Critics of Gandhi	28	7	1	5	41
Foreigners and others	15	5	—	1	21
Total	94	39	5	13	151

While 89 interviewees said that over-population is a major problem faced by India which is already a poor country and which would be rendered more so if population isnot controlled, as many as 47 held that other ways are not practicable. Two social workers said that it improves the general health both of the mother and the children and that it proves that woman is much more than a mere child-bearing machine or instrument. So far as the reason for the disapproval of the programme are concerned, only 4 agreed with Gandhi in maintaining that India is not over-populated; one of them an Ashram inmate gave it as the sole reason.

Twenty-eight held the view that family planning leads to immorality. Out of these, 5 were Ashram inmates, and 5 women associated with Gandhi, 3 active participants in the freedom movement, 3 constructive workers and 2 women social workers. One of the respondents specifically stated that the programme would lead to spiritual, mental and physical bankruptcy of Indians and therefore defeat its own purpose. Amongst the 29 who held that self-copntrol should be the only way to control population, 6 were Ashram inmates, 6 critics of Gandhi, 3 constructive workers, and 2 social workers. Twenty-four objected to the programme on the ground of its being too expensive and modern methods of birth control being harmful for health. Thus, it is obvious that a majority of the interviewees did admit that India is over-populated.

Again, even the followers of Gandhi did not completely reject the family planning programme. Though 28 did say that family planning leads to immorality, it may be noted that it is not equivalent to saying that birth control by unnatural means is immoral. Many orthodox Hindus and Christians believe that since all life emanates from God, children should be looked upon as gifts from God and that abortion which amounts to taking living beings life should be taboo. Catholic women in France, Italy Ireland and the USA protested against this stand of the Church. As a result, the supreme court of the USA granted the right to abortion in December 1972. While women have, thus, won a legal battle, they will still have to be prepared to put up a hard fight against the tradition-bound orthodox sections of social set up.

Suggestions

Gandhi's suggestion to women was not to rely on men but on themselves and cultivate complete fearlessness and inner strength. Education, according to him, was the most important instrument for bringing about the desired change. "Education," he said, "is essential for enabling wemen to assert these natural rights, to exercise them wisely and to work for their expansion."[32]

Then existing system of education as Gandhi saw it had three major defects—it was based on foreign culture,was lopsided in asmuch as it ignored the culture of the heart and the hand confining itself only to the head; and was being imparted through an alien medium which was responsible for causing a brain-fag. One of the major devices by which he tried to revolutionise the system was giving a key place to handicrafts in his new scheme of education and make the children realise the dignity of labour right from their infancy.

This he thought, would serve a double purpose. Apart from paying for education and relieving the economic burden of the government, it would also teach the children an occupation that would help them in becoming economically self-reliant in their later half of life. Though equipping the students for earning their livelihood constituted an important part of the new scheme of education, its ultimate aim was nothing less than character building and prepare of an integrated man - a man possessing both intellectual abilities and qualities of the heart like compassion, moral courage and the ability to forget oneself in working for higher ends.

These targets were common both for men and women students. The aim of education for women in India was to enable them to work freely with men. In the first conference on educational reform, women themselves had wanted that "moral training based on spiritual ideals should be made compulsory for all schools and colleges".

No one however, not even women, demanded a way of education that would enable women to question men's superiority or to claim equal rights. What men wanted was that as a result of education, women should be enabled to become companions and helpmates of their any husbands in facing the vicissitudes of life. While Gandhi believed that men and women are equal in status and are complementary to each other, he was definitely of the opinion that home-life being the special area of women, they should be specially equipped for domestic duties including the upbringing and education of children very much as men should be equipped for activities outside home. His advice to the educated women was to protect the best traditions of Indian culture rejecting that which is base and appalling and refusing to ape the manners of the West.

Also, one of his expectations from the educated women was that they should have no attraction for jewellery. Once, addressing women college students, he observed, "Your parents do not send you to school to become dolls; on the contrary, you are expected to become Sisters of Mercy."[33]

Again, attempt was made to elicit the opinion of the interviewees regarding giving special education to women and Gandhi's view on it. Three of them (2 Ashram inmates, and an eminent educationist) clearly said that Gandhi never emphasised special education for women whereas 81 said his emphasis was fully justified, and 46 said it was partly justified. Eleven were of the opinion that Gandhi was not justified in emphasising special education for women and 10 did not give answer. Even those who favoured special training in child care, mother-craft and such other subjects for girls maintained that those with special aptitude and ability for specific subjects should be given all facilities to pursue training in those subjects. Some of the main reasons given by those who favoured different curricula for boys and girls were that their natural abilities and aptitudes are different from those of men and so are their functions. Their plea was that except girls with exceptional abilities, others should not waste their time and energy in learning subjects which do not help them anyway in life.

One social worker who also was an active participant in the freedom struggle stated, "I remember that when the Gujarat Vidyapeeth was started, Gandhiji called me to discuss the curriculum I had suggested for a women's college I started in Ahmedabad and the impression left on me is that he wanted different subjects to be taught to boys and girls." Anyway, all were agreed that Gandhi did not believe in debarring anyone, boy or girl, from developing other special talents. As against this, two constructive workers who had also worked as education ministers in the states viewed that what Gandhi wanted was not different curricula for boys and girls but only different treatment of certain subjects in the same pattern of education. This opinion seems to be nearer the truth inasmuch as he felt that once the division of spheres of work is recognised, the general qualities and training required by both boys and girls are the same.

Legal provisions is another remedy suggested for the amelioration of women. Gandhi was definitely of the opinion that women should labour under no legal disability not suffered by men but he had no illusion about legislative measures. He knew well that the base of the evil lies much deeper in man's greed for power and in mutual lust. The best remedy, according to him, therefore, lay in creating strong public opinion against the evil practices and in women learning the lessons of self-help. He wanted them to refuse to be slaves either of their own whims or fancies or of men and lead a pure life. He agreed that man was primarily responsible for making woman weak but taking women particularly the more enlightened among them to task for allowing this state of affairs to continue, he asked them a very pertinent question. "... Many women always throw the blame on men and save their consciences. Do the enlightened amongst them not owe it to their sex as also to men whose mothers they are to take up the burden of reform?"[34]

Economic Independence of Women

> *...spinning will remain womens' speciality. ...spinning is essentially a slow and comparatively silent process. Woman is the embodiment of sacrifices and, therefore, non-violence. Her occupations, must therefore be as they are, more conducive to peace than war—*
> *M.K. Gandhi*

The spectre of the stark poverty of a very great majority of his countrymen pained Gandhi deeply. In order to find a solution for this problem as also to revolutionise life in the villages, he presented the economy of the spinning wheel and supported *khadi* as an industry supplementary to and co-extensive with agriculture. He was convinced that very much as the loss of the spinning wheel brought about India's slavery, its voluntary revival will lead to its freedom; and women, in his view, were best suited to take up spinning and the propagation of *khadi* and *swadeshi,* i.e., goods manufactured in India. Gandhi did not favour women going out for their livelihood as he regarded their duties at home as important as, if not more important than, men's duty to earn.

Women thus had to supplement and complement the work done by men. This, however, should not be taken to mean that he was opposed to women taking up work; he only wanted them to do it without disturbing the home. He wanted them to take up some work which would supplement the earning of the family and spinning, according to him, was perhaps the best work they could undertake. Apart from supplementing the family income, it would go a long way in bringing about a total metamorphosis in the lives of women. He described the spinning wheel as a 'widow's loving companion'. He was also of the view that *charkha* will enable women to safeguard their virtue.

Thus, he recommended it specially to the fallen women and pleaded with them to turn a new leaf in their lives. Perhaps this is the reason why as many as 40 interviewees held that helping women to be economically independent was one of Gandhi's great contributions towards their emancipation and

30 opined that women's taking to *charkha* was one of the most efficient means to achieve this task. In the 19th Century, it was not thought respectable for women to work. Even as late as 1935, they were excluded from important services like the civil services, the medical services and the police service.

Trying to remove this discrepancy, the Indian Constitution says, "there shall be equality of opportunity for all citizens in matters relating to employment or appointment to any office under the state."[35]

Despite the fact that women have taken to many professions, including legal, medical, administrative and others after independence, teaching is by far the most dominant sole area of employment for them. Of the total persons engaged in the teaching profession 28.6 per cent are women. This may be because women have an instinctive quality to teach and also because, for long, teaching as a profession for women has received approval even from the traditional society.

The medical profession too seems to have a great attraction for women. Of the total persons involved in this 19.6 per cent are women. It is difficult to say whether it is the social status and prestige enjoyed by a doctor, especially a woman doctor, or the ideal of service inculcated by Gandhi, the hope of high earning or the romance of healing the is the chief cause of this attraction. So far as social work is concerned, it may be remembered that Gandhi laid great stress on it and wanted women to take up one of the activities under his constructive programmes, consisting of communal harmony, removal of untouchability, prohibition, khadi, village industries, village hygiene sanitation, new or basic education, adult education, women's uplift, education in health and hygiene, encouraging provincial languages, popularising national language, economic equality, welfare of kisans, labour welfare, tribal welfare, service of lepers and student welfare. Many more women are employed now as compared to pre-independence days. Female employment increased from 8.62 lacs in 1971 to 19.5 lacs in 1986.

In the private sector also it increased from 10.67 lacs to 13.07 lacs during the same period.

Khadi and Small Scale Industries

After agriculture, cottage industries have been the mainstay of our villages for centuries. However, after the advent of British rule, these industries decayed as the policy of the British Government was to see that the village industries got destroyed so that Manchester and its machines could flourish. This led to large-scale unemployment and underemployment of artisans adept in these age-old industries. Gandhi labelled *khadi* as the livery of freedom and left no pains to revive village industries and propagate *swadeshi* in dress and spirit. Though *khadi* was thus closely linked with the freedom struggle in the initial stage, in 1925 a different organisation.

The All India Spinners Association was established with a view to encouraging hand-spinning and hand-weaving. Ten years later, The All India Village Industries made to organise industries like, beekeeping, handmade paper, palm gur, ghani oil and others. It was only after independence that concerted efforts were made for the development of *Khadi* and village industries in line with the directive principles of State Policy included in the Constitution which uniquely lays down that "the state shall endeavour to secure, by suitable legislation or economic organisation or in any other way, to all workers, agricultural, industrial or otherwise, work, a living wage, conditions of work ensuring a decent standard of life and full enjoyment of leisure and social and cultural opportunities and, in particular, the state shall endeavour to promote cottage industries on an individual or cooperative basis in rural areas.[36]

Along with creating employment opportunities in the rural areas at a low capital cost, village industries are helpful in developing local initiative, and a spirit of self-reliance and cooperation among the general. Other advantages of these industries are that they offer employment at the place of residence of the artisans and compared to other industries they require a shorter gestation period.

Also being small, there is higher scope for participation by the artisans in them than in large-scale industries. If, therefore, they are equipped with modern technology, they are bound to prove useful in the industrialisation of the rural sector.

Keeping in view all these advantages, the Government of India evolved a policy for the development of *khadi* and village industries and tried to link it up with planning. In the first Five Year Plan, the development of khadi and village industries was regarded as a conjunct to the development of agriculture and the emphasis of the government policy was on maximum utilisation of the idle hours of the agriculturists.

The plan had much of what Myrdal terms 'the fragrance of vintage Gandhism' in it. The authors sought to further rural uplift and enhance the level of rural employment by resuscitating the sagging arts and crafts but they desired that such renovation occurs primarily within the defined corpus of village self-sufficiency. On the recommendation of the Planning Commission, an autonomous body called All India Khadi and Village Industries Board was set-up in 1953. Realising the importance of small-scale and cottage industries, in 1956, the Industrial Policy Resolution of the Government categorically stated that small-scale industries "provide urgent large-scale employment, offer a better method of ensuring a more equitable distribution of national income and facilitate an effective mobilisation of resources of capital and skill which might otherwise remain unutilised. Some of the difficulties that unplanned urbanisation tends to create will be avoided by the establishment of small centres of industrial production all over the country.[37]

Accordingly, in 1957, a statutory status was given to the Khadi and Village Industries Board. As a result, the Khadi and Village Industries Commission was formed to plan, organise and implement programmes of development for Khadi and cottage industries including hand-spinning and weaving on handlooms, processing of cereals and pulses, *ghani* oil, manufacture of canegur and khandsari, palmgur making, cottage match, cottage soap, manufacture of shellac, collection of forest plants and fruits for medical reasons, bamboo and cane-work, manufacture of gum and resins, manufacture of katha, handmade paper, bee-keeping, cottage-pottery, flaying, curing and tanning of hides and skins, and cottage leather industries, fibre alongwith than coir manufacture and other waste products, lime manufacturing, blacksmithy, carpentry fruit processing and fruit preservation and manufacture of household utensils in the metal of aluminium. During the Second Five Year Plan which attached greater importance to promotional than on the protective aspects

Table 4.3

Number and Percentage of Women Workers to Total Workers in Every Industrial Category and Percentage of Women Workers in Every Category to the Total Female Workers

Industrial Category	*Workers in thousand*		*Female workers as percentage of workers*	
	Total	*Female*	*Total workers in each factory*	*Total female workers*
(a) Primary Sector (1 to 4)	92,522	14,932	41.6	33.2
1. Cultivators				
2. Agricultural labourers	55,500	20,768	20.9	46.1
3. Live stock, Forestry, Fishing, Hunting and Plantations, Orchards and allied activities	4,993	833	2.2	1.9
4. Mining and Quarrying	1,264	163	0.6	0.4
(b) Secondary Sector (5-a & 5-b)				
5. Manufacturing, Processing, Servicing and Repairs				
(a) Household industry	7,712	2,064	3.5	4.6
(b) Other than household industry	17,432	1,598	7.8	3.6
(c) Tertiary Sector (6 to 9)				
6. Construction	3,565	358	1.6	0.8
7. Trade and Commerce	13,930	917	6.3	2.0
8. Transport, storage and Communications	6,069	170	2.7	0.4
9. Other Services	19,530	3,170	8.8	7.1
Total of all categories	2,22,517	44,973	20.2	100.00

Source: Census of India 1981, Series-I, India Part II, special Report and Tables Based on 5 per cent Sample Datas size Registrar General and Census Commissioner for India, New Delhi, 1984, pp-6-9 and 24-27 (Tables).

of rural industrialisation, the emphasis was on extending work avenues and with it progressively raising the standard of living of the artisans and bringing about a more balanced and integrated rural economy.

The Third Plan emphasised the need of positive correlation between old and fresh industries and recommended an integrated approach. The Fourth Plan drew special attention to regional disparities in the development of *khadi* and village industries and the necessity for special efforts in backward areas. The Fifth Plan spoke of the needs of traditional artisans who were getting displaced and suggested larger deployment of industrial finance for village industries in the light of the expansion of the banking structure after nationalisation. The feeble exercises initiated in the Second Five Year Plan and continued in the Third Five Year Plan to integrate khadi and village industries with the longer programme of rural development came to an abrupt end with the abandonment of the Community Development Programme and the dismantling of the block machinery in most of the states.

During the latter half of the Fifth Plan, the Planning Commission began to show a marked preference for the beneficiary-oriented approach and self-employment in the anti-poverty programmes. This trend of thinking received a boost in the Janata period (1977-79) when some state governments revived the evocative term 'Antyodaya' which was coined by Gandhiji himself. When one is called upon to identify the poorest of the poor and help him receive viable self-employment through the acquisition of assets like tools and equipment and through training, one is compelled to choose a simple craft or a village industry, if the selected person has the will to be an artisan.

Accordingly, the Sixth Five Year Plan laid down specific targets for village industries to be developed under the Industry, Services and Business Sector, i.e., ISB of Integrated Rural Development Programme (IRDP). Out of the 600 families selected in each block, at least 50 were thus required to be assisted to take up village industries. The Seventh Five Year Plan recorded that the target through Part I of ISB Sector could not be achieved in the Sixth Plan for various reasons. Nevertheless it reaffirmed broadly the approach under IRDP. The financial arrangements made available by the Government to the Khadi Village Industries

Commission for implementing its development programmes during the various plan periods are as shown in Table 4.4.

Table 4.4
Public Sector Outlays and Plan Provisions for Khadi and Village Indians

Plan Duration	*Public sector Outlay*	*Public Allocation for KVI*	*Funds made available*	*Col. 3 as % of Col. 2*	*Col. 4 as % of Col. 3*
First Plan	1,960	15.00	11.58	0.8	77
Second Plan	4,672	83.78	78.71	1.8	91
Third Plan	8,577	92.40	86.90	1.1	94
Annual Plan 1966-67 to 1968-69	6,757	53.05	53.05	0.8	100
Fourth Plan	37,250	180.00 +	118.20*	0.06	66*
Annual Plans 1978-79 to 1979-80	24,192	154.20	154.20	0.6	100
Sixth Plan	97,500	480.00	521.72CC	0.5	109
Seventh Plan	1,80,000	540.00		0.3 xxx	109

As far as employment of artisans is concerned, the Commission provided employment to 18.01 lac persons in 1971-72 which increased to 233.72 lacs in 1979-80 and the target for 1990 was 400.00 lacs according to the Seventh Five Year Plan. Among these, 9.63 lacs were employed in the khadi programme in 1971-72 whereas in 1979-80 the figure went up to 11.20 lacs, and the target for 1990 was 20.00 lacs according to the Seventh Five Year Plan.

Similarly 8.38 lac people were employed in the village industries in 1971-72 which went up to 16.13 lac persons in 1979-80 and the target for 1990 according to the Seventh Five Year Plan was 30.00 lac persons, if possible. Majority of women work in the rural unorganised sector which mainly includes nine employment systems viz. agriculture, dairying, fisheries, small animal husbandry, art and handicrafts, sericulture, handlooms and social and agro-forestry. The sex-wise break-up of the first eight of these systems is shown in Table 4.5.

Table 4.5
Number of Men and Women in Large Employment Sector

Sector	*Males*	*Females*
Agriculture	754.70	18.70
Dairying	50.00	750.00
Fishries	18.00	10.00
Small Animal Husbandry	20.00	150.00
Khadi and Village Industries	19.90	17.00
Handicrafts	22.00	5.40
Sericulture	12.00	8.00

* *Source:* Natikonal Perspective Plan for Women, Ministryof Human Resources Development, Govt. of India, 1988, p. 26.

Here it may be noted that 17 lac women are employed in the Khadi and Village Industries as against 19.90 lacs of men and that a vast majority of the interviewees were of the opinion that the attempts of the KVIC to reduce unemployment and provide work to women were praiseworthy. It is assumed that khadi and rural industries equipped with modern technology, apart from providing a ground for rural industrialisation, will also help to reduce some of the evil effects of large-scale industrialisation like proliferation of slums, unplanned urbanisation and social and health hazards and the like. Though women are increasingly taking to various professions, it is not always that they get the right type of occupation. Age-old prejudices still continue and so is about discrimination against them. The Commission on the Status of Women appointed by the U.N. stated in its report that women (all over the world) continued to be subject to unequal treatment with regard to employment opportunities, betterment and remuneration.

Duration of work, holidays, leave and other matters related to the employment of women are regulated by the prevailing rules. Employment of women at nights is prohibited. In agricultural sector women work for shorter hours as compared to men. This is in keeping with the practice followed in other countries of the world. As mentioned in the National Perspective Plan for women, segmentation in the labour market, adverse implications of technological growth for women, lack of unionisation of women workers, absence of a purposeful human resources development policy aimed at improving women's employability through training and lack of a national labour policy encompassing workers in the unorganised sector are the leading factors affecting women's employment status.

This way, by and large, Indian women have performed their double function as house-keepers and as careerists well and creditably. If measures like diversification in agriculture and other main sectors of rural employment, proper training in skills and management are adopted they would fare still better; but they must bear in mind Gandhi's advice that their work should never be allowed to come in the way of their job as house-keepers, mothers, moulders of future generations and builders of the country.

Political Empowerment

The Hindu society towards end of 19th century had been open to women. Still women had to continue agitation for getting their due. It may, however, be noted that the struggle of the Indian women was not as severe, nor was it assertively feminist as in some of the western countries. It was at last, in the year 1917 that a deputation waited on Montague and Chelmsford under the leadership of Sarojini Naidu and submitted a memorandum which contained demands for better education, improved health, maternity benefits and the equal franchise rights as would be extended to men. In as much as it demanded the abolition of disqualification of sex in the legislative and administrative spheres, it marked a distinct landmark in the history of women's movement in the country.

It was resolved that the same tests be applied to women as to men in regard to the franchise. When their expectations did not bear fruit, many leading women's organisations lodged vocal and voluminous protests. The question, however, was left to be decided by the provincial legislative councils. Madras decided in side of women in 1921; other provinces followed suit in 1926, and the discrimination against women disappeared in all the provinces. By 1929, they were enfranchised on the same terms as were applied to men and became great units in the life of the nation.

With Gandhi's magic touch, the ancient walls of tradition crumbled as women—the helpless victims of cruel customs—came out of the close precincts of their homes in hundreds and thousands and became valiant soliders of the freedom struggle. Renuka Ray correctly observes: "the most momentous change in the position of women in India was due to the efforts of Mahatma Gandhi, who, in launching his campaign of non-violent, non-co-operation in the struggle for India's freedom ignored both law and custom of specially calling upon women to participate ... No legislation could have been more sweeping or more effective than the Mahatma's call, which levelled the barriers of established customs almost overnight."[38]

Time to test the strength of women came when, in 1913, Gandhiji launched passive resistance in South Africa. Gandhiji invited women to join the movement to resist unjust marriage laws as they were directly connected with the subject. Women from 'Tolstoy Farm' were only too glad to participate in the struggle. Fatima Mehtab and her mother were the first Muslim satyagrahis to be sent to prison. Even Kasturba willingly joined the Satyagraha. Women expressed exceptional bravery. Some of them were illiterate and could not read newspapers. But they knew that India's honour was at stake. Their going to jail was "a cry of agony and prayer offered from the bottom of their hearts." Then it was here that Gandhi first saw the high potentialities of women in a non-violent struggle. Paying a rich tribute to Valliamma, a girl of 16, who succumbed to jail hardships, he wrote "She built her temple of service with her own hands, and her glorious image has a niche even now reserved for it in many a heart; and the name of Valliamma will live in the South African Satyagraha as long as India lives".[39]

During the days of the Champaran Satyagraha in India in 1917, women had lent a helping hand to him by organising literacy classes and doing other constructive work. Also, in the Ahmedabad labour movement of 1919, Ansuyaben Sarabhai fought a brave battle on behalf of the workers even against her own brother. In spite of women having thus proved their ability and sincerity to work for the cause of freedom and justice, initially, he was reluctant to allow them to take active role in the Salt Satyagraha of 1930. No woman was included in the original band of 78 volunteers in the historic Dandi March which began on March 12 from his Ahmedabad Ashram.

Quickly reacting to this attitude of his, the Women's Indian Association protested against their exclusion on the ground that in a non-violent struggle, any discrimination on the ground of sex was unnatural and liable to work against the awakened consciousness of women. Gandhi advised them to confine their participation to the picketing of liquor-shops and foreign cloth shops, but it did not satisfy them. So he was compelled to permit them to fully participate in the Satyagraha. He also named Sarojini Naidu as his next successor after Abbas Tyabji and she carried out her purpose with rare distinction. Once he had given the long-awaited signal for the starting of Satyagraha on 6 April, 1930 by picking up pinch of salt from the seashore of Dandi, women in their thousands strode down to the sea, carrying sea-water in pitchers of clay, brass and copper with a view to prepare contraband salt and auction it for fancy rates—an unusual way of breaking the nefarious salt law.

They thus took struggle to a higher moral level and turned it into a 'beautiful epic, instead of an armed conflict with the mighty British Empire describing how the unlettered, untrained women of India fought with courage and fortitude and made-law-breaking universal Kamaladevi Chattopadhyaya says, "Women turned every home into sanctuary for the law-breaker. They lent sanctity to their act by their purity of spirit. Even the mightiest military power cannot cope with a struggle that has its being in the sacred precincts of the home."[39]

They marched in processions, and organised *vanar senas*-the monkey army and *maniar senas*-the cat army of young children and *prabhat feris*-early morning processions luring the people by their sweet melodies to join the righteous struggle started by Bapu. They addressed public meetings, sold prescribed literature and came forward to face all sorts of atrocities including inhuman treatment by the officers and imprisonment.

Number of women worked as 'dictators' of the war councils. Some of the devices used by the police to terrorise them were to drive them in deserted jungle in a van and release them at dusk, turn water-hoses against them, bring mounted cavalry to trample on them, throw mustard, pepper and chilli powder in their eyes, jeer at them, abuse their husbands and snatch away their babies. In spite of this in the first ten months of the struggle, nearly 17,000 women were convicted and sent to jails. Dhondo Keshav Karve, the founder of the first and sole women's university in India, on his return from Japan witnessed a phenomenon which brought tears of joy in his eyes.

He saw hundreds of women high and low, old and young moving towards the sea from the crowded streets of Bombay. As they advanced in an orderly manner to the sea and broke the salt law, he astonished, "what decades of my work and work similar to mine has failed to achieve, this wizard of Sabarmati has achieved by a single stroke of imaginative action". This was the method which Gandhi employed. Whether it was in the sheltered shade of his Ashram or on the burning sands of the seashores at midday, he would call girls and women, fill them with enthusiasm and inspire them to work for a great cause. O. Malley observes, "The call of Mr. Gandhi for active support from women in his campaign appealed at once to their sense of nationalism and to the spirit of selfless devotion which is characteristic of Indian womanhood. They came out of *purdah* in thousands, and thousands have remained out of it. There are great public gatherings of emancipated women which would have been unthinkable twenty yeas ago".[40]

The cause being Indian, and the objective being freedom, it had none of the man-woman antagonism that has characterised the women's movement in America. As a matter of fact, men were its great supporters. As many as 111 and 66 interviewees respectively stated that making women participate in the freedom struggle and work shoulder to shoulder with men and enabling them to divorce fear of every kind were Gandhi's most important contributions to the emancipation of women. As one interviewee said "we found in him not only a 'Bapu', a wise father but what is far more precious a mother before whose all-embracing and understanding love all fear and restraint automatically disappear". As per one of Gandhi's critics, Gandhi should be given the fullest credit cor encouraging women to accept responsibilities and helping them to develop qualities of leadership. So far as the means adopted by him for achieving this target are concerned, 46 and 44 respectively asserted that inducing women to court imprisonment and picket liquor shops were the two most powerful means used. In the year 1942, when World War II came to India's doorstep, Gandhi passionately urged Britain to leave India. Gandhi gave a mantra for the non-violent soldier of freedom-"do or die".

He asserted, "We shall either free India or die in the attempt." This served as a signal for a reign of terror in the country. Gandhi, the arch-rebel and the accredited leaders of the nation were put under arrest; India's national pride rose in revolt and all groups of the society-peasants and workers, lawyers and students, young and old men and women - not only thundered out a warm welcome to the mass movement but also actively participated in it. Women not only adopted the old tactics of taking out processions and shouting slogans and organising meetings but also took a leading part in the underground movement which included activities like running a secret Radio, making bombs, raiding police stations, blowing up government buildings and all others.

Like the enthusiasm of the people, the repression resorted to by the government also knew no bounds. As Gandhi wrote to the British Government it was the "leonine violence" unleashed by the government which gave birth to violent responses from the people. Not only were unarmed bands of women volunteers teargassed and lathi-charged without warning but women in several parts of the country were also humiliated, injured and raped by the soldiers. Gandhi wanted that the women of India should have as much share in winning the war as men. He expected much of them and they did not disappoint him; they came forward to give all that they had - their wealth and strength, their jewellery and skill, their mark for the success of the struggle. He had once said that it is possible that in this peaceful and non-violent struggle, women might win the race leaving man trailing behind. Women of the country proved this beyond any doubt. One of the questions put to the respondents was whether Gandhi's attitude towards women would have been the same even if the struggle led by him were violent. Sixty-one respondents said that the struggle being violent or non-violent would not have made any difference in his attitude whereas 64 said it would have; 23 did not respond. One stated that he was not very certain and 2 interviewees - including one constructive worker - almost frowned at the investigator saying that she should realise that Gandhi and violence could never go together and hence it was futile even to think of this kind of a possibility. The heroic role played by women in all the struggles for freedom right from 1919 to 1942 heralded the dawn of a new age which culminated in the independence of India finally in August 1947. The Constituent Assembly which met in 1946 to draft the Constitution of free India had some eminent women members in it. Ever from the first general elections, several women contested seats both for the Lok Sabha and the Vidhan Sabhas of the states in all the elections held till now as will be seen from the following table :

Table 4.6

Year	*Total No. of Candidates*		*Total seats won by Women*	
	Lok Sabha	*Vidhan Sabha*	*Lok Sabha*	*Vidhan Sabha*
1951	51	216	19	81
1957	70	490	27	197
1962	68	233	36	154
1967	69	230	31	90
1971	86	–	21	–
1972	–	351	–	154
1977	70	272	19	146
1980	142	–	28	–
1982-83	–	241	–	44
1984	164	–	42	–

It is a matter of happiness that we are far ahead of countries like Egypt, Iraq and Ethiopia and even USA where there are only 2 women members in the Senate. However, it cannot be denied that we have yet to travel a long way before we can compete with nations like the USSR (where women constitute one-half of the membership of local Soviets and 28 per cent of that of the Supreme Soviet), Czechoslovakia, Yugoslavia, Sweden and Israel where the participation of women comes up to more than 20 per cent. At the State level too, the percentage of women legislators went up from 2.74 in 1952 to 5.9 in 1967 though in

1977, it once again dropped down to 3.9 per cent. However, in the year 1987, it went up again to 8.6 per cent.

Women have also been given representation in the ministries in many states and mostly put in charge of portfolios like education, social welfare, local government and public health and family welfare. Though, by and large, the urban woman is comparatively more assertive about her rights than the rural woman, at present, women are included in the cabinets in number of states.

At the local level too, women are coming forward to shoulder the responsibility of administration. It is reported that a village panchayat in a village in Saurashtra entirely manned by women managed the affairs of the village successfully and well for one full term. Despite women having shown such rare ability to hold the most responsible positions, the number of seats occupied by them in the Vidhan Sabhas, the Lok Sabha and Ministries is very small compared to their total population. Membership of political parties is one more criterion for determining the political status of women. Their record in this regard is very poor. Though exact figures are not available, it can be presumed that in no party do women members go beyond 12 per cent of the total membership.

A number of active women political leaders and members of political parties both in India and abroad feel that the main reason for women being reluctant to contest elections is a well thought discrimination on the part of men who lead political parties and wield a decisive influence so far as the final selection of party candidates is concerned. This was borne out by the UNESCO survey on the political role of women performed in Germany, France, Norway and Yugoslavia as also in all the general elections in India since independence. As Duverger points out "in the realm of politics, the promotion of women comes up against a barrier of male opposition."[41]

Undoubtedly men leading political parties deny this charge and assert that it is mainly the difficulty of getting sufficiently qualified women candidates rather than their prejudice against women, which is responsible for fewer number of women candidates. It may also be noted that women members of the Lok Sabha and Vidhan Sabhas have, on the whole, given a good account of themselves, by actively taking part in the debates and made a substantial contribution to discussion in the legislatures on matters of general interest like corruption, fair deal to members of the scheduled castes, development of backward parts and specially on matters pertaining to women like dowry, right to succession, right to seek divorce, special facilities for education and others. So far as demonstrations and mass movements matter, women have generally participated in them though not in a large number. However, their participation in movements like the 'Chipko' movement against deforestation and in acts of demonstrations concerning women's problems like dowry, rape, price-rise affecting housewives and other problems has been really noteworthy. In the state of Maharashtra an Anti-Price-Rise front organised under the able leadership of Mrinal Gore, Ahilya Rangnekar, Pramila Dandavate, Susheela Patel and others did laudable work not only in focussing the attention of the government on the hardships of the women who are house-wives but also in spreading political consciousness among women. In Bihar too, women played a prominent part in the movement against the corrupt Ghafoor ministry. Commenting about this *The Times of India* reported, "A remarkable feature of the movement is the active interest taken by women who rarely stir out of their homes. In the first week of the month 15,000 women joined a procession.[42] Numerous of them were behind prison-bars and faced government repression with extraordinary courage and fortitude. Awakening about their political rights especially as manifested in voting can well serve as one of the measuring rods for judging whether women are politically emancipated or not. In a survey on the changing status of women, it was observed that 82 per cent of women knew about their political rights and that the average of their percentage of voting was higher than that of men and women put together; in some groups, it reached as high as 92.24 per cent.

This perhaps was mainly due to the influence of urbanisation and education.

However, there is no denying the fact that the gap between the voting of men and women voters has narrowed considerably during the last 20 years as indicated by the Table 4.7:

Table 4.7

Year	*Electorate**		*Votes Polled*		*Percentage*		*Difference*
1952	*Men*	*Women*	*Men*	*Women*	*Men*	*Women*	
1952	94461	77286	51128	28132	55.0	37.1	17.9
1957	99968	89443	55984	35405	56.0	16.6	16.4
1962	113944	102428	70703	47764	62.1	46.6	15.5
1967	129569	119434	86460	66264	66.7	55.5	11.2
1971	145000	135000	101600	81000	69.7	60.0	9.7
1977	120100	108305	72073	52280	60.01	48.40	11.61
1980	136103	124995	80600	59642	59.21	47.71	11.50
1984	134122	107123	Not available		68.17	58.6	9.57

* Number in millions.

In 1952, 37.1 per cent of women went for the pollsas compared to 55.0 per cent of men. In 1971, these figures rose to 60.0 per cent and 69.7 per cent respectively and the gap between the voting of men and women voters narrowed down from 17.9 in 1952 to 11.6 in 1977 and it reduced down to 9.57 per cent in 1984. Though it is well known that election manifestoes are read only by a very small section of (both men and women voters) and that they do not affect their decision to vote to any appreciable extent, all political parties vie with each other in winning the votes of women by including special provision therein for the emancipation of women and pulling them into the political community. Some even bracket them with backward classes. Thus, the entry of women into the political struggle has had a far-reaching effect both on the policies of the political parties and the bias of their propaganda. So far as administrative services are concerned, Plato said long ago that there is no special faculty of administration in a state which only a woman has because she is a woman or which a man has by virtue of his sex, and that the gifts of nature are alike diffused in both. Even the UN Declaration of Political Rights expressly says that 'access to public service is a political right.

Though women have entered the services, they are far behind men as will be seen from the following table:

Table 4.8

Services Sector	*Men*	*Women*	*Total*
Indian Administrative Service	4209	339	4548
Indian Police Service	2418	21	2439
Indian Foreign Service	480	53	553

Thus, it is, however, heartening to note that for the first time, a woman was included in the Personality Test Board for the IAS Officers in 1974 and that in the list of successful candidates selected for the examination, there was steep rise in the number of women chosen, it being 37 out of a total of 170. This may be explained by the fact that 'the few women who managed to break the barriers of prejudice and join the IAS demonstrated clearly that whatever their male colleagues do, they could do even better", therefore justifying Gandhi's implicit faith in them. Even among Judges there are 12 women-Judges (including one in the Supreme Court) out of the total of 380. However, traditional prejudices still exist and come in the way of women's active participation in politics. One of the suggestions put forward to remedy this situation is reservation of seats for women at all administrative levels. Gandhi, who stressed on selection being made on the basis of merits, however, would not have quite approved of this suggestion. In answer to a question on the advisability of taking more women on various elective bodies, he gave a visible reply, "I am not enamoured of equality or any other proportion in such matters. Merit should be the only test. Seeing, however, that it has been customary to decry women, the contrary custom should be to prefer women, merit being equal, to men even if the preference should result in men being entirely displaced by women. It would be a dangerous thing to insist on membership on the ground merely of sex".

In conformity with his attitude of encouraging a feeling of self-respect and self-confidence in women, he further asserted, "Women, and for that matter any group, should disdain patronage. They should seek justice, never favours".[43] This way, his advice to women was to assert their rights without being aggressive, to understand that there could be no rights without responsibility and to rely on their own inner strength instead of the charity of men.

Impact of Gandhi's Efforts on the Present Status of Women

There is no doubt that the status of women in India has changed but not fully; it is in the process of being changed. The rate of change is slow and unevenly distributed. So, we have a picture of peculiar contrasts. On the one hand, there are women who occupy the highest positions in many fields; on the other a vast majority of them—especially in the rural area—are illiterate and thus exploited.

Position of Women at Present

As far as the social field is concerned, the overall situation is far from satisfactory. So far as child marriages are concerned, in a survey carried out in 1967-68 it is stated that "nearly one-fifth of the girls from the age-group 10-14 were married and that an appreciable number of parents, especially in the rural areas still prefer getting their daughters married before they reach the age of puberty".[44] Probably, the violation of the law being made a cognisable offence will go a long way in creating public opinion against this evil practice. Kapadia has the same sorry tale to tell regarding dowry. "Ill-assorted marriages" pays he, "have at times resulted from the practice of dowry. Education, instead of eradicating the evil has worsened it to a candalous proportion".[45]

To curb this evil, the Dowry Prohibition Bill penalising the giving and accepting of Dowry was passed in 1961 and yet the custom persists in many parts of the country, for unlike as in a country like Israel there is a great laxity in the implementation of the law. So regarding polygamy is the Hindu Marriage Bill of 1955 outlawed polygamy, enforced monogamy and conferred equal rights of divorce on both men and women and yet it is a known fact that physical ill-treatment and exploitation by husbands and the relations-in-law make many women seek shelter in rescue homes. Sometimes, they even seek refuge in death as revealed in a study of the incidence of suicide among men and women conducted by the Government of Gujarat State during 1960-64.

As Judith Brown the great advocate of women's liberation states, "The married women... is locked into a relationship which is oppressive politically, exhausting physically, stereotyped emotionally and sexually, and atrophying intellectually".[46] Here, it may be noted that polygamy still persists among the Muslims as it has a religious sanction behind it. Though there is a demand for a uniform civil code from many progressive quarters, it is opposed by the orthodox sections of the Muslim society and the Government does not have the courage to antagonise these sections. The Hindu Marriage Act allows divorce on ground of adultery, change of religion, lunacy, incurable disease, desertion and others which hamper joint living and companionship among the marriage partners.

This law is certainly a step forward in the direction of women's emancipation mainly because it assures a stable and progressive climate in the country, but a divorced women is still looked down upon and frowned at in the society. She is regarded more or less as a non-person. The plight of the widow continues to be pitiable as social restriction and the stigma attached to remarriage either forbid a new life for her or make it utterly disgraceful and humiliating.

Family Welfare and Foetal Termination

Biggest problem of India is that of population explosion. Ever since the First Five Year Plan period, the government has been spending a substantial amount on family welfare planning programmes. In the Fifth Five Year Plan also, a provision of Rs. 516 crores was made for this purpose. However, because of the age-old prejudices against family planning ingrained in the society, the efforts of the government and the social reformers have failed to hold the imagination of the people. Their experience has been frustrating and their efforts abortive. In a survey of the family planning work done in the clinics of Greater Bombay in 1963, it was seen that the percentage of married women who had visited a family planning centre was as low as five. This may be explained partly due to illiteracy and partly due to the attitude adopted by certain orthodox religions towards abortion. Countries like Korea, Thailand and Singapore have made more satisfactory results in the field of family planning-probably due to the higher rate of literacy prevailing in these countries than in our country as also that existing in countries like Pakistan, Afghanistan and Indonesia where a large proportion of the female population is illiterate. No doubt, an all-out endeavour was made to implement this programme vigorously during the emergency, but due to over-enthusiasm of some of the policy-makers and the coercive tactics adopted by the relevant bureaucrats, the whole programme boomeranged. Many orthodox Hindus and Christians believe that since all life emanates from God, children should be considered gifts from God and that abortion which amounts to taking of human life should be tabooed. Catholic women in France, Italy, Ireland and USA protested against this stand of the church.

As a consequence, the Supreme Court of the USA granted the right of abortion in January 1971. Though women have thus won a legal battle against discrimination, they still have to be prepared to put up a tough fight against the tradition-bound orthodox sections of the society. In India, abortion was legalised in 1971 by Medical Termination of Pregnancy Act. So far as the political field is concerned, even though the representation given to women in legislative bodies and public services is inadequate and their political participation much below men, it is true that more women are taking to public life now than in the pre-Gandhi era. Gandhi would have expected women to wield power with a sense of closer kinship with the understanding of the troubles of the less fortunate among them. He wanted them to realise that political power emanates or rather should emanate from moral power and supremacy.

This, howevel, does not seem to have come fact. It is certainly a 'painful end' to the glorious role assigned to women by him. In the economic field, women work mostly as unskilled labourers in both the rural and the urban areas. Also, the avenues for work given to them are much less than those given to men and discrimination against them both so far as the nature of work and the wages given still present.

Undoubtedly, the situation is not much better in the West inasmuch as the European woman, in spite of the remarkable strides she has made in the last 60 years has to rest happy with playing a secondary role in society. In West Germany for example female domesticity is still favoured again, women are under-represented in the legislative bodies of most of the European nations. Though more women go out to work than in the past, their proportion has increased only marginally in Britian and other countries. The discrimination in wages also persists in many countries of the world including USA, France, and Japan. In answer to a question whether women in India enjoy equal status with men today, 78 said that they did and 48 that they did not.

From amongst the different sections of respondents it was only among the constructive workers that a majority held the view that they did not enjoy equal status with men. The general feeling seemed to be that though there was progress towards equality, much left to be done to ensure complete equality. One noteworthy feature is that sc far as the condition of women in the rural areas is concerned, a majority of the respondents expressed doubt about women enjoying equal position as will be revealed from Table 4.9. So far as the reasons for their answers are concerned 85 respondents were of the view that it was mainly due to Gandhi's efforts that women enjoyed equal status. The other causes in order of priority were the work done by social reformers (74), equal rights being guaranteed by Indian Constitution (73), the work done by educational institutions (72), and women's organizations (69) connection with foreign countries and western education (61) and the policies followed by the Congress governments (35).

It is significant that Gandhi's efforts ranked first and the policies of the Congress Governments just the last among different reasons given. Some of the other reasons mentioned by a couple of interviewees were courage and skill shown by women in all professions and Gandhi's regarding women true custodians of culture. The reasons given by those who held that women do not enjoy equal status today were that women themselves being a tradition-bound (91), illiterate (84) and financially dependent on men (84) are reluctant to assert their rights, and that age-old customs still have a firm grip on people's minds (81). Fifty-nine were of the opinion that it was mainly ignorance of constitutional rights given to them which was responsible for this state of affairs whereas 36 said that women do not enjoy equal social status because people and especially present-day leaders have forgotten Gandhi, 31 of these believed that it was the government instead of the people who had forgotten him.

However, only 17 accused the government of being apathetic towards women. Some of the other reasons given were lack of employment opportunities, lack of women's organisations especially in rural areas and too much involvement in domestic affairs on the part of women. Thus, though the respondents were more tilted to give credit to Gandhi than to the government for the improvement in the status of women, they did not throw the blame for non-improvement on the government as is natural from 'apathy of the government towards women' being mentioned as a cause by just 17 respondents as against 91 who held the women themselves responsible for the unequal treatment meted out to them by social set-up.

Views of the respondents regarding position of women in the villages being bad is confirmed both by government and active social workers involved in community welfare work in rural areas. Writing about women's welfare in development project, P.P. Naidu wrotes "In most cases they (villages) are still very backward and ignorant relying on age-old customs and traditions. This is very true with regard to womenfolk whose conservatism is proverbial. While our women are no doubt repositories of our true culture, they are also the repositories of worn-out beliefs, meaningless customs, unwanted practices and unbelievable superstition. They form nearly 50 per cent of our rural population. Whatever facilities are provided for cultural and social development, they are not directly shared by the growing girls and women of the rural community. The village may advance economically as a result of improved agriculture, better cattle, good roads and marketing facilities, the results of which perhaps may be seen, so far as the women and children are concerned, in a few more jewels adorning them, but by and large they would still remain what they were, conservative, ignorant, superstitious. Homes will still be managed on the conservative line; children will be brought up in the traditional style,nutrition and food-values will remain ununderstood... In short their outlook does not change with the changed atmosphere".[47]

Among respondents, one constructive worker asserted that unlike the past, thanks to Gandhi's efforts, now women can move about freely even in villages. Another went a step further and said that women in the villages enjoy greater freedom than

Table 4.9
Opinion that the Women in India Enjoy Equal Social Rights and Status as Men

	In cities				In Villages				
	Yes	*No*	*Party*	*N.R.*	*Yes*	*No*	*Party*	*N.R.*	*Total*
Family members	2	—	—	—	—	2	—	—	2
Ashram inmates	6	9	1	1	1	15	—	1	17
Women associated with Gandhi	1	5	2	—	1	6	1	—	8
Active participants	13	7	2	—	3	14	1	4	22
Constructive workers	10	5	2	1	4	8	5	1	18
Non-Gandhian turned Gandhian	1	—	1	—	—	2	—	—	2
Women Social Workers	10	4	6	—	2	13	3	2	20
Critics of Gandhi	26	9	6	—	4	32	5	—	41
General and Foreigners	9	9	2	1	—	18	1	2	21
Total	78	48	22	3	15	110	16	10	151

those in cities. The position, however, was stated thus by an educationalist, Gandhiji succeeded in raising the status of womeh inasmuch as he made them fearless without making them obnoxious in the eyes of men and conscious of their rights, without making them oppressive. He made them conscious of their strength and personality but he was not completely successful in raising the domestic or social status of women in villages".

As far as Gandhi's contribution to raising of women's status is concerned, whereas 55 asserted that he was fully successful in raising their status, 90 held that he was partly successful. Six did not respond but it is very significant that not even a single respondent was of the opinion that his efforts failed completely. Also, there was no doubt in the minds of 98 respondents about the fact that women would not have enjoyed the status they enjoy at present but for Gandhi's attempts towards their liberation. As against this only 35 including 10 social workers, 5 freedom fighters and 5 constructive workers held that they would have as would be seen from the following reply to the question, "Do you think women would have enjoyed the status they enjoy today but for Gandhi's attempts towards their emancipation?"

Table 4.10

Respondent Category	*Yes*	*No*	*N.R.*	*Party No.*	*Total*
Family members	—	2	—	—	2
Ashram inmates	4	11	2	—	17
Women associated with Gandhi	3	4	1	—	8
Active Participants of the movement	5	16	—	1	22
Constructive workers	5	12	1	—	18
Non-Gandhian workers Gandhian	—	2	—	—	2
Women social workiers	10	6	4	—	20
Critics of Gandhi	5	30	6	—	41
General and foreigners	3	15	3	—	21
Total	35	98	17	1	151

Inevitable truth that the critics of Gandhi feel that but for his efforts, women would not have enjoyed equal status goes to prove that even in their perception there is no doubt that he used his redoubtable influence on the masses to liberate women from the handicaps and hardships suffered by them in the tradition-bound Indian society.

Other Social Reformers and Gandhi

In this part, an attempt was made to find out how the interviewees rated Gandhi vis-a-vis other social reformers who worked for the emancipation of women. Not only did he score the highest but there was a very wide margin between him and Raja Ram Mohan Roy who came second. Ninety-six out of the 136 who responded gave him first preference as against 18 who voted for Ram Mohan Roy. This shows how highly his contribution was rated by the respondents. As far as the second and the third choices are concerned Maharshi Karve and Raja Ram Mohan Roy were preferred to others as can be viewed from the following table:

Table 4.11

	Gandhi	*Raja Ram*	*Maharishi Karve*	*Vidya-Sagar*	*Madam Annie*	*Pandita Ramabai*
First Preference	96	18	12	5	3	2
Second Preference	18	22	40	14	12	7
Third Preference	11	18	23	16	18	18

In the views of a reformer, "Whereas other reformers touched only a microscope fringe of the many problems had to face, and their efforts were piecemeal, Gandjhiji tried to bring about a total revolution in their lives by trying to change all aspects of their lives." In the idea of the another social and political worker, the difference between Gandhi and other reformers was that whereas others tried to seek an intellectual solution to women's issues, Gandhi emancipated them emotionally. Still another asserted that unlike some of the other social reformers, Gandhi never borrowed ideas from the West and did not become a crusadar for women's rights but attempted to emancipate them by teaching them to rely on their gentleness and inner strength.

The same idea was put slightly differently by another respondent who held that while other emancipators were social reformers Gandhi was a spiritual reformer. One respondent illustrated the difference by the following interesting. One respondent illustrated the difference by the following interesting example. "Every emancipator who has worked for the emancipation of women has been great. So far as education for women goes, Maharshi Karve would stand first followed by Ramabai, Ranade and Naniben Gajjar. But for bringing women out of *purdah* and helping to banish fear from their minds, Gandhiji stands first. It was lay in their gentleness, dedication, tolerance and maternal love and that they could be a force, for establishing a non-violent society. I am reminded of the story of a lion's cub who was in a group of sheep. It used to imitate all that the lambs did. Once the sheep were confronted with a lion. Frightened beyond their wits they started running helter-skelter but the cub tried to join the lion and to recognise his own strength. In the same way Gandhiji made women realise their strength and helped them to break the traditional bondages which kept them down."

Right now, today, a woman seems to be facing a most challenging period in history. She is on an adventure and there are many pitfalls in her way one of the most significant among them being non-acceptance of equality on the part of men, whose attitude reinforces her deepest insecurity and feelings of worthlessness. Another hurdle is the persistent of the conventional attitude of women themselves. A woman wants to have a career of her own and yet does not wish to give up her responsibility as a wife and a mother. Even in a country like China, the government does not appear to have been able to free women from their traditional subjection to undeniable male chauvinism. Thus, even though constitutional and legal equality may have been granted to women, it is not yet ingrained in the thoughts of men and women and if not overt at least a hidden discrimination still persists against her.

Solutions

Here are certain important solutions suggested by the respondents to remove the discrepancy and give equal opportunities to women to become complete and separate human beings not competing with men but cooperating with them to set up an egalitarian and equalitarian social order are: (i) education, (ii) legislation, (iii) work by women's organisations.

I Education

Opening more schools especially separate schools as also hostels for girls in future parts, awarding special scholarships and freeships, giving attendance prizes, organising educational broadcasts and developing media of communication like the radio, cinema television programmes etc. were advocated to enhance the educational prospects of girls. In New Zealand teachers are made to serve for a three-year term in rural areas for being eligible for salaries above a certain level. In Australia 'single teacher' schools are promoted. In our country the village teacher should be encouraged to act as a real catalytic agent for the rural society.

Though as Gandhi maintained, home-making should be regarded as an occupation that enables a women to make her contribution to national development in a significant manner, alongwith providinjg these and other facilities, attempts must also be made to provide chances to women who have been generally treated as non-persons till now to become independent and complete human beings and to equip them for the new roll they are expected to play in today's world. An issue that is often raised in this connection is whether there should be special courses for girls like home science, family life and others. In 1968-69, the National Council for Women's education tried to prepare curriculum including courses in family life, education and simple agricultural activities. Unfortunately, however, it has not been implemented.

Again, in the field of vocational education, training in small-scale industries, handicrafts, social work and public health may provide good outlets for girls. Opening of industrial agencies and polytechnics especially in rural areas has to be stressed. It needs to be realised that women cannot and should not be made to rest content merely with playing the inside role by remaining behind the four walls of the home but should be afforded equal opportunities for the outside role. Not only must need for the education of girls be recognised but all possible attempts should be made to remove discrimination in any shape or form-whether it be in the field of providing physical amenities or providing the right type of courses.

As the National Committee on Women's Education observes: "The problem of the education of women is so vital and of such great national significance that it is absolutely necessary for the centre to assume more responsibility for its rapid development."[48]

II Legal Provisions

Another remedy is legislation. Many laws have been passed with a view to improve women's status. Some of the more important among them are The Hindu Marriage Act of 1955 increasing the minimum age of marriage to 15 for girls and 18 for boys; the Hindu Succession Act of 1956 providing for women becoming equal owners of property with men; Law on the Suppression of Immoral Traffic in Women and Children Act of 1952, making immoral traffic in women a punishable offence; The Special Marriage Act of 1955 and the Dowry Act of 1961 prohibiting dowry. They are, however, not implemented properly and hence have not been able to produce the desired effect. Gunnar Myrdal rightly observes: "There have been revolutionary changes in the legal status of women in India but only in the exceptional instance there been any significant change in their actual condition . . ."[49]

During the last decade not much has changed, particularly in the rural areas. Despite this yawning gap between the legal enactments and stark reality, as many as 60 respondents suggested this way out, 7 of them holding that it is the only remedy that can be effective. As against this there were 38 who suggested founding of more organisations—especially women's organisations as the sole remedy; 43 others recommended it alongwith others measures like education and legislation.

III Some Suggestions

More put forward by the respondents for improving the lot of women were educating public opinion and especially men to Grant equality of status to women, giving publicity to the achievements of eminent women especialy in areas which are considered to be men's preserves, reserving jobs in village and cottage industries for mothers and giving them social education and appointing a minister preferably a female minister to look after the welfare of women and take concrete steps to raise their status as has been done in France.

We came across scholars who maintain that though women in India in the post-independence era are certainly more conscious of their rights than in the past, on the whole, the Indian feminist movement lacks vigour and momentum inasmuch as women's agencies have not launched mass movements protesting against non-implementation of legal measures favouring them or non-enactment of progressive bills. This, for them, "is the basic weakness of the women's emancipation movement".[50]

Agitation by 12 respondents was suggested agitation as the sole remedy and 35 as one among others like education and legislation for the betterment of women's condition. As against this, one educationalist suggested that Gandhi's revolutionary style being organic and its pace evolutionary, in the ultimate analysis, it is only the establishment of a non-violent social order and an integrated society and not agitation for redressing any particular grievance that will ensure the desired change. More than anything else, it was self-restraint which was stressed by Gandhi. "The movement of non-cooperation is nothing, if it does not purify us and restrain our evil passions,"[51] asserted he. As one of his family members observed, "Bapu raised women of India to an extremely high level from the degraded state they used to be in. Rama, it is said, transformed one Shalya (stone) into Ahilya (the pious woman) but Bapu transformed of Shalyas into Ahilyas and if we follow his teachings, the transformation would continue."

To conclude the chapter, there have been changes in the Indian society since Independence. It is sure that they are not sufficient but they are certainly significant and indicative of progress. Though the Gandhian influence is not easy to discover in these challenges. Gandhi's contribution to the change cannot be ignored as he left no stone unturned to spread consciousness among the people about their rights. As Unnithan rightly says, "The main contribution of Gandhi is not so much in the realm of effecting actual social changes in awakening social consciousness about the necessity of change."[52] Among some of Gandhi's ideas which have not been opposed and found favour both with the government and the people are those regarding the status of women. This is clear also from the fact that the response to the question: "Do you think following Gandhiji's teaching will help to improve India's condition in general and women's in particular? was significant inasmuch as 131 which included 37 of Gandhi's critics replied in the affirmative as against 8 who gave a negative reply. Among these were ione social worker as against 14 of them whose response was positive and 2 against Gandhi. Twelve did not respond.

While commenting on this point G. Ramchandran asserts, "The gap today is not between Gandhiji at the back and the younger generation in the front. The gap is really between Gandhiji in front and younger generation at the back. Can the younger generation catch up with this man marching towards a great destiny for mankind through his programmes and through his philosophy and word."[53] An internationally reputed author and educationist asserted, "Gandhiji's teachings, in principle, are as relevant today as they were during his life and would have been a couple of centuries ago. However, they will have to be amplified and even modified very much as the principles of multiplication and division which cannot be changed but whose application may be adjusted wherever necessary according to the time so that an attempt may be made to implement them instead of dismissing them as impractical".

Therefore, there is no doubt that as a result of the efforts of Gandhi and other social reformers, the position of women in India hs changed and is still changing. Women's freedom is now an accepted fact at least in theory, and her future appears to be full of hope and promise. The gloom of the past is being slowly dispelled. However, a long and tortuous distance has to be traversed before the ignorant non-descript women of the past give place to the women of the future, who would definitely be healthier, happier, freer and more responsible members of the socciety the real better halves as Gandhi wanted to become.

References

1. Altekar, A.S., *The Position of Women in Hindu Civilisation,* p. 36.

2. *Ibid.,* p. 5.
3. *Ibid.,* p. 254.
4. Sen Gupta, Sankar, *A Study of Women of Bengal,* p. 85.
5. Quoted in Mazumdar, B.B., *Heroines of Tagore,* p. 124.
6. Ghose, J.C. (Ed.), *English Works of Raja Ram Mohan Roy,* pp. 363-64.
7. Quoted in Shridevi, S., *A Century of Indian Womanhood,* p. 30.
8. *My Story, the Autobiography of Hindu Widow,* p. 28.
9. *Ibid.,* p. 18.
10. *Ibid.,* p. 20.
11. *HIMSELF—The Autobiography of Hindu Law,* pp. 79-80.
12. Altekar, A.S., *op. cit.,* p. 206.
13. Natesan, G.A., *Gopal Krishna Gokhale's Speeches,* pp. 882-83.
14. Chattopadhyaya, Kamladevi and others, *The Awakening of Indian Women,* p. 25.
15. *Ibid.,* pp, 32-33.
16. Mazumdar, B.B., *op. cit.,* p. 276.
17. Andrews, C.F., *Mahatma Gandhi's Ideas,* pp. 320-40.
18. *Young India,* 21-10-1926.
19. Tendulkar, D.G., *Mahatma,* Vol. VII, p. 184.
20. Gandhi, M.K., *Navjivan,* 8-7-19285, as quoted in *Tyagmurti and Other Essays,* (Gujarati), p. 85.
21. *Young India,* 21-6-1936.
22. *Harijan,* 23-5-1936.
23. *Young India,* 26-6-1920.
24. Gandhi, M.K. *op. cit.,* pp. 3-4.
25. *Young India,* 5-8-1926.
26. Gandhi, M.K., *op. cit.,* p. 413.
27. Kalapi, Kalapi No Kekarav (Gujarati) To Widow Sisterm Baban, p. 70.
28. *Harijan,* 15-9-1946.
29. *Young India,* 8-10-1925.
30. Gandhi, M.K., *op. cit.,* p. 215.
31. *Harijan,* 21-11-1936.
32. Gandhi, M.K. *Women and Social Injustice,* p. 5.
33. *Ibid.,* p. 179.
34. *Ibid.,* p. 4.
35. *The Constitution of India,* Article 16.
36. *The Constitution of India,* Article 43.
37. Draft Fifth Five Year Plan, p. 21.
38. Ray, Renuka, *The Background of the Hindu Code Bill, Pacific Affairs,* Vol. XXV, No. 3, September, 1952, pp. 268-277.

39. Chattopadhyaya, Kamaladevi, *The Struggle for Freedom, Women of India,* (ED), Tara Ali Baig, p. 19.
40. O'Malley, *Modern India and the West,* pp. 693-94
41. Duverger, *Political Role of Women.* UNESCO, 1955, p. 125.
42. *Times of India,* 13-5-1974.
43. *Harijan,* 7-4-1946.
44. Hate, C., *Changing Status of Women,* p. 264.
45. Kapadia, K.M. *Marriage and Family in India,* p. 128.
46. Brown, Judith, *"Toward A Female Liberation Movement,"* as quoted in *Women's Liberation in America, Span,* January, 1974, p. 23.
47. Naidu, Smt. P.P., *"Women's Welfare in Development Project,"* as quoted in Unnithan, T.K.N., *Gandhi and Free India,* pp. 151 52.
48. *The Education and Advancement of Women,* UNESCO, Paris, 1970, p. 24.
49. Myrdal, Gunnar, *Asian Drama,* Vol. II, pp. 764-65.
50. Desai, Smt. N., *Women in Modern India,* p. 258.
51. Gandhi, M.K., *The Women,* p. 165.
52. Unnithan, T.K.N., *Gandhi and Free India,* p. 223.
53. From a speech delivered on All-India Radio, Gauhati, on January 25, 1974.

5

Dalit Women in Politics

When we talk of vulnerable sections of the Indian society, we also mention those who are at the bottom of caste hierarchy but even more vulnerable are women of those lower castes. This chapter is focussed on these Indian women—dalit women. The confusion centres around the connotation of the word 'Dalit' which was originally used as a Marathi and Hindi translation of English term 'Depressed Classes.' There are varieties of nomenclatures such as Untouchables, *Harijans,* Depressed Classes, Dalits, servile classes, down trodden weaker sections, Panchamas, Atishudras, Avarnas and the Scheduled Castes. The term 'Depressed Classes' refers to those castes who are among the lowest rung of the Hindu caste hierarchy and whose touch and proximity is considered polluting by the caste Hindu.

This is a British innovation from the article written by Dr. Annie Besant in the *Indian Review,* February 1909 titled "The Uplift of the Depressed Classes." Further, the term 'Depressed Classes' was mentioned in the Census Report, 1921, but the castes regularly called the 'Depressed Classes' were not defined and it was used before 1930, but since the enactment of the Government of India Act, 1935, they are consistently referred to as the 'Scheduled Castes' popularly known as (SCs). This term was coined by the Simon Commission, 1928 and subsequently the British Government issued the Government of India (Scheduled Castes) Order, 1936, specifying some castes and tribes. The category of the Scheduled Castes was known as the Harijans, that is, the children of God—a term coined by Mahatma Gandhi in 1933. Some leaders of the aforementioned castes regard the Harijan nomenclature pejorative and they prefer to be called 'Dalit', that is, oppressed. Since then the term has undergone a drastic change and this oppressed section of the Indian society has decided for themselves 'a new identity', 'a revised self-image' to indicate their lack of belief in being polluting and their inclusion in the Ambedkar movement, their sense of denial that their condition is the defect of the caste system and to assert their rights and denial of being subordinated by the religious, social or economic status.[1]

The Dalit Panthers, once a militant organisation had used this term and has expanded its scope as it defines "members of the Scheduled Castes and Scheduled Tribes, neo-Buddhists, the working people, the landless poor peasants, women and those who are being continuously exploited politically, economically and in the name of religion, are called Dalits."[2] Through this asserted identity, the Dalit Movement took itself "towards status improvement vis-a-vis social mobility among Dalits and shaping their agitational sensitivity and assertion for achieving the rights of equality and equal opportunity, self-respect and respectful identity."[3] This may, the Marathi word 'Dalit' was chosen by this section of the society itself and is used proudly. Even in the English Press this word has to be used without translation only. "None of the normal words as Untouchables, Scheduled Castes, Depressed Classes, etc. had the same connotation. *Dalit* implies those who have been broken, ground down by those above them in a deliberate and active way. There is in the word itself an inherent denial of pollution, Karma and justified caste hierarchy."[4] Professor Gangadhar Pantawane, the famous founder-editor of *Asmitadarsh* (Mirror of Identity), the chief organ of Dalit literature, defines the words as follows:

> "To me Dalit is not a caste. He is a man exploited by the social and economic traditions of this country. He does not believe in God, rebirth, the soul, holy books teaching separatism, fate and heaven because they have made him a slave. He does believe in humanism. Dalit is a symbol of change and revolution."[5]

In this manner, the definitional perspective of the word 'Dalit' is wide enough to address the oppressed sections of the society and it includes in its paradigm not only those castes which are oppressed for centuries but all those who are subject to excesses thereby including women as a 'category' cutting across the caste, creed or community lines because it is a proven fact that almost half of the humanity in this nation has been subject to subordination at various levels.

Another definitional perspective that needs equal attention is that of political participation. As a matter of fact, in the developing societies like India, political participation is not confined to a relatively limited set of acts like exercise of franchise campaigning or participation through very formal institutions but it certainly has a wider context which refers to any voluntary action, successful or unsuccessful, focussed or unorganised, episodic or continuous, employing legitimate or illegitimate methods, intended in influencing the choice of public policies, the administration of public matters or the choice of the political leaders.[6] What is of crucial importance in terms of political participation is the vision to relate oneself with the larger social movement for equality and justice.

This kind of political participation requires a large level of mass mobilisation with very clear understanding of one's socio-political context, a bold and committed leadership and mutually confident and transparent organisational structure which can associate people in different manner formal and informal as well. Having such a kind of understanding of political participation one wonders whether women as a category have the required level of political participation in their movements which are differently termed as fragmented, sparse or even fizzled out.

Whereas the role of women in the changed domestic and global perspective has been considered most important to the political life of our society, it is the sphere of socio-economic liberty, equality, and decision making where they have to carve out a meaningful space for themselves. Though constitutional safeguards and progressive legal enactment have endowed juridical equality but the right to similar status and opportunities in education, law and political participation influencing the key decisions having serious imprints on socio-economic structures have till date a distant dream that needs urgent attention.

We find that the majority of the womenfolk, particularly in rural India, are operating in a closed social system where they are inferior to their male counterparts in almost every sphere of their lives and are left with no option other than the 'kitchen affairs' to display their skills. The situation of Dalit women is more precarious and what is even worse is that they have to face two-way simultaneous oppression; one, from their male counterparts in their own family and kinship as well as from the upper-caste males, and second because of their so-called low status in the caste hierarchy. There are numerous examples in our country where women of the lower castes are being exploited in different ways including physical but the level and degree is minimum or sometimes absent and people do not have the will to protest against the shameful and heinous acts of physical violence.

Though with the expansion of the communication technology cases of exploitation are coming to light but the punishment and deterrents are not working somehow and many a time the culprits go scot-free. It is now largely accepted that assertion by women for their rights and admissions in civil society is of utmost importance for the overall development of the democratic fabric of our society. But its proper execution is sometimes understood in a diffused manner by the government and other institutions. The concerned agencies shirk their responsibility towards them and only a wish well which does not augur well for the outlook of a mass-based women's movement. They tend to ignore that specific socio-economic structure of our society where the nature of women's inferiority adversely affects the forms, character and effectiveness of their participation. In fact, political equality is meaningless where the mass of the population suffers from poverty, continuous threats of starvation, absence of health and inequality of class, status and power. It is more so in the case of women who suffer from another dimension of inequality, namely, the weight of traditional attitudes that consider them physically and socially inferior to men.[7]

Women's participation in the political process is central to their struggle against oppression. All the different aspects of women liberation rely on their articulation to express their demands and aspirations politically associating themselves with the larger movements of liberation, equality, liberty and justice. Issues about women emancipation have to be addressed in almost all fields and only through consistent organised political behaviour and action can they achieve their goal in the social, cultural, religious and economic fields; whether it is health, employment, education and training or demands for their basic rights, it is through collective endeavour that they can achieve their specific objectives. Political participation in India, particularly by women, has been considered in the narrow sense of participating in the elections and casting their votes. Party politics is not the mere expression of political participation. People's organisations and movements both at the grassroots and macro levels for transformation of society and women's liberation are to greatly recognised. As was pointed out earlier there are various levels of political participation, institutional and non-institutional as well as formal and informal. Thus, all these issues have to be seriously considered and only then can a comprehensive approach to the women's development emphasising on the issues of education, employment, health, nutrition and empowerment be decided leading towards women's empowerment thereby making an empowered society at large. Amidst this background we shall now focus on the crucial issues or concerns which definitely need urgent attention. First of all, the chief task of the women movements, specifically of the Dalit women's movement, is to fight for economic and social equality, not only formal equality as we know that equality before law is not necessarily equality in fact.

Women's movements which are necessarily an important component of the larger mass movement must address the issue of equality alongwith justice. For achieving this goal they must be aware themselves and of society and also its context. These women have to struggle at two basic levels: one, they fight for their social recognition as an equal human being in the Indian social system dominated by the caste hierarchy and, two, for the recognition of their rights alongwith the greater movements for women emancipation. Their struggle has to be two-fold making their movement more complex and requires a holistic approach. What is more significant here is that women's right to organise and struggle against their oppression must be linked to the question of the democratic rights of the people and strategy should be evolved to delineate their participation in the movement in a more active manner.

One more issue concerning women's political participation is their household and child-rearing responsibilities and tasks. Lack of maternity and child-care facilities not only prevent women from participating in productive labour but are a hiderance to their participation in public life. The State policies have been ineffective in addressing this problem and are hampering their development. Alongwith this they need to participate in the administration of the private and public affairs. Here we must concentrate on the life-skill development where both the genders should equally participate on mutual basis.

One of the leading causes of gender discrimination is the negative attitude created among both boys and girls at an early age. Gender discrimination at the societal level begins at birth and is powerfully reinforced at different stages. Even children starting school at the age of five already have a gender identity and hold stereotypical assumptions about different gender roles of majors as well as themselves. Gender relationship in our society have been stereotyped in a characteristic way, in which men dominate and women are subordinated. The women is supposed to perform all domestic task and is generally not assigned a decision-making or important role in day-to-day life. There is a tacit gender based division of labour which determines who does what, when and where. Gender identity is among the first and far-reaching identities that a human being acquires, and this is overshadowed by traditional gender roles. The application of traditional gender roles paves way for many forms of differentiation and discrimination between men and women.

In order to achieve gender equality, a vital component of the overall strategy of securing social equality and social justice, education has to be interventionist, empowering and reflective of social reality. The education system, its curriculum and its teachers have a prominent role in evolving a future generation inculcating a spirit of equality among children and sharing responsibilities equally. Here the role of the life-skill development becomes more important. Life-skill development mainly includes:

1. Strengthening financial management where women are given more autonomy and freedom to manage the financial affairs of the family life;

2. Health of family and child care where the male counterparts have a very important role to play as child rearing is not only the women's responsibility; but the man's as well;
3. Nutrition, cooking; and
4. Day-to-day house management and related household tasks which should be performed mutually and should be shared.

Concerned with the above issues is the major concern for a dignified human life.[8] Every individual must enjoy a dignified life and not be subjugated or a subordinated nor made to lead a life that is appropriated by the male-dominated social system. We must strive for a society that should work out for the dignity of the individual and everyone should be so nurtured that she/he should have respect for the human life and should appreciate equality, liberty and fraternity in his/her life approach. This can be an ideal but not unachievable if the whole society works collectively and consciously for its attainment.

This goal needs a serious introspection on the part of the each individual and the entire structures of the social system to impart training towards that direction. This also demands same commitment and more so in shedding down one's own prejudices and inhibitions regarding gender, caste, colour, creed and region, etc. There are other issues of equally utmost significance which also need thorough analysis but it is the limitation of this book.

The crucial issues of equality (social, political and economic), managing household and child-rearing responsibilities, life-skills development and a dignified human life are dealt with touching upon the issues of education, health, nutrition, employment, etc. which clearly need further attention. Analysing these issues at length one dwells on the double strategy which has been phrased in the idea of employment where empowerment means a restructuring of gender relations within both the family and in society at large and it is society's recognition of women's parity vis-a-vis men as independent human beings which will bring the real change.

Empowerment is a continuous process encompassing several mutually reinforcing components that are ushered in by an increased politicisation and participation in the public affairs. If politics means power then women must achieve power. They must achieve power themselves and with their own struggle.

They must fight for their recognition as an equal partner of social life. Dalit women in particular have to fight against oppression in more active and better ways. They have to fight against the caste system and against the male-dominated patriarchal social structure. At the primary level, they have to associate their movement with bigger anti-caste Dalit movements[9] while at the secondary level they have to align themselves with the feminist movements.

The task is definitely a tough one but hope sustains, though in a fragmented manner when in the Marathi literature Dalit women have challenged male supremacy and also the caste system. In other areas of human life politics, training, management, development, etc. women are becoming aware of their rights and they are in the continuous process of defining and re-defining their self-image and striving for autonomy and freedom. What is needed at this decisive time is a gender-sensitive approach towards overall human development and I think one important change or step that can be taken immediately is to question one's own conscience for human equality which will undoubtedly culminate in the continuous process of women's empowerment. If our democratic fabric has to be enriched then a comprehensive approach to equality has to be developed ensuring democratisation, decentralisation and transparency in the private and public affairs which will lead towards the establishment of an egalitarian society and will have a fruitful transformation of social structures.

References

1. Zelliot, Eleanor, *From Untouchable to Dalit: Essays on the Ambedkar Movement,* Delhi: Manohar Publishers, 1992.
2. Manifesto of Dalit Panthers.
3. Ram, Nandu. *Beyond Ambedkar,* Delhi: Har-Anand Publications, 1995, p. 87.
4. Zelliot, Eleanor, *ibid.,* p. 267.
5. Zelliot, Eleanor, *ibid.,* p. 268.
6. Weiner, Myron "Political Participation: Crisis of the Political Process" in L. Binder *et al.,* Eds. *Crisis and Sequence in Political Development,* Princeton: Princeton University Press, 1979, p. 164.
7. Committee on the Status of Women in India, 1974.

8. For more detail please see a very powerful impression in Dalit Literature all over India which, inherently, is a protestant literature and on visions a society where each individual enjoys a dignified human life.
9. Omvedt, Gail, *Dalits and the Democratic Revolution: Dr. Ambedkar and the Dalit Movement in Colonial Delhi.* Delhi: Sage Publications, 1994.

6

The Commencement of National Level Womanhood

Of course, it is very difficult to say when the seed of womanhood was sown and when it started sprouting but we can say that the organised efforts started with courageous Indian women like Pandita Ramabhai. And then, a direction was given to it by Mrs. Annie Besant. Today, Indian women are able to not only vote with men without any disparities, legal level, but can also be elected in political offices as per Indian Constitution and supplementary laws. Still, in true sense, they are yet to achieve complete equality but at least they are on the way. Thanks to freedom struggle who pulled women at least out of their four walls and extended them strength to fight for themselves as well as for the nation.

National Level Womanhood

Is not it next to impossible for people who are nationals of small nations, such as the English, the Dutch, the Norwegians, the Spanish, the Japanese, to imagine, still less to understand, the vast extent, the immense population, the variety of ethnological types, the range of climatic conditions, the multitude of different languages, the contradictions of rituals, included in the subcontinent known as India? What a problem is the attempt to create a United States of Europe! Yet India is as expanded and as complex as Europe, excluding Russia!

It may have been that during the thousand years of Buddhism in India, unity came to a widespread area of this great land and its ancient religion-loving people, but we are without its complete history.

We do know that the attacks from the 8th century onwards from Arabia, and those of the Persian-Moghuls from Iran and Iraq, broke up whatever unity may have bound together the followers of the gentle Buddha. Certainly by 1500 A.D. there were as many separated and diverse states in India as there are nations in Europe today. Five hundred years of Muslim rule gave Hindi-Hindustani as a language to three-quarters of the population of India, and with it an approach to a national unity and at least a double national consciousness.

It remained as one of the achievements of British rule in India that by its educational policy it made English the sole medium of Higher Education for a unified British Government over the whole expanse of India, and sowed the seed of a single national awakening which has become so strong as to challenge the existing stage of political affairs. Until very recently the women of England knew little or nothing of the women of Belgium, and the women of Finland little of the women of Spain. So also there was ignorance of one another between the women of the state Punjab and the Malabar Coast, between the Bengals and the women of Kashmir.

The speed with which India has become welded into one national unit is one of the miracles of modern history. In the sphere of womanhood and its rapid evolution in the last 50 years, the commencement of a consciously fostered unity of Indian womanhood began from about 1914 when Dr. Annie Besant entered Indian politics and made a memorable series of public lectures in Madras City entitled "Wake up, India!"

These resonated throughout India in a clarion call to the Indians to work out their own salvation by freeing their girls from illiteracy and child marriage, by freeing their untouchables (since re-named Harijans by Gandhiji) from all religious and social degradations, and by freeing the whole nation from foreign rule. A wave of fresh enthusiasm then swept over the country for political freedom; and from the beginning it was connected with a realisation that it should be freedom for women as well as for men. There had been women members of the Indian National Congress since inception; but from the time that Dr. Besant formed the Home Rule League, there was an accentuation of the political oneness of India, and linked with it the desire and the means for members of different geographical and linguistic areas to know one another personally, to mingle in great groupings, focussed in single outstanding magnetic personalities, but each of such groups accepting as its definitive circle the letter and the idea "All-Indian." There probably had existed right down the ages of Hindu India a unity of the Hindu people which felt itself and was self-conscious to a greater or lesser extent through the pilgrimages to the many holy shrines, to cover which necessitated visiting all the four corners of this wide and varied subcontinent.

Any pupil studying history can see the same essentials of life and experience demonstrating themselves over and over again in slightly different guises. They are the alterations of fashion in the expression of the mind of masses of people.

For instance, one sometimes thinks that our present ideas that reading, 'riting and 'rithmetic, are the only bases of education, are only transient fashions of thought; that previous civilisations had other methods (some by the ear alone, others by plastic symbols or pictures alone, or perhaps by even more occult systems), and that education which is to us to-day so important may be superseded. Similarly, the concept of nationalism, of unity on ethnological, geographical and linguistic bases may also prove to be only a passing fashion.

At the beginning of the awakening of women's responsibility for public service this organisation took a valuable historic part. Its afternoon sessions were held in Branches as far apart as Srinagar, Madras, Calicut, Tanjore, Bezwada, Bombay, to take at random some of its 87 Branches between 1920–1930. It was meant in all its varied activities to serve the country, that country which a few years before had not emerged in the heart as India the Motherland.

The National Liberal Association included men and women, decidedly intelligentsia, and highly official. The Brahmo Samaj Women's Branch was acting more in Bengal than elsewhere. There were the Seva Sadans of Poona and Bombay, the Bharata Stri Mahamandal. Among all of them there was a certain uniformity of search for a single formula of service. But more was needed. In between 1910 and 1926 there came to India from London the Secretary for India, the Honourable E.S. Montagu, to survey righteousness of the Indian claim for Home Rule.

Different movements popularly created an all-India unity and strength amongst little girls of Blue Bird age, girls of Girl Guide years, and path finders for these—the fine bands of Rangers. These all built up a desire and organisation for open-air life and detailed usefulness and general knowledge through Badge Tests which made parents leave loose their bonds of conservatism, has given young people greater freedom of movement and more civic and First Aid usefulness than earlier, and instilled a discipline which is linked to nationalism and internationalism. In different Provinces women banded themselves for social work, education, economic and religious purposes—The Bombay National Council of Women, the Seva Sadan of Poona and Bombay, The Saroj Nalini Dutt Mahila Samitis, and the Bharata Stri Mahamandalam of Bengal, the Arya Sama of the Punjab and United Provinces, the Mahila Seva Samaj of Mysore, the many Women's Clubs for recreation. Then the converging process started which brought all these diffused energies to a point of focus.

The following is the genesis of that Conference—Again as in 1883, Bethune College, Calcutta, prepared the platform for advance. At its Annual Prize-giving, the Bengal Inspector of Education threw out a challenge to wome to inform about the country what kind of education they wanted for girls, and not to be content with leaving the making of curricula in the hands of men. A couple of write ups by Mrs. Huidekoper on this challenge were given in *Stri Dharma,* the monthly magazine of the Women's Indian Association.

In (1929) the political awakening of the masses was upon India in the non-violent Non-cooperation movement. Coming out of it an agitation about the political status of Indian women in any proposed Reform. The Viceroy procured the inclusion of women delegates to the Round Table Conferences. Between 1931 to 1933 the Conference gave splendid leadership on the entire question of the views of women on franchise eligibility. All-India womanhood, through the Conference, opposed communal electorates, "reserved seats" for women, and "wifehood" eligibility. It favoured literacy qualification, and all terms of equality with men voters, but considered adult suffrage the only satisfactory answer of all the suffrage problems. Indian women are still entirely dissatisfied with the present franchise conditions for women.

It fostered all indigenous trades and industries, Swadeshi and Khadi, and encouraged the revival of Indian culture by holding exhibitions of articles, pictures, folk dances, folk rituals, belonging to India's age-old tradition and civilisation. With the fast rise of political consciousness, and the growth of awareness amongst the masses of the condition of subjection of India to a foreign Government, the great majority of delegates moved towards the realisation of the fundamental neccessity there is for India to emerge as a self-governing, independent nation.

Thus, to conclude, pilgrimage of manhood at freedom front as well as political front has been a tough but bold journey. Though they could get their rights to vote on equal footing with men very late, i.e., in late 1930s but the beginning at last, had an end and opened doors for them in elected offices. In the general elections of 1937, though very low, but women held leading position 'as legislators and ministers. But there was still a long way to go and even today, they are yet to reach their destination.

7

Environmental Management

When we talk of women's participation in societal matters, the most important aspect is their participation in the management of Environment. This chapter gives an insight into the evolution of a bond between women and environment. The chapter also brings to light managerial skills of women in various cases of environmental management.

Environmental Management (EM) is everyone's concern both at the national and the global levels. The objective of EM, however, varies from one society to another. In developing countries like India the main purpose of EM is more to secure the present with the concern about the future. Thus, EM deals with maintaining the sensitive balance between short and long run objectives and goals (Agarwal, 1992). The connection between women and EM gained attention when it became apparent that the twin crises in ecology and development are closely linked. The topic of women and EM encompasses *inter-alia,* such different areas as agriculture, water, energy and forestry. Consequently, today we are witnessing a remarkable convergence of policy objectives between themes of EM, sustainability and the empowerment of women. This chapter seek to examplify that women are grassroot natural environmental managers. The discussion identifies current challenges, constraints and opportunities for policy and action programmes in the context of the contribution that women can make in EM in India. The linkage between women and EM is now increasingly acknowledged and understood. More and more women are perceived as a vital part of the solution to the crisis, as *environmental managers.*

The truth that women have many relevant skills and possess the knowledge essential for the care of the environment, is being recognised. Women constitute the majority, as users and managers of natural resources. They are also the leading gatherers of food, fuel, water, fodder, medicinal plants and raw materials. Through practical experience, they have gained a vast knowledge of various types of plants, kinds of fuelwood, types of soil and agricultural practices necessary not only for survival, but for the well-being of their families too and also of communities.

Definitions of Environment and Environmental Management (E&EM)

Let's first see the meaning of environment. It has been defined as an aggregate of all the external conditions and influences affecting the life and development of an organism. The external conditions can be natural or man-made. The natural environment includes flora and fauna, soil, air, water, etc. whereas, built or man-made environment consists settlements in which human activities are carried, alongwith the human population and their cultural heritage. Jolly (1978), considers that management of environment should reflect balanced view of the physical, biological and social environment.

As per Cairns (1991), EM may be viewed as a proactive or preventive measure that maintains the environment in good condition for a variety of long-range sustainable uses. He has suggested that EM may be regarded as coordinated control, direction, or impact of all human activities in a defined environmental system to achieve and balance the broadest possible range of short and long term objectives.

Thus EM is not fragmented decision-making where only one use is kept at a time, but an amalgamation of variety of uses. Lal (1995), has proposed that EM can be viewed in terms of the three different perspectives, viz. ecological and technological, socioeconomic and institutional. The ecological or technological perspective focuses on productivity, socioeconomic perspective stresses equity, while the institutional perspective is concerned with stability. Further, he has indicated that as per the objective of EM, at different points of time different approaches were taken up for managing the environment.

Looking into the Past

When we peep into history the UN Conference on Human Environment held in Stockholm in 1972, was instrumental in focusing world's attention on environment. Alongwith this, the declaration of International Women's year in 1975 and the "Decade of Women" (1975-85) further highlighted the relationship between women and environmental concerns. In the words of Shiva (1992), "Women environmental action in India preceded the UN Women's Decade as well as the 1972 Stockholm Environment Conference. Three hundred years ago more than 300 members of the Bishnoi community in Rajasthan, led by a women called Amrita Devi, sacrificed their lives to save their sacred 'Khejri' trees by clinging to them. With that event begins the recorded history of Chipko" (p. 67).

Concerns for Environment

In our country, EM is a concern of not only the planners and scientists but also of legislators and politicians. The Indian democratic system has chosen the instrument of law as a major device for EM which has become a matter of great concern for the people. Within the duration of five years of the U.N. Conference on Human Environment at Stockholm in 1972, the Constitution of India was amended, among the other things, to include safety of environment as a constitutional mandate.

The Constitution (Forty Second Amendment) Act of 1976 has made it a fundamental duty to protect and improve the natural environment. It is also interesting that India took note of integrating environmental aspects into planning during the course of formulation of its Fourth Plan (1969–74), at least three years ahead of U.N. Conference on Human Environment. The impact of these international and national events can be seen both, at the academic researchers' and policy-makers' levels. The researchers have gone away from preoccupation with the role of women within the family and informal sectors, whereas, policy-makers have begun to shift their focus from universal concern of welfare orientations to the role, skill and sensitivity approach in support of women. As a result, in the last two decades, a number of articles and books have been published dealing with various aspects of women and environment like, "Role of farm women in animal husbandry programmes" (Puri, 1974); "Women power in agriculture" (Chakravarty, 1975); "Water resources development and rural women" (Agrawal, 1991) and on specific subjects like "Women in forestry" (Saksena, 1987); and *Women and the Environment* (Sontheimer, 1991).

Female and Male Participation in Environmental Management

We find strong dichotomies between men's work and women's work. In agriculture, men generally have the primary responsibility for land preparation and irrigation. Women, on the other hand, fertilize the fields, plant and transplant crops, weed and harvest.

During peak labour times, both men and women work together. Animal husbandry task is also divided on gender lines. While men have the primary responsibility for grazing and pasturing the livestock, the women collect fodder, care for animals, make dung cakes and milch the cattle. They are also responsible for grazing the animals in agricultural fields and homestead land. In forestry, women manage for diversity. They prefer tree species which are based on multiple usage within the household, including food, fodder, fuel, medicine and income needs. Men's preferences are more often based on usefulness as timber, either for construction purposes or for sale. The collection of water for domestic purposes is also the primary responsibility of women. They collect water early in the morning and late evening from various sources like wells, tube-wells, rivers, etc. either near or away from home.

Men seldom collect water during necessity while in addition to their major involvement in agriculture and resource management, women take responsibility of domestic chores including food processing, cooking, and child care, etc. In times of hunger or economic hardship, women seek short-term migrations to supplement household incomes. During food deficiency or economic stress men frequently go for seasonal migration.

Women interact primarily with family and neighbours, whereas, men interact generally within and outside the community. In this division of labour between the two sexes, the work of collecting cooking fuel, fetching water and cattle care bind women more intimately with the natural resource base than men.

Environmental Resources Managed through the Better Half

Significance of women in managing environmental resources and their active role as managers of natural environment has been widely recognised. As managers of households, livestock, farmers and suppliers of food, fodder, water and fuel, they interact intimately with their environment. Women manage a huge range of activities connected with the natural resources. They play important roles in farming, agricultural management, food processing, health of the domestic animals and safety of family health.

Women's Fourfold Performances

While uncovering critical links between women and EM, it would be useful to classify women's role in four main categories: *consumers, producers, reproducers* and *managers*. Obviously, there is considerable overlap between these roles reflecting multiple duties that women must perform. For example, women in economically active age-groups are likely to fall in all the four categories, while female children would fall only in the first. Women of the child-bearing age who are neither economically active nor are housewives would only come under the third category. The fourth category includes women of all ages, as they are the practitioners of the principles of management.

(a) As Consumers: This category includes women's consumption patterns relevant for determining their impact on the environment. It should be examined in the following areas : (i) self-sustenance, (ii) sustenance of those for whom women are responsible, such a family/household members etc., and (iii) consumption which is unwanted for survival. This category accounts for the impact of decisions and activities, determined essentially by women's status—which lead to consumption—on environment and environment's reply which has implications for EM.

(b) As Producers: This group includes women in economically active age-groups, i.e., women in agriculture (including animal husbandry and fishery) sector, rural and informal sector including cottage industry and handicrafts. The aspects relevant for analyzing the consequences on environment of women's productive activities are : (i) quality and intensity of views on natural resources and man-made inputs employed

in production (ii) techniques of production and (iii) modes of disposal of unusable by products through the act of production.

(c) *As Reproducers:* In this specific category includes women of child-bearing age who are actual contributors, or have the necessary requisites for contributing to population growth (through fertility). The impact of this female role on the environment takes place through population growth.

(d) *As Managers:* This particular section comprises women of all ages. They manage the environment by a set of decision-making stages, which link people and the issues. The five decision-making steps for EM are: exploring, analyzing, setting goals, action and evaluation (Brown, Smith, Wiseman and Handmer, 1995).

Stages given above are similar to the basic steps of general management which includes planning, organising, coordinating and control. Before deciding the options, an exploration of the important influences is required. Then, analysis of a wide range of information helps the manager to identify the main players and resources. This enables to set practical action to achieve realistic goals. Evaluation of results of the action involves considerations of the interests of the key players and the steps to be taken in coming times. Also, the five elements in stages of managerial process applies to women of all age-groups. For example, in *tendu* leaf plucking (leaves which are used for *Bidi* making) young girls of 8 to 10 years of age are taught by the elders to look for better quality leaf, then, after exploring analyze and sort the leaves to be bundled together, thus setting the goal. The elders, above 25 yeas of age, then count the bundles and pack them to take it to the *phad* (collection centre) and afterwards, evaluate the amount of the money earned for the labour. Another example is that of *sal* leaf plate, *kurchi* and *sal mala*-making industries in West Bengal where young girls go alongwith their eleders to collect the suitable *sal* leaves and *kurchi* and then are given training to make the *sal* leaf plates, *kurchi* and *sal mala.* Women of 25 to 40 years of age-group, then grade the leaf plates and bundle them according to their quality and carry them to the market for selling.

Process Involved in Management

Present interest in women and EM is growing, but the paucity of knowledge on the linkage involved requires that more attention should be paid. The means of identifying the linkage between women's role and EM depends to great extent on the theoretical framework, policy objectives and mandate for action. The environmental management processes been outlined in Figure given below. As agent of social change, women operate at three specific levels, or dimensions in the management of environmental resources.

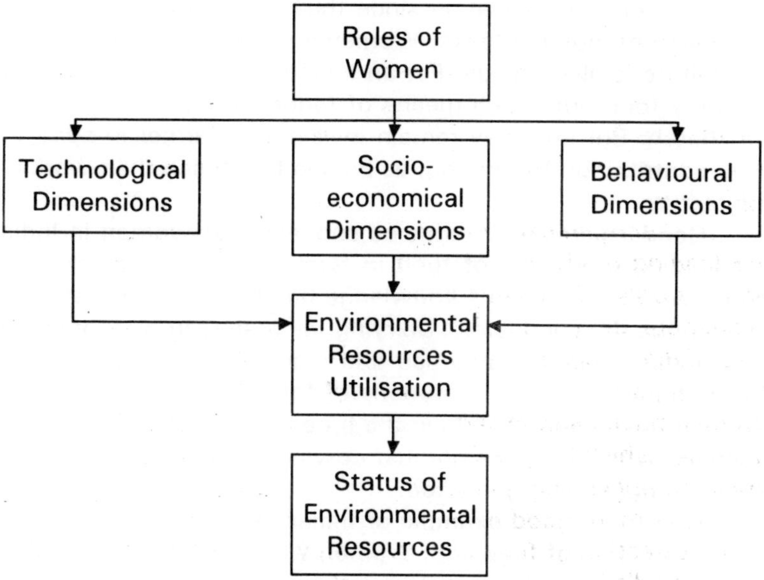

Environmental Management Processes (Rodda, 1991).

(A) Dimensions of Behavioural Aspects

"At the micro level it is increasingly understood that in most countries women have the primary responsibility of the management of the natural resource base. They are custodians of indigenous knowledge . . ." (Sharon Capeling-Alakija, Global Assembly of Women and the Environment newsletter, 1992).

In each culture, there is a form of environmental behaviour that more or less protects the natural environment. In forestry too women's knowledge is crucial in use of biomass for feed and fertilizer. Similarly, fuelwood collection is the primary responsibility of women. Women will hardly cut a green, growing tree, for they know the value it will bring when it reaches maturity. Frequently it is the case of women training their own behaviour in accord with nature, as they know that to do otherwise means starvation of their family, irrespective of whether or not they are the head of the household.

As is evident by now, women have been the custodians of biodiversity in most cultures. Being selectors and preservers of seed which conserves diversity leading to balance and harmony. Their work and knowledge is focal to biodiversity, conservation and utilisation since they work between *sectors* and perform multiple tasks. Women's work and knowledge in agriculture is also unique. For an Indian women farmer, rice is not only food but also a means of fodder for cattle and straw for thatch. But still they remain invisible as farmer in spite of their contribution to farming, as people fail to see their work in agriculture.

Gender-perspective studies suggest that women in India are leading producers of food in terms of value, volume and hours worked. Women's knowledge has been the mainstay of indigenous dairy industry. Dairying, as managed by women in rural India, embodies practice and logic rather separate from those imparted in the institutions of formal education in India. Women have been experts in the breeding and feeding of farm animals, which includes not just cows and buffaloes, but pigs, chicken, ducks and goats too.

One more good example of Indian women's competence in the selection of firewood. Women who collect firewood can very well distinguish between variety of wood that will burn for longer or shorter duration. They can differentiate fuelwood which can provide quick heat, those which offer long lasting low heat, and those which smoke. They also have knowledge regarding the taste of bread cooked on different types of fuelwood. They are also familiar with the huge range of biomass species and have in-depth knowledge and know-how about their properties and uses.

When it comes to the management of fuelwood species, successive generations of older women have taught expertise younger women in the art of lopping and pollarding (Shiva, 1988). Further, according to Shiva women are naturally or instinctively closer to the forest and preservation is part of the feminine ethos.

(B) Economic and Societal Dimension

Various developers, planners, bilateral and multilateral organisations are especially concerned to work against the Third World women's productive capacity. There are many economic constraints on women's participation in EM. They have less access to producing cash crops as they are wanted to produce for the family's subsistence. Women are not very much aware about cash crop culture or chemical fertilizers but are often required to repair their deteriorating effects.

Arable lands are exploited for monocropping from which women have not got any benefits. For example, in India crops like soyabean, sugarcane, etc. are cash crops which are grown on a large scale with massive use of chemical fertilizers and pesticides. The returns are profitable, and are controlled by the menfolk. However, when deteriorating consequences of such practices are encountered, it is women who are asked to repair the deteriorating effects.

It is seen in India that after excessive use of chemical fertilizers the soil is rendered useless, then the women are directed to put cow-dung manure in the field to restore fertility. On the other hand, women always use natural resources available to them for agricultural production, which is important to them. Obviously EM is central to women and they can provide useful advice and information. Women also face special constraints with regard to land and natural resources particularly, limited property and political rights. With regard to private land, women have very limited legal rights and legitimized claims. Women only exercise tenuous claims to produce from forest and common property resources, despite their role as primary collectors and managers of biomass. The tenuous nature of women's rights to land directly affect their economic position.

(C) Scientific and Technological Dimension

Number of the EM techniques women apply are traditional. These involve the selection of drought and pest resistant tree species, the conservation of genetic diversity and species of nutritional and medicinal value. The saving of energy and the use of wastes are also significant for them.

Other techniques include measures to conserve soil and water by terracing and trapping the natural stream. The technology involved in the EM operates more on crisis basis rather than on preventive measures. Technologies evolved to manage environment, usually do not meet women's need in developing their local capacity and enhancing self-reliance. Besides, due to want of access to credit they do not receive technology, tools, equipment, fertilizers and technical help. One example to illustrate the technological development which has undermined women, is very well observed where the threshing machine, power tiller, harvester, sower, etc. are introduced in an Indian village.

Women, who earlier used to control these agricultural operations, get fewer opportunities of employment after mechanisation of the agricultural labour. Moreover, the work of these women is now directly controlled by the men, thereby the women lose their status, power of decision-making and suffer financially also. While, innovations and technologies are steps towards development, the design of the equipments should be gender sensitive so that women could also operate them. Another example is that of handpump technology that has changed now in support of women. Earlier it was only men who could repair the handpumps when out of order as pipe fitted in it was too huge. But now, designing of handpump pipes which can be assembled has enabled women to approve them.

Factors that Affect Participation of Women in Managing Environment

(a) Entry of external agencies. Involvement of women in EM is reduced with the stepping in of external agencies. Conservation and development intervention success is linked to their degree of local control and commitment. The highest success rates are achieved by community started projects followed by local, national and international NGOs. National governments have occasional success but majority of them do not meet their objectives. Success is at least achieved by multilateral organisations because of distance from stake holders and large bureaucratic regulatory and planning organisational base. It must be seen that technologies developed to utilise environmental resources are steered toward meeting women's needs, developing their local capacity and increasing community self-reliance.

(b) Understanding the local system and priorities. Who have no access to credit, skills and training or technical assistance that could make their work more productive and remunerative. Women have an important stake in the decisions and practices which directly influence environments. A thorough understanding of local EM system, community organisation and local priorities is an essential ingredient of almost all successful initiatives (Mukherjee, 1995; Menon, 1995).

The initiatives must be entirely locally driven and this must be accomplished with a commitment of significant resources in terms of personnel and time. It is essential for a women to be present in the team mobilizing local knowledge through participatory rural appraisal techniques, to establish local contacts. Ignoring local condition can quickly lead to failure of well-planned project.

(c) Women in the position of decision makers and policy makers. Greater recognition of and support for the largely unheralded role of women as environmental managers is needed. Women should be assisted financially to play their role in more productive and beneficial way. This would ensure more fruitful use of their time and wider opportunities to participate in the planning and decision making which affects them and their families. Present management at the local level is grossly neglected and the potential at the managerial and policy-making level remain largely generalised.

Hence, dispute about women's essential role as managers of their environment, as well as their perspectives is largely omitted from macro level and community decision making processes, which affects environmental outcomes.

(d) Fragmented vs integrated approach. Women feel more comfortable with small scale multisectoral projects which are better managed with more benefits to them (Pinto, 1995). Significant result could be attained by targeting an area or community rather than a sector by incorporating local initiatives. Sectoral approaches increases the chances of success by providing flexibility, particularly in establishing points of introduction. Institution should be built with fragmented approach which is more efficient than the integrated multiagency approach. For overall success of EM by women, they should be integrated at all levels and decision-making and control of resources should be strongly delegated to them.

(e) Financial inputs. These inputs have obvious implications for women's involvement, because beyond a certain level external inputs result in reduced diversity and resilience of the local area. Moreover, women who are conservative and shy by nature withdraw from such efforts as their institutions are not compatible with excessive external intervention into the indigenous and locally available techniques and resources. Large scale commercial production through mechanisation and external inputs shakes both women and environment.

(f) Unification of women. Most environment training programmes whether in agriculture, forestry, energy or water sectors include token or very less participation from women. But in view of connections between environment and women, more attention needs to be focused on involving women in large numbers in decision-making, planning and management. Planners still prefer to address women in specialised women focussed programme (Pradhan and Rankin, 1990).

They are often seen as part of the problem, seldom as part of solution. Yet, success in EM intervention is dramatically increased with awareness of gender issues and full integration and unity of women. Experience shows a direct relation between project success and the level of women's participation, when the latter is high the former is also high but it is the other way round when women's participation is low (Singhal, 1995).

To sum up the chapter, women are not a new dimension in EM. They have an important managerial role to play vis-a-vis the environment and merit special consideration in development and conservation policy. Primary stress needs to be placed on understanding the tremendous diversity and institutional framework to ensure visibility. Women's integration into government initiatives builds sustainability across many sectors, and may be strengthened through community organisations, achieve access to resources, and recognition of their vital role. What is needed is structural and attitudinal change in institutions including new management systems in human, financial and environmental resources. In the end, it may be concluded that, "women have a vital role in environmental management and developmental management. Their full participation is therefore essential to achieve sustainable development".

References

Agarwal, A. (1992). *The Price of Forests.* New Delhi: Centre for Science and Environment.

Agrawal, B. (1981). *Water Resources Development and Rural Women.* Mimco.

Bishnoi, R.S. (1987). *Conservation as Creed.* Dehradun, Jugal Kishore, Letter from Gandhi to Mirabehn, 16 Jan. 1948.

Brown, V., Smith, D.I., Wiseman, R. and Handmer, J. (1995). *Risks and Opportunities: Managing Environmental Conflict and Change.* London: Earthscan Publications.

Cairns, J. (1991). *Integrated Environmental Management: The Need for Integrated Environmental Systems Management.* Michigan: Lewis Publishers.

Chakravarty (1975). Women power in agriculture. *Kurukshetra,* 24-28.

Jolly, V. (1978). The concept of environmental management in D. Bandhu, V. Bhardwaj and J.L. Bhatt (Eds.), *Managing the Environment* (pp. 23-47). Delhi : Indian Environmental Society, University of Delhi.

Lal, J.B. (1995). Perspectives on resource management. National Workshop on "Biodiversity Conservation in Managed Forests and Protected Areas", Indian Institute of Forest Management, Bhopal, 29-01, November-December.

Menon, A. (1995). Constructing the local, decentralizing forest management: *Economic and Political Weekly,* 26 August.

Mukherjee, N. (1995). Forest management and survival needs: Community experience in West Bengal. *Economic and Political Weekly,* 9 December.

Nagbrahnain, D. and Shreekant, S. (1983). Women's drudgery in firewood collection. *Economic and Political Weekly,* 1-4 January.

Pinto, M. (1995). Development through improvement of women in India. *Kurukshetra,* 9-12.

Pradhan, B. and Rankin, K. (1990). Conceptual perspectives on women's role in mountain resource management. In *Perspectives on the Role of Women in Mountain Development.* ICIMOD, Kathmandu.

Puri (1974). Role of farm women in ancient husbandry programmes. *Kurukshetra,* 22-29.

Rodda, A. (1991). *Women and the Environment.* New Jersey: Zed Books.

Sachchidananda (1994). Women, environment and development. *Trends in Social Science Research, 1* (1), 71-79.

Saksena, N.C. (1987). Women in forestry. *Social Action, 37,* April-June, 150-173.

Shiva, V. (1988). *Women Ecology and Survival in India.* New Delhi: Kali for Women.

Shiva, V. (1992). *Staying Alive: Women in the Forests.* New Delhi: Zed Books, Kali for Women.

Singhal, R. (1995). Behavioural factors in institutional effectiveness. Unpublished Report, Indian Institute of Forest Management. Bhopal.

Sontheimer, S. (1991). *Women and the Environment: A Reader Crisis and Development in the Third World.* London: Earthscan Publications.

8

Family Welfare

They say that it is a woman who makes or mars a family and this is absolutely true about her role in family planning and family welfare. A woman is always accused for having unwanted extension in a family but infact, it is the man, her husband who forces her to have more children and sometimes, mother-in-law who wants a male heir for her family. Despite the truth that wife has almost no say in family planning, when it comes to contraception or even extreme step of sterilisation, it is woman only who is pushed forward. Govt. figures have also proven that both in practicing contraception and using other family planning methods, number of women is much higher than their male spouse. In the present chapter, we are throwing light, on the basis of facts and figures, on rate of women in family planning.

As per the statistics of 1991 census, India's population is 844.3 million—a substantial increase from 342 million in 1947 and 683.3 million in 1981. We will cross the mark of a thousand million by the turn of twentieth century at the current level of growth and would be double of that in the next 35 years. We are increasing at a rate of 16 million a year, 47,871 per day. 48 births are taking place each minute. Within 2.4 per cent of the world area, we are supporting 16 per cent of the world population. The implications of this are drastically disastrous.

The family Welfare Programme was launched in 1951. The clinical based approach was extended to include an extension approach in the Second Five Year Plan. In 1977, the Department was renamed to be known as the Department of Family Welfare by integrating the Mother and Child Health Services.

The National Health Policy clearly spelt out the various demographic goals to be achieved by the year 2000 A.D. These also included infant mortality rate of 60, growth rate of 1.2 per cent (with the birth rate of 21 and death rate of 9), Couple Protection Rate (CPR) of 60 per cent and NRR, i.e., Net Reproductive Rate of one.

The Universal Immunisation Programme was launched in 1985 as a Technology Mission and aimed at immunising all children within the requisite age group and all expectant women. This Universal Immunisation Programme (including oral dehydration therapy) has now been integrated with the safe motherhood and child survival programme by adding of control of severe Respiratory Infection in the programme. An extensive infrastructure was also proposed to be set up during the 7th Five Year Plan with the goal to establish the sub-centre (SC) for every 5000 population in normal areas and 3,000 population in tribal and tough problem areas; Primary Health Centres (PHCs) for 30,000 in normal area and 20,000 in hilly and tribal areas and Community Health Centres (CHCs) for 1,20,000 in generally normal areas and 80,000 in hilly and tribal areas. However, the growth rate has just started coming down. Actually, it kept increasing from 1.33 per cent in 1941 to 2.11 per cent in 1981-91. This was of course, as the death rate fell at a greater pace from 31.2 per cent in 1941 to 9.6 per cent in 1991 and birth rate only fell from 45.2 per cent in 1941 to 29.9 per cent in the year 1991.

It is surprising that the exponential growth rate has fallen for the first time to 2.11 per cent in 1981-91 from 2.22 per cent in 1971-81. It is 2.03 per cent as per 1990 SRS Survey.

Introduction of Balance Sheets

This programme consists of both success and failures. In a democracy and in such a sensitive area, a programme cannot be enforced. 130 Million births have been averted infrastructure of 1,30,978 sub-centres covering almost the entire country has been created and 22,059 PHCs and 1923 CHCs. The birth rate has come down to 29.9 per thousand in 1990 compared to 41.7 during the decade 1951-61.

At the beginning of the programme in 1985-86, vaccine coverage levels ranged between 29 per cent for BCG and 41 per cent for DPT. By the end of March, 1991, the coverage levels got better significantly. It is estimated that 98 per cent of infants were immunized with DPT3 and OPV3; 97 per cent infants with BCG and 89 per cent with measles immunity vaccine. 78 per cent of pregnant women were immunized with Tetanus Toxide. This may, infant mortality rate has notably come down to 80 in 1990 compared to 114 in 1980. The CPR has also reached 44.1 per cent. The total fertility has come down to 4 in 1988 against 5.97 in 1960. On the side of the losses, we find that the birth rate is still very high particularly in the Central region. The stress was also more on sterilisation and not on spacing methods which resulted in people adopting the methods after reaching required family size.

The impact has not been the same in all States and the progress in States like Kerala has been remarkable with the growth rate coming down to 1.31 per cent. Despite all this, the growth rate is as much as 2.37 per cent in the States like Madhya Pradesh. Similarly in Tamil Nadu, the growth rate has been 1.39 per cent as compared to a growth rate of 2.47 per cent of Rajasthan and 2.26 per cent of Uttar Pradesh. Similar has been the case with other parameters in this regard.

Table 8.1

Sl. No.	*State*	*Growth Rate 1981-91*	*Birth Rate*	*Death Rate*	*Infant Mortality Rate*
					(SRS–'90)
1.	Rajasthan	24.7	33.1	9.4	83
2.	Madhya Pradesh	23.7	36.9	12.5	111
3.	Haryana	23.3	31.8	8.5	69
4.	Uttar Pradesh	22.6	35.7	12.0	98
5.	Bihar	21.1	32.9	10.6	75
6.	Punjab	18.5	27.6	7.8	55
7.	Tamil Nadu	13.9	22.4	8.7	67
8.	Kerala	13.1	19.0	5.9	17

Concept of Family Welfare has also been perceived generally as a Government's programme, more so a Central Government programme. It has not been adopted by the people and came to be known as a programme of their own where they would demand services. Also the infrastructure created has not been able to cater to the entire area particularly the difficult area.

Contributory Factors

In this whole process, the Planning Commission has estimated that the goals of NRR 1 would be achieved between 2006 and 2111 A.D. against the goal that was set for 2000 A.D. It would be feasible to achieve it earlier through a new thrust and dynamism; through a total commitment. Experience of the past 41 years has revealed that population relies on various social, political and economic factors. Broadly we could say that it depends on the following five factors given below:

1. Social factors for example, female age at marriage, female literacy, women's status in society etc.

2. Infant Mortality Rate; on prospects and possibilities of child survival.

3. Level and quality of out-reach of services; improved contraceptives and easy availability; better infrastructure.

4. Strong political will and administrative support; Tamil Nadu has demonstrated how political will and administrative support can help to accelerate rate of fertility decline.

5. Popular Participation; unless demand is generated from the people themselves, this programme which involves highly personal and intimate aspects of their lives cannot be thrust on them.

The Role of Women in Family Planning and Welfare

It is universally accepted that the life throughout the hemisphere begins with woman. In India, women have been worshipped in the form of goddesses for years. Giving the daughter away in marriage is regarded as an extremely noble deed. However, it is ironical that the female foetus is often aborted. Earlier there was practice of abandoning or killing of girl child soon after birth in some regions and societies. But now that it is possible to know the sex of a child before birth, many well-educated and so-called modern people also take recourse to destroying the female foeting. Though the law of the land bans the practical of sex determination tests, the practice goes on unabatedly and unashamedly. Medical community does it to rake in the moolah and people for want of a boy child.

Women face discrimination in education, in food, in clothing, in medical attention and certain other sectors especially in our rural and backward areas. If generalisations are permissible, it can be stated that where prosperity is greater, women's status is also higher. In our family welfare programme, we find the parameters directly linked it are female literacy and age at marriage of a woman. These linkages can be seen in a comparison of the growth rates and parameters of certain States in India.

Table 8.2

Sl. No.	*State*	*Age at Marriage*	*Female Literacy*	*Growth Rate*
1.	Kerala	21.8	86.9	19.0
2.	Tamil Nadu	20.3	52.3	22.4
3.	Rajasthan	16.1	20.8	33.1
4.	Uttar Pradesh	16.7	26.0	35.7

Importance of the effect of age at marriage on the growth rate has been established by many studies. Mr. S.B. Mukherjee in his book has shown that if the age of woman at marriage is 19 years, total fertility would decline by about 1. He has also established the secondary decline in the birth rate because the next generation of women would be ready for child bearing late. This will account for 2 point decline in the birth rate beginning after 16 years. Thus, after 25 years, the birth rate will come down to 25 per cent, if no woman is allowed to marry before the age of 18. Aggarwala in his book has calculated that Indian birth rate might be reduced as much as 30 per cent by 1991-92 if all Indian women are married after the age of 19. P.P. Talwar and K.C. Seal have stated in their book have said that the change in fertility would be 10 per cent to 50 per cent if the age of marriage were to be raised to 20 from the then average level of 16 years of age. If we go through an arithmetic impact of age of marriage on population growth shown on a hypothetical model made by Rami Chhabra the final that the productivity through three generations:

High Maternal and Infant Mortality

One more extremely adverse effect of low age of marriage is the high maternal mortality and infant mortality rate. In India, 43 per cent of female deaths in ages 15 to 24 are due to reasons associated with pregnancy and child birth. A further break down of causes of deaths in the 15-19 year age group is not available. Still, in Bangladesh, 6 out of every 10 women deaths in the age 15-19 were due to pregnancy and child birth. This study in Bangladesh also shows that MMR was twice as high for women under 20 years against the age group of 20 to 24 years. The study revealed that maternal deaths would fall by 20 per cent if child birth were within the age of 20 to 39.

Gautamala has observed that if there were no births to women outside the age of 20-29, maternity deaths would fall by one third. As we have already said, closely associated with maternai mortality is the infant mortality rate. In a study conducted in Delhi, neo-natal mortality was more than double amongst below twenty mothers compared to 20-24 years old and neo-natal mortality was about 80 per cent higher. The table below also shows the infant mortality in different States in our country which is evident.

Table 8.3

Sl. No.	*States*	*Age at Marriage*	*I.M.R.*	*Growth Rate*
1.	Kerala	21.82	17	1.31
2.	Punjab	21.07	55	1.85
3.	Uttar Pradesh	16.71	98	2.24
4.	Madhya Pradesh	16.56	72	2.37

Renowned author A.S. Altekar in his book **Position of women in Hindu society** claims that in the ancient times in India, the girls were not married early and child marriage is a comparatively latest phenomenon adopted in the 13th century as a result of Muslims rule. According to him, the religiously prescribed minimum marriage age for women during vedic times was 16 years. However, it has widely been accepted that ancient Hindu scriptures sanctioned child marriage stating that a girl should be married before she attains puberty. The close relation of age of marriage with birth rate and growth rate internationally has already been acknowledged.

Table 8.4

Sl. No.	*Countries*	*Female age of marriage*	*Birth*	*Growth Rate*
1.	India	18.0	37.2	2.11
2.	Japan	25.1	11.0	0.40
3.	China	22.4	21.0	1.40
4.	Singapore	26.2	18.0	1.30
5.	Indonesia	20.0	29.0	1.90

Along with this the linkages of literacy rate and IMR with growth rate are also very well established.

Table 8.5
Female Literacy Linked to Growth Rate

Sl. No.	*State*	*Female literacy*	*I.M.R.*	*Growth rate*
1.	Rajasthan	20.84	83	2.47
2.	Uttar Pradesh	26.02	98	2.24
3.	Bihar	23.10	75	2.11
4.	Kerala	86.93	17	1.31
5.	Himachal Pradesh	52.46	75	1.77
6.	Tamil Nadu	52.29	67	1.39

Contraception in Practice

There is no doubt that woman has had a very strong role to play in controlling her fertility. It has been established that where she has a role in getting an income, she has a say in her reproductivity. Though the proportion of women in labour force is very low, her role in practicing contraception still remains high. Out of the couple protection rate in India which is now 44.1 per cent, the break up is as below :

Table 8.6

Method	*Couples effectively protected as on 31.3.91*
Sterilization	30.3 per cent (24.6 per cent Tubectomy 5.6 per cent Vasectomy)
I.U.D.	6.7 per cent
C.C. Users	5.1 per cent
O.P. Users	2.1 per cent
Total due to all above methods	44.1 per cent

Figures establish that out of the total of 4,121,980 sterilization performed in 1990-91, 3,872,963 were Tubectomy and 249017 Vasectomy, thus resulting in 94 per cent of sterilisation being on women. In any country, one of the factors of progress is the ratio of female to males. In India, if we peep into the decadel history, a peculiar phenomenon emerges :

Table 8.7

Year	*Female Ratio (per 1000 men)*
1901	972
1931	950
1951	946
1961	941
1971	930
1981	934
1991	929

Though between 1901 and 1971 it kept declining, the ratio of women to men started going up in the last decade (1971-81) which was a welcome sign. Its decrease in this decade (1981-91) has been noted with great concern and is one of the reverse trends noted in the census. There is also a sharp North-South divide which is less than 950 and above 950 and can be seen in the table given that follows :

Table 8.8

Region	Sex Ratio of Female to 1000 Males	Male Probability of dying by age of 5 as compared Female
North		
Punjab	888	0.87
Haryana	874	0.81
Uttar Pradesh	882	0.83
Madhya Pradesh	932	0.96
Rajasthan	913	0.90
South		
Andhra Pradesh	972	1.05
Tamil Nadu	972	1.13
Karnataka	960	1.01
Kerala	1040	1.01
All India	**929**	**0.93**

As per statistical information, the proportion of men to women per thousand in developed countries is as follows :

Table 8.9

Country	Male Ratio
India	929
U.S.A.	1050
United Kingdom	1049
Canada	1020
Germany	1080
Austria	1096
France	1048
Italy	1057
Switzerland	1045

Thus, anyone can well say, without any fear that it is ironical situation indeed. Women who provide the mechanism for the birth of human beings, need protection, as if they are infact an endangered spicies. The worst enemy of women has found to be women herself in the role of mother-in-law demanding a male heir or dowry. A woman in the Indian sociological framework is seen in the traditional role-loving, sacrificing, giving up her requirements for others in the family. The image of a typical *Sati Savitri* receives a lot of appeal in the cinema also which promotes the requirement of men. We need to get the women out of the image and look at her interests as a human being. We need toi merge the girl child in the mainstream of development, looking into her dreams and wishes, her complexities and constraints, all of which together mould her outlook on life. We also need to address her special physiological and psychological requirements to prepare her for mother-hood. Swami Vivekanand had said that "Educating a man means educating an individual while educating a woman means educating a family". One could even go further and say that looking after the interest and development of women would contribute to a better tomorrow for the Nation and in the present context, her wisdom will contribute a lot to prosperity and development of a nation but planning her own family and thus checking fast population growth.

9

Female Labour Force

When we talk of women's performance, we tend to bend towards the glorification of women but it is almost ignored that their performance as well as outcome gets affects due to wrong attitudes towards their work, intentional partialities and incorrect policies. Women at employment/work force have been the greatest victims of this threefold victimisation. Unequal wages for equal has, if been principle of unorganised sector, keeping them away from key position has been the motto of organised sector. In short, whether organised or unorganised sector, public or private, women have always been victims of double standards one for them and the other for their male counterparts. This chapter throws light on some of these aspects and suggests some steps to raise from the present situation by skill upgradation of women and many more.

The significant role of women in the Indian labour force and their contribution to the national economy has been established beyond doubt. Women engage in a huge variety of occupations, especially in the unorganised sector. In the rural unorganised sector, women take care of cattle, sow, transplant and harvest, weave and work on handlooms and produce handicrafts mostly as low paid wage earners, or as unwaged family workers. Alongwith this, in the urban informal sector, women work as petty traders and producers selling and preparing a wide variety of goods, such as vegetables, fruits, flowers, cooked food, groceries, etc., or work as domestic workers. In both the rural and urban regions, they are engaged as construction workers.

In addition, women spend on an average 7-10 hours a day on domestic activities as well as collection of fuel, fodder and water, and child care. The large amounts of time and energy expended on these domestic acts, however, remain invisible as no productive economic value is attached to these tasks. Nor has any major attempt been made to improve women's access to technology aimed at reducing drudgery in the domestic chores performed by them.

I. Analysis of Ground Realities

Extent and nature of work of women. Correct data on the extent and nature of women's work is an essential pre-requisite in the development of employment policies and programmes. Data about the employment of women in India is currently available from six main sources. There are (a) The decennial population census, (b) Surveys undertaken by the National Sample Survey Organisation (NSSO), (c) Research conducted by the Directorate General of Employment and Training (DGE&T) and Labour Bureau, (d) Yearly surveys of industries compiled by the Central Statistical Office (CSO), (e) Periodical reports from the State Governments and (f) Dependent studies conducted by the Central and State Governments, universities and research agencies/institutions.

As we all know, the decennial population census provides valuable information on important areas, such as work participation rates by age, sex and occupation for both rural and urban areas. These statistics are available on an All India basis and for individual States upto the village level. The census also provides information about the levels of employment and other work related aspects.

NSSO produces comprehensive and detailed data on structure and changes brought in the labour force by relevant socio-demographic variables with a series of quintenniel surveys from 1972-73 till date. The Thirty-second (1977-78) and Thirty-eighth (1983) rounds have collected valuable data on the attitudes of women for work and other related aspects.

The DGE&T and the Labour Bureau have continuously collected large information related to the organised sector and the implementation of labour laws. The latter also conducts occasional field studies on selected subjects of national importance. The Labour Bureau has brought out a useful reference document entitled "Statistical Profile on Women Labour". It provides details regarding the population of workers, their average daily employment, sex-wise employment in factories by extra-ordinary/normal weekly hours, live register and placement data, minimum and maximum wage rates for workers by sex and age on the ground of occupational wage surveys, statistics on social security and information on factories providing creche facilities.

The yearly survey of industries (CSO) gives information on employment by sex and data on emoluments with respect to large scale factories. Some organisations under Central or State Governments, universities, research organisations and individual scholars have also been making micro studies concerning the socio-economic characteristics of workers and other problems.

But the tragedy is that the comparability of data on employment from these sources is, however, limited because of conceptual differences in the definition of workers and lack of uniformity in classification of workers by educational level, sex, etc. The work force participation rates written in successive census are not comparable either as the definition used in each census has been changing. In the 1961 census, any person engaged in gainful work for even an hour per day of the larger part of the working season was counted as worker, whereas in 1971, the person was asked as to what his/her major activity was and he/she was classified as worker or non-worker accordingly. This main activity concept of workers reduced substantially the participation rate of females. In 1981, the concepts of 'main worker' and 'marginal worker' were adopted. As per the 1981 census, the 'main' worker has been defined as a worker who has worked for the major part of the reference period, and the 'marginal' worker was he/she who had worked not for the major period but nevertheless had done some work in the reference period. Then standard definition used by the NSS provides data for 'useful status,' 'weekly status', unemployed'. 'Useful status' measures the usual activity status-employed or unemployed or apart from the labour force—of those covered by the survey. Thus, the activity status is determined with reference to a longer duration than a day or a week. 'Weekly status' is determined with reference to a period of preceding seven days. A person who reports having done work at least for one hour on any day during the reference period of one week while pursuing a gainful occupation was fit to be employed. A person who did not work even for one hour during the reference period but was seeking or available for work was said to be unemployed. In 'daily status', activity of a person for each day of the preceding seven days is recorded. A person who worked at least for one hour but not more than four hours was considered as employed for half a day. If the person worked for four hours or more within a day, he/she was considered as employed for the whole day. Those with jobs for less than half the days in the preceding 365 days are regarded as unemployed with 'usual status'. The 'weekly' employed are those with less than one day's work in the preceding seven days and the 'daily' unemployed with less than half a day's work in the week preceding the survey. In this situation the employment of women is almost under-estimated in many of these sources. Often women themselves would report unemployed in case they were not cash wage earners. The manner in which women's productivity is interpreted is also responsible for underenumeration of the women workforce participation. In quantifying labour days of employment female and child labour is often changed into equivalent adult man days, though the converse factors vary from source to source and region to region. Such an assumption is all untenable. A woman often earns half the wage earned by a man for an equivalent of a day's work, but not because her productivity is less. The wages given to women is determined not by economic criteria but is an outcome of the cultural attitudes, social practices and power structures in society. Some review of the relative evaluation of different operations in any sector is called for to redefine equal remuneration for work of equal value.

II. Women's Work Participation Rate

Here, it would be important to analyse the changes in female work participation rates over a period of time so as to evaluate the impact of various programmes on female employment. The main limitations in such comparison is due to the changes in the definition of employment. General inferences may be drawn from Table 9.1 below keeping in mind the conceptual limitations.

Table 9.1
All India Level Crude Work Participation Rates, 1971 to 1981 (Furnished by Census and NSS)

	Rural India		*Urban India*	
	Male	*Female*	*Male*	*Female*
(a) Main Activity				
1971 Census	53.62	13.36	48.80	6.65
1981 Census	52.62	16.00	48.54	7.28
1977-78 NSS	62.25	28.82	56.29	13.81
(b) Modified Main Activity (Including Marginal Workers)				
1972-73 NSS	63.84	35.53	57.09	15.53
1977-78 NSS	64.06	38.48	57.48	17.80
1981 NSS	53.80	23.18	49.07	8.32
1983 NSS	63.23	38.74	57.71	17.13

Sources (i) Census of India, 1981, Series I, India, Primary Census Abstract Delhi 1983
(ii) NSS, Sarvekshana, April, 1986, page S-III.

Referring to the 'main' activity, the participation rates for rural females in 1981 are noticeably higher than in 1971, whereas only a marginal hike is evident with respect to urban females. The NSS work participation rates for females show much higher participation rates instead of the census for both rural and urban females. This is due to differential base figures used in the calculations. The NSS data employing the perception of modified main activity (including marginal workers) shows an upward trend in the work participation rates between the durations 1972-73 and 1977-78. The work participation rate of 1977-78 is roughly approximated in 1983 even after recording a fast decline in 1981.

We notice a downfall in the self-employed category and an increase in casual labour for both male and female workers except for a slight decrease in 1983 for women casual worker category. The Regular Salary and Wage Work categories, however, declined substantially for females in 1977-78 but has since shown an increase in 1983. According to Census data,

Table 9.2
Age Based Worker Participation Rates Census Main Activity, 1971 and 1981

(per cent)

Age group	*Rural Males*		*Rural Females*		*Urban Males*		*Urban Females*	
	1971	*1981*	*1971*	*1981*	*1971*	*1981*	*1971*	*1981*
1	*2*	*3*	*4*	*5*	*6*	*7*	*8*	*9*
0-11	7.56	6.30	3.05	3.53	2.75	2.46	0.82	0.88
15-19	62.31	58.19	18.80	22.77	28.32	31.54	5.51	6.19
20-21	86.56	82.71	20.58	24.29	67.49	63.35	9.54	9.29
25-20	95.45	92.79	22.16	26.14	90.54	86.78	11.68	12.17
30-39	97.61	96.71	23.78	28.45	95.45	94.93	13.11	15.14
40-49	97.62	97.25	24.43	28.90	95.15	95.40	14.53	15.34
50-59	95.50	94.08	21.08	23.94	87.85	86.86	12.71	12.42
60 +	77.52	67.59	11.19	11.29	55.35	47.49	6.46	5.75
All ages	53.62	52.62	13.36	16.00	48.80	48.54	6.65	7.28

Source: Census of India, 1981, Series I, Paper 2 of 1983, Key Population Figures Based on 5 per cent Sample Data, Delhi, 1983, Table 15.

age specific participation rates show that women's participation increased for all the age groups 60+, and the increase was found in the age group 30-39 and 40-49 for rural females. The NSS data show enhanced participation of women in all the age groups, but unlike thue census do not recommend a special increase with respect to the two age groups.

Table 9.3
Sex-specific Distribution of Workers by Type of Employment Analysis

Sl. No.	*Men*			*Women*		
	1972-73	*1977-78*	*1983*	*1972-73*	*1977-78*	*1983*
1. Self Employment	65.90	62.77	60.40	64.48	62.10	62.21
2. Regular Salary/ Wage Work	12.06	10.57	10.77	4.08	2.84	3.10
3. Casual Labour	22.04	26.66	28.83	31.44	35.06	34.69

Source: NSS, *Sarvekshna,* Vol. IX, No. 4, April, 1986.

The Census trend data reveal that more and more women are joining employment after completing the child bearing age. This may imply greater reliance by working mothers on older children to help bring up younger children and points to the urgency of extending of supportive serivces to working women.

(A) Number and Composition of Women in Labour Force. In this context, the size and composition of the female labour force are a reflection of their overall submerged socio-economic status. In extreme terms the female labour force has grown from an estimated 78.6 million in 1973 to 88.9 million in 1978 and 99.4 million in 1983 or otherwise, an average annual addition of 2.1 million.

In proportional terms, however, their participation rate has gone down dramatically from 33.7 per cent in the 1911 Census to 20 per cent in the 1961 Census. Even following the new and larger definition of work, the female participation rate between 1971 and 1981 has registered just a marginal improvement from 12.06 per cent to 13.99 per cent. The size of women's representation in the total labour force has also reduced from

34.44 per cent in 1911 to 31.53 per cent in 1961, and 17.35 per cent in the year 1971 (*Source :* Table I, p. 153 of Report on Status of Women). Sectorwise composition of women workers reveals an ever increasing process of marginalization of female, with agriculture accounting for 80 per cent of the employment in 1971 as against 73.9 per cent in 1911 and 79.6 per cent in 1961. Female workers in industry declined from 14.7 per cent (1911) to 10.5 per cent (1971) and in the service sector from 11.4 per cent to 9.4 per cent in period of 1911 and 1971. Though in the decade 1971-81, some marginal improvement has been recorded in the ratio of female to male workers. The comparative participation level of males and females in the primary, secondary and tertiary sectors in the primary, secondary and tertiary sectors in 1971 and 1981 reveals that the percentage of female workers to total workers grew in each of these sectors during the decade 1971-81. Among females, the proportion of those engaged in the primary sector declined by 1.4 per cent, whereas it is increased by 1.2 and 0.2 per cent respectively in the secondary and tertiary sectors. The percentage growth in employment in secondary and tertiary sectors in case of females nevertheless has been less than that of their colleagues.

Apart from this, the organised sector in India (which consists of public sector and non-agricultural private sector establishments) absorbs less than one-eighth of the true work force of the country. Of this, the share of women as of 1978 was 12.4 per cent. Women's employment in the organised sector increased from 19.30 lakhs in 1971 to an estimated 33.41 lakhs in 1986. Whereas the growth rate of women's work in the organised sector has shown a steady increase, their proportion in the total public sector work force has remained almost constant while within the organised sector, female employment in the public sector increased fast from 8.62 lakhs in 1971 to 19.50 lakhs during 1986. In the private sector too, women's employment improved, although at a lower rate (from 10.67 lakhs in 1971 to 13.07 lakhs in 1986). The number of women job seekers through employment exchanges went up from 11.25 lakhs in 1975 to 50.98 lakhs in 1986. The percentage of placements, on the other hand, increased from

1975-1982, but declined in the following years, i.e., 1983-1986.

(B) Female Labour Force in the Unorganised Sector. Larger number of women are to be found in the vast rural and urban unorganized sector. As per an estimate by the National Commission on Self Employed Women, 94 per cent of the total female workforce operates within this greatly exploited sector. Employment in this sector is characterised by low pay, long hours of work, low productivity, low skills and absence of job security.

There are few labour or trade unions/organisations to facilitate the mobilisation of women workers and include them into a conscious workforce. This is due to the varied nature of occupation in this sector, inadequate legislation and useless enforcement of legal safeguards to protect these workers, particularly, in regulating their work conditions. Traditional socio-economic relations that take place in this sector defy categorisation into 'employer', 'employee', 'labour', 'capital', 'rent', and 'interest' based relationships.

Among the major reasons for women's work becoming increasingly limited to the unorganised sector is that women lack the opportunity to gain skills and training which could facilitate occupational shifts. This is related to the prevailing social relations between men and women as well as the full structure of the economy. Since women have to bear the major burden of domestic chores, which in a poor household is time taking and labour intensive, they do not have the time and opportunity to acquire skills and training for better job.

Low skill learning among women and their consequence relegation to jobs which are labour intensive, time consuming and arduous is then exploited by their unequal access to technology. Huge share of employment in the rural unorganised sector is held by women. Employment of women in the rural unorganised sector is concept, traced to nine employment systems. These are agriculture, dairying, small animal husbandry, fisheries, social and agro-forestry, and sectors like khadi and village industries, handlooms, handicrafts and sericulture.

The first five sectors are broadly classified as agriculture and others allied occupations; the last four are categorised as village and small industries sector. The sex based break up of employment in eight of these systems for which data is available is as follows in the table 9.4:

Table 9.4
Number of Men and Women Employed in the Large Employment Systems

(in Lakhs)

Sl. No.	*Women*	*Men*
1. Agriculture	18.70	754.70
2. Dairying	750.00	50.00
3. Fisheries	10.00	18.00
4. Small Animal Husbandry	150.00	20.00
5. Khadi and Village Industries	17.00	19.90
6. Handicrafts	5.40	22.00
7. Sericulture	8.00	12.00
8. Handlooms	29.80	44.80

Source: Different Departments of the Government of India.

Despite the fact that investment outlays in these sectors command high priority, and several government programmes exist to boost the productivity of said sectors, most endeavours are focussed on men and male producer organisations. The programmes themselves are executed mainly by male bureaucrats and male extension workers. Women are viewed as indirect beneficiaries through the male members of their families, and not as participants and target groups. Most of the jobs in these sectors are low paid and accomplished by women.

It is also a recognised fact that women are gradually being displaced from some of these sectors in context. Structural problems have risen in the rural unorganised sector as a result of the hierarchical style of land ownership, the nature of land relations, and gender division of labour and the credit system. There is a tight-class-caste relationship in the ownership of land which works to the disadvantage of the economically weaker sections and more specifically against women. Construction labour is a fairly large sector of casual work, employing women in substantial numbers while the construction labourers are engaged on a casual basis (daily or piece rate), many of them have long years of experience in this field of work. Quite a few are initiated as youngsters, moving from one project to another, often migrating to distant and strange places, constantly dependent on the contractors to hire them. The use of contractors to mobilize labour for this sector has followed the age old method of recruiting by "credit tying" and "loan bondage" methods that are routinely used to utilise migrant labour for the seasonal harvesting operation in high growth areas.

The exploitation of these workers thus starts with the methods of their recruitment. Their services are hired by sub-contractors who most often obtain their labour from backward rural regions where unemployment is high. Sub-contractors obtain work from the main contractors on a piece rate basis but gives to the labourers on a daily money basis. This enables them to keep their profit margins high at the expense of labour. Ideally, construction workers ought to be recruited through a workers' board or social work organisations and trade unions.

There is a need to form such union or bodies that could organise groups of migrants workers to press for enforcement of minimum work conditions like right wages, maternity benefits, medical facilities, creches, etc. Domestic work offers another major avenue of employment for women and girl children. It is the most accessible avanue of employment for female migrants and urban poor women. This group of workers, as others in the unorganised sector, has remained grossly unrepresented in the national data systems. Of all the services in India, household service is the most unregulated and disorganised. The major constraints are an absence of a written contract for work and protective rules and regulations.

The highly personalised nature of the work further complicates the situation. The percentage number of young unmarried girls as domestic workers, many under the age of ten, who are initiated mainly as a help to the mother has increased fast. An estimate in 1977-78 (Sarvekshana, 1987) reported 1.68 million female domestic workers as against 0.62 million male workers. The spreadover of working hour for full time living in domestic workers is known to be 12 to 16 hours. The immediate task is that of ensuring them dignity and security at work and regulating work conditions an organisation and protective legislation. Simultaneously, they must be provided with opportunities to seek alternate employment by giving skill training and education.

Very recently, the National Commission on Self-Employed Women and Women in the Informal Sector has gathered exhaustive data and analyses on these sections of women workers including specific groups live women in the primary sector in mining, tobacco and beedi work; handlooms, handicrafts and garments; women vendors and street hawkers, construction workers, and domestic workers, etc. While analysing the status of these group of workers in the structural purview of existing macro policies and existing legislation, the National Commission makes various recommendations for their safety and empowerment.

(C) Female Force in the Organised Sector. The organised sector accounts for approximately 10 per cent of the female labour force. Employment avenues in the governmental and public sectors and the private corporate are limited in view of the general constraits on the dictates of market mechanisms which are prejudical to women. Given these facts and based on the performance in previous decades, it is unlikely that this sector can offer much relief by way of increased employment potential to women.

(D) Hurdles. Despite the fact that whether in the unorganised or the organised sector, women workers face several constraints which is known for their low status as workers. Their lack of access to productive inputs such as raw material, credit, technology, training and markets are main impediments. Despite legislation, women's right to land deeds and pattas continue to be overlooked contributing to their marginalisation. As a result, women are increasingly compelled to migrate both, rural as well as urban regions on a temporary, seasonal or permanent basis. In addition to their lack of adequate skills and resources they may face extreme adjustment problems due to differences in religion, language and socialisation as well as separation from their families. The condition of migrant women needs attention.

When we talk of economic strucutre, in the Indian economy, women are concentrated in occupations which are usually at the lowest rung of the ladder. In number of occupation they work in arduous and less skilled areas of work. For example, in the construction of industry men perform bricklaying while women carry bricks and mortar; women carry soil while men do the digging; women workers transplant paddy, weed, reap, pluck vegetables and bundle the harvest produce while men plough and sow the seeds. In terms of access to skills, women are always employed in monotonous, low skilled and low wage sectors.

In terms of access to credit, while low interest credit through the Differential Rate of Interest (D.R.I.) scheme is available to women. In reality, the need for collateral, cultural and other obstacles faced by women in dealing with bank staff, low priority for small loans in banks, etc., have led to a very low level of utilisation of this type of institutional credit by women workers. Unfortunately, gender differentiated data about women's use of bank credit is not available nationally which could yield a more precise picture.

In the situation of absence or lack of enforcement of social and labour legislation hampers women's access to basic employmnt benefits. These factors together contribute to the insecurity of women and strengthen their inferior status as workers.

III. Reasons for Low Participation Rate of Women in Employment

Not any single factor, but a combination of social and economic factors are responsible for the low participation rate of women. The most critical ones are :

(a) Sectionalisation in the labour market which works against women;
(b) Negative implications of technological growth for women;
(c) Absence of unionisation of female workers;
(d) Non-availability of a purposeful human resource development policy aimed at improving women's employability and productivity with training; and
(e) Ideological ambiguities and lack of a National Labour Policy encompassing workers in the unorganised sector.

(A) Sectionalisation or Segmentation of the Labour Market. This leads to two major types of discrimination viz., (i) Wage differentials between men and women; (ii) Discrimination in terms of concentration of women in specific sectors (primary sector) and in certain types of jobs or operations. In the agricultural sector, for instance, the majority of women are seen to be concentrated in lower paying operations.

In the informal sector, women almost uniformly get less wages than men. In the organised sector, about 90 per cent of women are known to be engaged in unskilled or semi-skilled activities. A fundamental economic force that keeps women's wages low is the gap between supply and demand for women's labour. In the past two decades, India's overall growth rate of 3.5 per cent per annum has not been high enough to create sufficient demand for labour (particularly female labour) and to provide productive employment to a labour force which is increasing at over 25 per cent p.a. Further, the capital intensive organised sector has been heavily male oriented, while number of the traditional activities which suffered from competition offered by the modern sector were those which engaged women workers.

(B) Consequences of Technology. As is evident to all, technological modernisation has further eliminated the traditional employment activity and adversely affected women. Examples of technological modernisation eliminating traditional activities are well known. Powerlooms have thrown about 84,000 women handloom weavers out of work in five States between 1961-71. Modern herbicides and rice mills have displaced women and eliminated their traditional incomes from weeding and milling.

Apart from straight displacement of labour in the short run, we find a number of other mechanisms through which technological progress has adversely affected female earning and opportunities. The demand from modern industry, for instance, pushes the price for raw materials beyond what conventional workers can afford (as in the case of bamboo basket weavers). Mechanised fishing displaced whole fishing communities. The rise in the water table because of increased irrigation leads to increased salinity of drinking water necessitating long trips to fetch drinking water.

Conversely, more pumping of ground water may lower the water table to such an extent that traditional wells fall dry. In more deforestation, linked to 'development', has often meant much longer trips for women to collect fuel, water and fodder. Reforestation has itself gone to favour cash crops over fuel and fodder and trees entailing further hardship for women. Last but not the least, adoption of new farming technology has significantly downgraded the input of women, largely on account of their limited education. It is thus essential to analyse technology/industrial/agricultural/environmental policy to assess the status of women workers.

(C) Lack of Unionisation of Women. Absence of organisation and unionisation hampers the bargaining position of women, especially in the unorganised sector, which refuses women all the benefits of collective action. Dispersed, unorganised and atomised they have no political power and without any bargaining strength. The unorganised sector presents a number of difficulties in implementing protective labour laws about wages, conditions of work, insurance, provident fund, maternity leave, creche facilities, etc.

The exploitation in this particular sector is only marginally under the purview of laws. Hours of work are long, wages are poor, conditions are hazardous, benefits are non-existent and wages are below survival needs. Channeling inputs such as literacy, health, family welfare services, etc., is also highly difficult in this sector. As a result, there are marked disparities between women in the organised and unorganised sector of industry. Apart from all this inter-state, inter-urban disparity in the nature and structure of wages and other benefits are considerable and support 10 per cent in the organised sector as against the 90 per cent women workers in the unorganised sector. Investment policies also continue to award low priority to the unorganised sector.

(D) Non-availability of a Systematic Training and Human Resource Development Policy. Among the major hurdles to the development of employment opportunities for women is the lack of adequate training. The objective of training is to develop employable skills that can generate better income and improve the status of women workers. At present in most of those occupations where women are employed in large numbers, such as agriculture and construction they work as low paid unskilled labourers with almost no training facilities available to upgrade there skills. Even the existing training programmes are primarily aimed at men creating further imbalances. Though certain facilities to train women in different skills through the industrial training institute or polytechnics and apprenticeship training under the Apprentice Act are available, there is no speical emphasis on the training of women which is packaged alongwith other inputs such as credit and marketing support. Moreover, current facilities largely cater to urban rather than rural areas. At present, the nodal department for women's development in the Government of India is the Department of Women and Child Development. Though it has a number of schemes such as short stay homes, working's hostels, women's development corporations.

Further, it is evident that the mixed programme such as the TRYSEM have not reached women as effectively as assumed.. Currently, there are at least 45 schemes in 17 departments/ ministeries of the Government of India catering to training needs of women but they do not present a systematic integrated approach to women's training. It is essential that such an approach be adopted and fostered. The focus of such training should be at those who are presently the most disadvantaged— i.e., the great majority of women engaged in the informal or unorganised sector and forming 90 per cent of the total female labour force. It should provide training to enhance productivity as well as explore new avenues of employment to facilitate occupational shifts wherever possible.

(E) Ideological Vagueness. Despite the fact that constraints are multifarious and real, there is difficulty in clearly understanding the problems at hand, mainly because the invisibility and under-recording of work done by women. In evolving suitable employment promotion interventions, a crucial issue has been the invisibility of female work as well as lack of comprehension and value added to numerous tasks they perform for their family. A conceptual framework for computing the value of such tasks is necessary.

The poor data base about the extent and nature of enployment of women on the one hand, and the absence of clarity on what constitutes work on the other, pretend for definite impediments in assessing women's actual productive participation in the economy. The low visibility of their productive quality is illustrated by the fact that only 14 per cent of the total female population in the country fell into the group of workers as per the 1981 census. Yet, both the Sixth and Seventh Plan documents clearly attest that there are large numbers of women whose work keep on to be unreported and invisible. It is this lack of adequate and accurate data which is one of the impediments to the introduction of informed policies for improving the employment status of women. Conceptual ambiguity in evaluating the employment status of women becomes a basis for lack of appreciation of and sensitivity to the problems which women come across, particularly in the vast unorganised employment sector.

This, in turn, leads to the virtual lack of strategies for improving conditions in this sector. Presently, support structures for employment like training, mobilization of workers, legal safeguards, as well as the institutional base for identifying new avenues of employment and more productivity for women are lacking.

IV. Strategies for Setting the Wrongs Right

Appropriate strategies are to be viewed holistically and not as isolated piecemeal actions. In order to truly be effective, the overall employment strategy for working women should be viewed as a package comprising employment opportunities, legal safeguards, training assistance and social services, awareness generation and mobilisation. Only then will a purposeful synergy be achieved. The corrective strategies are mainly addressed to the factors which have been reviewed earlier as constraints. Those strategies must aim to create new opportunities for employment of women, upgrade their existing employment conditions as well as productivity and employment potential, ensure in them a more articulate and conscious workforce, and assure them better status and recognition as workers.

(A) More Opportunities. It is true that in the organised sector, the employment potential for women is likely to grow very slowly, while there is a considerable scope for employment in the agricultural and service sectors. Diversification in agriculture and in the other leading sectors of rural development offers enormous potential for employment. Horticulture, commercial vegetable plantation, food processing, fisheries and poultry, agro industry offer ample opportunities to rural women.

Unemployed young women could be better trained in extension work for imparting the necessary skills in these activities. Besides, a variety of new occupations could be generated for women workers in the areas of agro-based industry, weaving, textile printing, ready-made garments, production of stationery material and preparation of indigenous herbal medicines and packaging, etc. Extension of the service in the rural areas is a need and reality offering scope for local women to be absorbed with the minimum training being given. Nurseries, creches and anganwadis also offer employment opportunities for a large number of women. The spheres of simple health care like immunisation diagnostic screening (testing of blood, etc.) and other health functions could be started for intermediary levels without affecting the overall standards.

These facilities are not currently available to poor families particularly in the rural parts. Middle level workers could be trained for employment in the provision of these services. There is an urgent need to diversity the prevailing occupational base so as to promote skilled employment on a wider scale. Currently, training is in traditional occupations like carpentry, welding smithing, tailoring, book binding, etc. which is also male oriented. Today it is necessary to provide training to women in such non-traditional fields as well.

An area based identification of potential occupational groups would have to be undertaken systematically in the different regions of the country in order to detemine the nature and size of avenues that could be made available. Effective linkages between metropolitan and large urban areas with the surrounding hinterlands is one more modality with considerable potential for employment generation.

The demand from these urban and metropolitan centres in the areas of food processing, packaging, transportation, storage and other services could open up bigger areas for production, processing and marketing, thereby providing employment opportunities in such areas on a large scale. Spread of small scale industries is widely recognised as a means of creating potential for employment. Suitable institutional mechanisms for the improvement of small scale industry need to be developed to assist in the provision of credit, supply of raw materials, monitoring of marketing and creation of skills necessary for these enterprises. Two of the important areas requiring immediate attention for the expansion of cottage industries are :

(a) Upgradation of skills in order to raise the status of workers to that of artisans and enhance the quality of products

(b) Education, training and organisations of workers for collective action on various aspects. Appropriate technologies and modernisation of their occupations would have to be inducted to push their income potential.

The role of middlemen who have been getting sizeable benefits disproportionate to their investment and attempts has to be reduced. Producer Co-operatives are one such strategy to reduce dependence. An appraisal is important to examine the viability/marketability of the trades for which training and assistance is being provided by the state.

(B) Skill upgradation. Well systematic human resource development strategy focussed on women is essential. Three levels of training are viewed viz. (a) The grass roots level; (b) The middle level; and (c) The policy and planning level. The course content of a training strategy should encompass five principal components as given below :

(i) Organisational and extension training.
(ii) Skill training.
(iii) Training of management and entrepreneurial.
(iv) Sensitisation programme for administrators/ implementors to women in development issues.
(v) TOTs, i.e., Training of trainers.

(i) Organisational and extension training. This particular component of training is to be geared to functionaries, catalysts, extension workers at the grassroots, middle and supervisory level staff, teachers, organisers of cooperatives, etc. It should aim at conscientization on legislation, environmental health, nutrition and sanitation, education and functional literacy, paralegal training and related aspects.

Strong group mobilisation, communication skills, skills needed for organisation and management will be stressed in this training alongwith functional knowledge. Particular attention will be paid to the attitudinal/behavioural component important for reaching programmes women at the grassroots.

(ii) Skill training. Here, we refer to skill training with special emphasis on the nine major sectors of women's employment like agriculture, dairying, fisheries, small animal husbandary, khadi and village industries, handlooms, art and handicrafts, sericulture and social forestry. This type of training will entail upgrading existing skills in these areas as well as training of women in right technologies.

It will be aimed at programme beneficiaries as well as catalysts/functionaries, extension and supervisory workers. All these skills need to be imparted on the widest scale to rural women in order to encourage them to attain household self-sufficiency as well as supplementary income. Also included will be the skill training in the urban/modern sector with relation to assembly, manufacturing and processing for larger industries as well as small scale firms. Wherever possible women's employability has to be enhanced in the organised sector as the employment conditions in the unorganised sector indicate the need for a shift in the occupational set-up. In generating such skills, care will be taken to ensure that the training imparted does not push women into sectors where mobility is not much, wages are low, health hazards are high, and worker benefits are not enforced.

(iii) Entrepreneurial and management training. Here we refer to taining in project formulation, monitoring, evaluation, information systems, credit/marketing management, and many other skills required to administer and manage projects, as well as supervisory and entrepreneurial skills. Such training could be imparted with the help of technical institutes (ITIs, Polytechnics, etc.) where special courses for training of female workers and entrepreneurs could be started.

In conducting such courses, banks, voluntary organisations and individual and public sector industries could be effectively utilised to help formulate viable entrepreneurial projects for the trainees. Special training programmes to improve rural entrepreneurship in particular would need to be designed.

(iv) Programmes for sensitisation of administrators/ implementators. For this, training should seek to achieve sensitisation of bureaucrats to the critical need to integrate women in development. The objective will be to evolve appropriate attitudes and knowledge for planning/monitoring/ implementing programmes and policies for women workers. Such training needs to be imparted through the training programmes of the Department of Personnel as well as numerous other governmental and non-governmental agencies.

A particular emphasis in this category of training must be to train the officers responsible for enforcement machineries at the Central and State levels, workers of quasi-governmental bodies, and voluntary agencies. A special agency, i.e., the Womens Division at NIPCCD is already undertaking sensitisation programmes for police officers/judiciary to the issue of atrocities against women.

(v) TOTs, i.e. Training of Trainers. Alongwith the training of trainers within the existing institutions and infrastructures, a special attempts should be made to train rural women as organisers and instructors in different sectors and trades so that they could train more women and ensure a multiple effect.

Keeping in mind the criticality of training for the development of women, setting up of a National Resource Centre for Women is imperative. By performing a coordinating/ interventionist role it would identify and strengthen existing governmental and non-governmental organisations to carry out training policy and programme research and information discrimination.

The Resource Centre would offer a new thrust for training and work towards translating national developmental goals into a systematic grid of programmes and various schemes for training in skills/knowledge/attitudes at different levels. To conclude, a preparatory step, it would be essential to identify and classify the various types of training institutions all over the country. Instances of such institutions* are agriculture and rural home science centres; schools of social services, khadi

*An exhaustive National Directory of such training institutions has been compiled by the womens division at NIPCCD.

and village industries, as well as vocational training agencies; universities, ITIs, polytechnics, agriculture and veterinary schools, engineering colleges, krishi vigyan kendras, etc. Right now, they have no special focus on training only for women, but these should take up new courses under a coordinated attempt, monitored and planned by the resource centre. In addition, newly established training and extension departments, as well as present training institutions, agencies, management bodies, and grass-roots organisations should be involved in giving training to women.

10

Woman Organisations

Women's organisations have been functioning since pre-independence days. The first modern organisation—The *Women's Indian Association* was started in 1917 by the great pioneer of women's cause, Margaret Cousins, in Madras undr the effective leadership of Annie Besant. Not only was it active from its very inception but it also worked on an all-India plane and had a non-sectarian character. As seen before, it was-mainly because of its efforts-supported by other leaders (both men and women) and associations that freedom struggle particularly to the programme of boycott of foreign goods, picketing of liquor shops and propagating of swadeshi. Since then its activities have gathered momentum.

It has not merely kept up the traditions of the pre-independence period by continuing its laudable work in different fields but also expanded its activities. It conducted programmes for relief and rehabilitation of the refugees in 1947, carried on strong propaganda in favour of the Hindu Code Bill, lent help in the implementation of the five year plans, carried on a constant campaign against social evils like early marriage, polygamy, *purdah*, dowry, prepared for the ground for the enactment of appropriate legislation, worked for better working conditions for women and played a significant role in spreading consciousness about their rights among women. The National Council for Women having its branches in all states also strives hard to help women of all sections to know and preserve their rights and to ameliorate their conditions. Their attempts are to make women and children healthy and happy, bold and self-reliant.

So far as education is concerned the S.N.D.T. Women's University occupies a pride of place; as from an institution which started with just 17 girls studying in small classrooms it has now expanded into a full-fledged university offering courses in disciplines, Arts, Education, Home-Science, Nursing and Library Science faculties and having a strength of 26,907 students in 29 colleges spread over Gujarat and Maharashtra.

Various agencies like the Women Graduate's Union cater more to the needs of professional women. They also help in educating public opinion on important matters concerning women like proper representation to women in state legislatures about the condition of women working in different fields, and in promoting contacts with international women's agencies. The Y.W.C.A. too has done significant work in this direction especially through international hostles. All these organisations have served as good training ground for several young social workers.

The *Hindu Women Rescue Home Society* started in 1927 has done commendable work in providing shelter to Hindu women and children in distress and tried to bring solace and ease in the lives of fallen women and deserted wives, despised widows and unclaimed orphans. Several other organisations too have done exemplary work in the fields of social education, rescue and rehabilitation of kidnapped women, help to widows and destitutes, giving shelter to orphans and young girls and educating them. The *Jyoti Sangh* and *Vikasgriha* of Ahmedabad and the *Sharda Sadan* of Pune from Western India deserve description for their work in this field.

Gandhi not only played a prominent part in training women for social work but also laid sound foundations of rural social welfare work. The *Kasturba Gandhi National Memorial Trust* set-up in memory of his wife Kasturba with the aims of providing education for women and children, medical and health services and socio-economic programmes to relieve economic distress has continued this tradition by taking upon itself the work of training *gramsevikas.* It is in charge of the entire training programme for village workers and midwives of the Central Social Welfare Board under the Government of India. Kasturbagram at Indore is the main training centre of the Trust, which trains grams sevikas, arogya sevikas, bal sevikas and angan wadi workers especially in rural India.

Undoubtedly, both these organisations were greatly influenced by Gandhi. The Kasturba Gandhi National Memorial Trust bears this view as will be clear from the replies they gave to the question regarding women's welfare organisations indicated below being influenced by Gandhi's teaching.

Rashtra Sevika Samiti

Rashtra Sevika Samiti was formed with the efforts of Vandaniya Laxmibai Kelkar, popularly known as *Mausiji.* It was formed in 1936 A.D. on the Dussehra day at Vardha. Mausiji Delivered that for the betterment of Hinduism as a society, it is necessary to form an organisation of Hindu women. While women is the pillar that supports a home, she is also the building block of a nation. With this idea in mind she sought the support of Dr. Hedgewar with his help this independent organisation could be formed.

Women have a different kind of field of action. Women are the link that which binds a society. If that link is weak, the society can never progress. Thus, it is necessary for the society to make women strong spiritually, intellectually, and physically. It is also necessary to make her aware about her duties to the nation. This sevika samiti was set up with all these objectives in mind.

A disciplined working of an organisation forms the basis of its expansion and efficiency. As our body needs food to remain healthy, same way character of a nation is built on the staple diet of spiritual purity of its citizen. And it is the mother who inculcates this purity into her children. The example of Jeejabai, the mother of Chhatrapati Shivaji is there for all to see and realise this.

Nation's building is the field of activity of the sevikas of this samiti. They have been helping the sufferers of national calamities in Bengal, Pune, Jabalpur etc. at various points of time with money, clothes, medicines etc.

The Samiti also runs educational institutions, yogasadhna centre, dispensaries, hostels, etc. at various places all over India. The Samiti is continuously expanding its scope of activities and is operation not only in India but also outside it. It is operational in ten other nations bearing the name, "Hindu Sevika Samiti".

The Samiti also publishes the following publications:

1. Sewika: Published annually in Hindi and Marathi
2. Varta: Published in Hindi, quarterly.
3. Dindarshika: A modern national panchang
4. Bhartiya Dainiki: Published annually.

This was the samiti which had been developing fast and its thousands of sevikas were working all over the country for the progress of the nation and its women. Now it is pertinent have to know in brief about the founder of this Samiti, by Vandaniya Laxmibai Kelkar. Laxmibai Kelkar was born in 6 July, 1905 in Detey family in Mahal area. Her childhood name was Kamal. Since her early age she was an exceptional child. She had the benefit of learning great virtues from her aunty known as *Dai* and *'Anna',* her father. She was particularly impressed by their selfless service to humanity an example of which she saw during the epidemic of plague. At the age of 14, she got married into Kelkar family and acquired the name Laxmibai Kelkar. Her husband Purushottam Rao was an anglicised man. He expect his wife to socialise with the ladies at the ladies club. Laxmi met the influential ladies than. As she was endowed with the leadership qualities, Laxmi soon made those women realise that it is a waste of time to play bridge while the country was bound in shackle. She was able to change their line of thinking and the ladies started reading newspapers, discussion on national issues etc. instead of playing cards.

Laxmibai held the view that service or sewa was the primary duty of women. She got around to working with RSS. Later she thought of setting up an independent organisation for women. It was decided to form a samiti that would be an independent entity and run parallel to RSS. 25 October, 1936 was the day. When 'Rashtra Sevika Samiti' was formed at an inagural function that was presided over by Shri Yadav Madhav Koli. A large number of women came out of the confine of four walls of homes to join it. Samiti turned into a training ground for women to would then into disciplined sevikas. Sevikas called Laxmibai as 'Mausiji' and soon she became Vandaniya Mausiji. Dr. Hedgewar was constantly guiding the working of samiti.

Other organisation that had the stamp of Mausiji include *streejeevan shakti,* form in 1953, *stree shaktipeeth* etc.

Set up in Maharashtra at Vardha, the samiti soon spread out of Maharashtra and as mentioned earlier, is engaged in upliftment of women and Hinduism all over India. Mausiji believed that through Shakhas, Sevikas could be trained to become able administrator like Sri Ram, Shivaji and Ahilyabai. Though the purpose of Samiti is not to acquire power but they should have the abilities to run administrative if the occassion demanded.

Mausiji left for her heavenly abode on 27 November 1978 but left behind a legacy that is to serve the cause of Indian women for a long time to come, in the form of Rashtriya Sevika Samiti. The work at Samiti goes on in order to fulfil the dreaming of Mausiji.

Central Social Welfare Board

Central Social Welfare Board started by Durgabai Deshmukh in 1953, for the first time joined together the government and voluntary social welfare efforts in the service of the welfare state. It has also been carrying out the work of welfare of women. Today it has become a big organisation working on all India basis. Outstanding women like Mridula Sinha have been associated with their organisation. The author herself is the chairperson of Delhi unit of this organisation. For the betterment of women's lot it is providing the following services:

(A) Education and Training

- (i) Condensed courses for education of women.
- (ii) Vocational training programme for women.
- (iii) Awareness generation programme.

(B) Support Services

- (i) Family Counselling Centres.
- (ii) Short Stay Homes.
- (iii) Working Women's Hostels.
- (iv) Creches.

Economic Empowerment

Socio-Economic Programme

The board gives grants to the voluntary organisations and NGOs to carry out the social work under its various schemes. Following documents are required to be submitted by the organisations applying for the grants.

(i) Copy of the Registration Certificate.
(ii) Copy of Memorandum of Association/Articles of Association/Bye-laws of the institution.
(iii) Detailed audited accounts of the institution of the previous 3 years.
(iv) Annual Reports of the previous 3 years.
(v) List of current Managing Committee Members.
(vi) Application form in the prescribed format duly filled in and signed by the Secretary or authorised office bearer of the institution.

Note. Accounts should be of the institution as a whole and not of any single individual programme.

The Central Social Welfare Board was established with the objective of developing the tradition of voluntarism in independent India and adding new dimensions to it in the context of the changing environment. On the one hand, the Central Social Welfare Board was given the responsibility of taking welfare services to the disadvantaged sections of society especially women and on the other hand, it was given the mandate of developing a nationwide infrastructure of voluntary agencies through which these services could be taken to those who needed them most. In this way, the Board took up the dual responsibility of formulating programmes fitting the changing values of life and of giving encouragement and guidance to voluntary organisations that would implement these programmes.

With the efforts of the Board, the activities of the voluntary sector have developed multi-dimensionally. There has been a qualitative change in the objectives and goals of this Sector. It has developed into the central supporting column of democracy. Today, it is playing a significant role in the task of social development. This sector has expanded its role in the formulation of government policies, programmes and their implementation.

The board also publishers two journals Samaj Kalyan in Hindi and Social Welfare in English. These are published to increase the public awareness about social issues and also for the publicity of board's programmes.

Following are the schemes of assistance run by CSWB

(i) Condensed Courses of Education for Women

Objectives. The scheme of Condensed Courses of Education for Women aims at facilitating social and economic empowerment of women by providing them with education and relevant skills. The scheme is specifically designed to help dropouts and failed candidates to complete their school education.

Eligiblity. The applicant institution should meet the conditions of eligibility as detailed earlier. In addition, the applicant institution should have had experience in conducting women welfare programmes/educational programmes. Registered social welfare organisations having experience in educational programmes and recognised educational institutions can apply for assistance. The scheme can also be run in aftercare homes and custodial institutions for women.

Description of the Scheme. Courses can be organised for women of the age of 15 years and above. The following types of courses can be conducted under the scheme:

(i) Two year non-residential education courses to enable women to appear for recognised primary/middle/matric/ higher secondary or equivalent examination, as private candidates. A component of skill development is also provided for in this programme of assistance.

(ii) One year non-residential education course for women who have failed in SSLC/Matric or equivalent examination, as private candidates.

(iii) The residential courses are also considered under Two year Condensed Course in Primary, Middle and Metric level courses wherever found necessary. No local candidates should be admitted as residential candidates.

Note: Selection of candidates is required to be done by a Committee comprising the Institution and the Principal/ representative of a local Government School of the Area where the course is to be held.

(ii) Vocational Training Programme for Women

Objectives: The Board provides assistance to organisations having the requisite capability, experience and infrastructure to provide vocational training to needy women of the age group of 15 years and above. The marketability of the skills and the capability of the applicant institution are the main aspects taken into consideration for providing assistance under this scheme. A suggested list of Vocational Training Programmes, which can be organised.

The prescribed schematic details of the Vocational Training Programme are as follows:

Eligibility. The applicant institution should meet conditions of eligibility. In addition, the applicant Institution should have had experience in conducting training programmes. The schemes can also be implemented in after-care homes and custodial institutions for women.

Description of Scheme. The duration of the course can vary between one year to two years. Training programmes of less than one year duration can also be considered. The number of candidates in a batch would be around 25 or multiples thereof. Preference should be given to destitute women, widows and women belonging to weaker sections, especially those belonging to SCs/STs and backward classes. The minimum educational qualifications for the candidate shall vary from course to course, but shall be clearly indicated by the applicant organisation in the proposal for sanction for grants.

List of Vocational Courses which could be Organised by Voluntary Vocations

Commerce and Business Related Vocations

1. Office Management and Secretarial Practice
2. Stenography
3. Insurance
4. Book Keeping and Accountancy
5. Banking
6. Data and Key punching process
7. Marketing and Salesmanship
8. Accounting and Auditing
9. Sales Representatives
10. Medical Representatives
11. Business Management

Engineering Based Vocations

12. Electrical Domestic Appliances-Servicing
13. Air conditioning and Refrigeration-Servicing

14. Domestic Electronic Equipment Servicing and Maintenance
15. Laboratory Instruments Servicing and Maintenance
16. Hospital Instruments Servicing and Maintenance
17. Furniture Design and Manufacturing
18. Electrical Equipment Maintenance
19. Watch and clock servicing
20. Repairs of Radio Transistors and Television

Textile Based Vocations

21. Handloom Weaving
22. Textile Bleaching, Dyeing and finishing
23. Tie and Die, Batik printing and Block printing

Chemical Based Vocations

24. Plastic Moulding
25. Rubber goods manufacturing
26. Ceramic Pottery
27. Soap and Detergent Manufacture
28. Leather Goods Manufacture
29. Sports goods Manufacture

Vocation Related to Home Science

30. Food Preservation
31. Bakery and Confectionery
32. Meal Service and supervision
33. Hostel and Hostel Management
34. Dieteties
35. Interior Decoration
36. Dress Designing and making
37. Designing, dyeing and printing
38. Canteen Management
39. Nutrition and Child care
40. Pre-primary Teacher's Training

Para Medical

41. Laboratory Technician
42. Nurse-aids
43. Physio-therapy Technician
44. Pharmaceutical Laboratory Assistant
45. E.E.G.-E.C.G., Angiometry Technician
46. Hospital House Keeping
47. Pharmaceutical Operator

Miscellaneous

48. Library Assistant
49. Tourist Guide
50. Photography
51. Commercial Arts
52. Aya and Sevika Training
53. Cottage/Agro-based Industry
54. Computer

(iii) Awareness Generation Projects for Rural and Poor Women

Central Social Welfare Board is implementing Awareness Generation Project programme with the aim of creating awareness in the community on issues relating to the status, rights and problems of women. Its main objectives are:

(i) To identify the needs of rural and poor women.

(ii) To increase women's active participation in fulfillment of those needs and in developmental and other allied programmes.

(iii) Orient the women through awareness camps in a manner in which they can involve themselves in efforts to meet their felt need in the area of social development and

(iv) To enable women to organise themselves and strengthen their participation in decision-making in the family and in the community to deal with social issues including atrocities on women and children.

(iv) Schemes of Vocational Training Programme for Women Under NWDC

Objectives. The Board has started providing assistance to organisations under the scheme of NORWEGIAN Agency for International Development (NORAD) from 1997-98 onwards for Vocational Training Programmes for poor and needy women both in urban slums and in rural areas. The Board provides assistance to organisations having the requisite capability, experience and infrastructure to provide Vocational Training in proposed trade to needy women of the age group of 15 years and above. The job potential, marketability of the skills, scope for self-employment and the capability of the applicant institutions are the main aspects taken into consideration for providing assistance under this scheme. A suggestive list of the Vocational Training Programmes, which can be organised.

Eligibility. The applicant institution should meet conditions of eligibility. In addition, the applicant institution should have had experience in conducting training programmes. The scheme can also be implemented in after-care homes, prisons for women and other custodial institutions for women.

Description of Scheme. The duration of the course can vary from trade to trade but in any case not exceeding one year. The number of candidates, duration of the course would be as per NORAD norms indicated in list below. The applicant organisation should give preference to destitute women, widows, women belonging to weaker sections, especially those belonging to SCs/STs and backward classes. Preference should also be given to women victims of riot affected areas and other natural calamities. The minimum educational qualifications for the candidates shall vary from course to course but shall be clearly indicated by the applicant organisation in the proposal for sanction of grant.

Following are the schemes for suppor services:

(i) Scheme of Short-Stay Homes for Women and Girls

The changing pattern of life, the rapid urbanisation and industrialization and the resulting migration from rural to urban areas, the spread of education among women and resulting problems of adjustment for first generation literates, rising cost of living and need for women members of the family to make an independent earning, creates problem which many women and girls do not find themselves adequately equipped to face. The break up of social institutions like the joint family contributes considerably in creating problems of adjustment for women and young girls. Cases of marital conflict and emotional disturbance occur. They require help and guidance to regain confidence in themselves to meet the situation and the acquire skills to become self-reliant and to develop, relationships with people that could help in the re-establishment of their status in the society. For meeting the situation, institutional services where counselling and guidance, medical and psychiatric check up; and treatment,, facility for development of skills and relationship are provided, could prove useful, in this line of thinking. Short Stay Homes have been established through voluntary organisations.

The Department of Women and Child Development, Central Social Welfare Board is giving grant-in-aid to voluntary organisations, to establish and run Short Stay Homes for women and girls, with a view to protect and rehabilitate those women and girls who are facing social, economic and emotional problems due to family problems, mental strains, social ostracism, exploitation or other causes or are being forced into prostitution and are in moral danger. The scheme provides following services/ facilities.

Temporary shelter to the needy women and girls from 6 months to 3 years. (1) Case work and counselling services, (2) Medical care and psychiatric treatment (3) Occupational therapy, skill development training and rehabilitation services (4) educational, vocational and recreational activities.

Children accompanying the mother or born in the home may be permitted to stay in the home upto the age of 7 years after which they may be transferred to children's institutions or provided foster care services.

(ii) Working Women's Hostels

The Central Social Welfare Board provides assistance to organisations to enable them to provide hostel facilities for working women. No grant will be given to institutions that have a building constructed with only govt. grant. After 5 years no grant will be given to any institution.

(iii) Creches

The CSWB provides financial assistance to organisations to set up creche units for the children of working and ailing mothers belonging to the lower income groups. Children of the age group of 0-5 years can be covered under this scheme.

Programme

Each unit consists of 25 children who are provided with sleeping facilities, health-care, supplementary nutrition, immunisation etc.

Schemes of Assistance for Economic Empowerment

Socio-economic Programme. Broad-based women's organisations can avail of grants from the Central Social Welfare

Board to assist women beneficiaries to set up agro-based units like dairy, poultry, piggery, goatery etc. and also utilise CSWB assistance to set up production units where women will be employed in large numbers. The Central Social Welfare Board has two different types of schemes of assistance under the socio-economic programme for these purposes.

(a) Assistance to Women's Organisations for setting-up of Agro Units

Scheme is under revision.

(b) Production Units

Conditions of Eligibility. As per eligibility conditions of Agro-based socio-economic programme.

Description of Scheme. A grant of upto Rs. 3.00 lakhs can be provided by the Central Social Welfare Board to facilitate the setting up of a production unit by the grantee institution. The grant is finalised on a case basis subject to a limit of Rs. 3.00 lakhs. The institution is also required to contribute a limit of 15 per cent of the project cost.

The Board's current chairperson Smt. Mridula Sinha is a diverse personality. She is an educationist, author, Leader, organiser and above all a social activist. Born on 27 November, 1942, she did her M.A. in psychology from university of Bihar, Mujaffarpur. She started out her professional carrier as a teacher. Smt. Mridula Sinha's husband Dr. Ram Kripal Sinha is an active politician. Smt. Sinha was interested in creative writing since her student days. She wrote short stories, novels and some thought provoking works. Her works include *Gharvas, Nai Devyani, Sakshatkar* etc. Through the character of her novels she brings up the problems of women in our society. That such a great personality came to be associated with central social welfare board, is something very good that happened to this organisation. She was given the responsibility of the board on 2nd November, 1998. After her take over this board has become an effective medium to highlight and tackle problems relating to women.

Central-Social Welfare Board—A Brief

- This organisation is an institution of the central government.
- This organisation offers, directions, guidelines, grants, assistance and various schemes to the non-government voluntary organisation.

- There is a Delhi Social Welfare Board working as its unit in the National Capital Region.
- Grants for the schemes of this board are given by the central government and expenditure in conducting the board activities is born by the state government.
- The board has an independent office and an advisory committee headed by a chairperson.
- Its various schemes include:
  - (a) Adult education
  - (b) Awareness generation programme
  - (c) Family welfare centre
  - (d) Working women's hostel
  - (e) Creche
  - (f) Vocational training centre
  - (g) Other socio-economic programmes.

Details of its major schemes is provided in this chapter. Grants given to voluntary organisation vary from Rs. 10,000 to Rs. 3,00,000. Editor is this book is currently the chairperson of Delhi Social Welfare Board. She is available to provide all assistance and can be contacted at the office for help.

Beneficiaries of Central Social Welfare Board Programmes

According to the annual report of central Social Welfare Board, the number of beneficiaries in 2000-2001 under it various programmes has been as under:

Sl. No.	*Programme*	*No. of Beneficiaries*
1.	Family Counselling	58480
2.	Short Stay Homes	6750
3.	Mahila Mandal Programme	64832
4.	Awareness Generation Programmes	76725
5.	Condensed Course Programme (2 Yr. C.C.)	14650
6.	Condensed Course Programme (1 Yr. C.C.)	5375
7.	NORAD	24540
8.	Creche Programme	2,31,625
9.	Demonstration Project	7470
10.	Working Women Hostel	1701

The above figures give us an idea how successful and popular are the various programmes of CSWB. And year the number of beneficiaries keeps on rising year after year. Grant-in-aids of CSWB bring in more and more participation of voluntary organisations, thereby increasing public participation in social welfare. Our country needs just that.

Addresses of the State Social Welfare Advisory Boards

1. Andhra Pradesh Social Welfare Advisory Board
   Gagan Vihar Building, Magazine Floor
   Infront of Gandhi Bhawan
   M.J. Road
   Hyderabad—500001
2. Assam State Social Welfare Advisory Board
   R.C. Barua Road
   Near Commerce College
   P.O. Barauni Maidan
   Guwahati—781001
3. Bihar State Social Welfare Advisory Board
   Barrack No. 9 'A', Old Secretariat
   Patna—800016
4. Gujarat State Social Welfare Advisory Board
   21, Ashok Nagar Society
   Near Bhatta, Sarkhej Road
   Ahmedabad—380007
5. Haryana State Social Welfare Advisory Board
   SCO 87-88
   II Floor, Neelam Cinema
   Sector-17D
   Chandigarh—160617
6. Himachal Pradesh State Social Welfare Advisory Board
   Sangla House, Khalini
   Shimla—171002
7. Jammu and Kashmir State Social Welfare Board
   Secretariat, Jammu—190001
   (In Summer: Srinagar)
8. Karnataka State Social Welfare Advisory Board
   No. 13, 10th Cross
   5th Main, 12th Block, Kumara Park
   West Bangalore—560020
9. Kerala State Social Welfare Advisory Board
   Sasthamangalam
   Thiruvananthapuram—695010

10. Madhya Pradesh State Social Welfare Advisory Board
Char Banglow Road
Civil Lines, Bhopal—462002
11. Maharashtra State Social Welfare Advisory Board
New Administrative Block
Stage-II, First Floor
R.C. Marg, Chembur (E)
Mumbai—400079
12. Manipur State Social Welfare Advisory Board
Paona Bazar, Imphal—795001
13. Meghalaya State Social Welfare Advisory Board
"Pyndem Villa", Bomfyle Road
Shillong—793001
14. Nagaland State Social Welfare Advisory Board
D Block, A.R. Road
Kohima—797001
15. Orissa State Social Welfare Advisory Board
Samaj Kalyan Bhavan
A/64, Nyaypalli
Bhubaneshwar—751012
16. Punjab State Social Welfare Advisory Board,
Quiet Office
No. 16, Sector-35A
Chandigarh—160011
17. Rajasthan State Social Welfare Advisory Board
D-87, Jhalani Bhavan
Meera Marg, Benipark
Jaipur—302006
18. Tamil Nadu State Social Welfare Board
485-B, Anna Salai, Nandanam
Chennai—600035
19. Tripura State Social Welfare Advisory Board
485, Akhaura Road, P.O. Agartala
West Tripura—799001
20. Uttar Pradesh State Social Welfare Advisory Board
Nari Kala Mandir Bhavan
6, Pandit Nagar
P.O. Aminabad, Lucknow—226001
21. West Bengal State Social Welfare Advisory Board
Bhawani Bhawan
Alipore, Calcutta—700027

22. Arunachal Pradesh State Social Board
Naharlagum—791111
Papumpare District
Arunachal Pradesh
23. Pondicherry State Social Welfare Advisory Board
27 (Upstairs) Willinoor, Main Road
Vivekananda Nagar
Pondicherry—605005
24. Delhi Social Welfare Advisory Board
Jeevan Deep
Sansad Marg
New Delhi—110001
25. Goa State Social Welfare Advisory Board
'Guru Nath Building'
Rau Da Qurem
Panaji, Goa—403001
26. Mizoram State Social Welfare Advisory Board
Khatla Chaunga Road
P. Box No. 178
Tuikhu Tiang
Aizawl, Mizoram—796001
27. Lakshadweep State Social Welfare Advisory Board
Kavarathy Islands (Via)
Cochin—682001
28. Andaman and Nicobar Islands State Social Welfare Advisory Board
Industrial Complex, Middle Point
Port Blair—744101
29. Sikkim State Social Welfare Advisory Board
Kazi Road
Gangtok, Sikkim—737101
30. Chandigarh State Social Welfare Advisory Board
Karuna Sadan Building, Ground Floor
Sector-11B
Chandigarh-160011

Sewa Bharti

Sewa Bharti was established in 1979 under the ritual guidance of third Sarsanghchalak of RSS Shri Bala Saheb Deoras. It has fast emerged as the largest non-governmental organisation in Delhi working in the slums and shantytowns. Out of an estimated 5.5 million of Delhi's 120 million population living in slums, shantytowns and unathorised and resettlement colonies, Sewa Bharti provides succour to over 3.5 million people through a wide network of more than 1,400 projects.

These projects targetting the economically weaker and socially neglected sections of our society range from medical assistance, creche, library, hostel, basic education, adult education, vocational and industrial training, upliftment of street children and the lepers in the capital. *All the services are offered free.* Through these projects Sewa Bharti aims at making the underprivileged sections of the society self-reliant in every aspect of their lives. The ultimate objective is to establish a casteless and classless society through service of the underprivileged class.

Sewa Bharti has successfully created an atmosphere of 'samrasta' (social harmony) in these slums and shantytowns through its various educational training, cultural and religious projects including 'Bhajan-Kirtan', annual Bharat Mata Pujan (worshiping Mother India) and 'yajnas'. Influential and prosperous sections of society also actively participate in these programmes.

Less to say, results speak of the works done by Sewa Bharti in the capital. Health and sanitation facilities in many of the slums adopted by Sewa Bharti have improved drastically. Thousands of unskilled and unemployed youth have now become self-reliant through the education of vocational and industrial training institutes run by Sewa Bharti.

Sewa Bharti, with its motto "NAR SEWA NARAYAN SEWA' (service of mankind is service of God). has succeeded in including in these people a sense of national pride moral esteem and humanitarian values.

The Delhi Government in recognition of the outstanding services rendered in the field of child welfare, gave awards to Sewa Bharti in the years 1991, 1994,1996 and 1998.

Future plans of Sewa Bharti include : computer training, motor driving training, mobile coaching center and a pathological laboratory.

Achievements

- 2500 young girls are trained in Cutting and Tailoring every year.
- 300 boys are provided technical training in Electrical and Electronics every year.

- 500 girls and boys are taught Shorthand and Typing every year.
- 268 promising boys of different castes and creeds belonging to 17 states are being provided free boarding, lodging and education in our residential school Sewa Dham Vidya Manor.
- 130 Gold, 105 Silver and 42 Bronze medals were won by the Sewa Dham's students in different All India Sports Meets
- 60-70 boys from very poor families are given free coaching, boarding and lodging in Chhatravas.
- A sum of Rs. 5,000 was collected by the old students of the Chhatravas for cyclone victims in Andhra Pradesh.
- 49 Students of our Coaching Centers got first, second and third position in their schools.
- 110 Adult dropouts restarted their studies in Xth and XIIth class under open school system.
- 16,000 children in the age group of 3-5 are given Elementary Education daily.
- 300 Street Children are now going to their respective schools.
- 155 issueless couples got babies from our Matrichhaya.

One lac slum dwellers get free medical aid through Sewa Bharti in 19 dispensaries and 20 Medical Centers, served by four Mobile Medical Vans.

600 people gave their blood in our Blood Donation Camps.

In the field of Lepers, Sewa Bharti got award from the Government.

Some other organisations of note that are doing work to contribute to women's cause include *Servants of People Society, Nav Jyotii Peace Foundation, Prayas, Jain Mahila Ashram* etc.

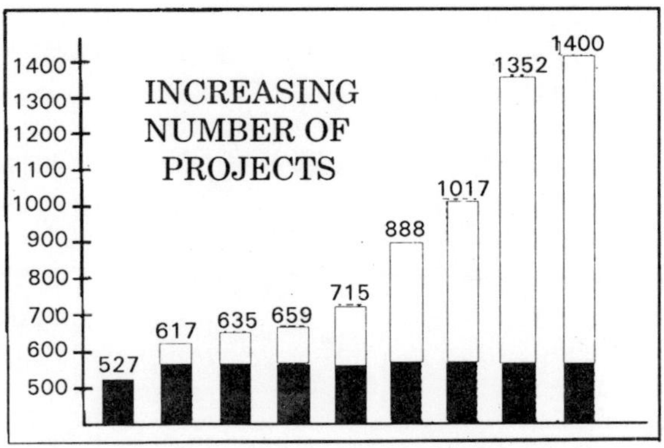

11

Domestic Role of Educated Working Women

When we talk of women's empowerment, the first thing that comes to mind of anyone is economic self-dependence and for that matter education of women is the first step in that direction. Highly educated working women have been pillars of strength for their families on financial front but this has, no way, got them rid of their day to day household responsibilities, more particularly taking care of children. Family enjoys the fruit of woman's assertiveness at workplace but at home, she is expected to be same conventional submissive housewife and a fully committed mother. What are those problems which a working women faces, and what can be possible solutions to her difficulties is the content of the chapter.

Women in the past days as also in the present have made choices which are ambivalent. Their decisions about expanding their horizons in various ways have brought them fulfilment no doubt, but it has cost them a huge part of their comfort, peace and leisure. These are reflected in increasing numbers of them going in for not only education at the primary and secondary levels, but more than this, at the levels of higher education, greater number joining the work force again, the increased percentages going to higher cadre jobs.

A Peep into the Background of Women's Education

There is no doubt that women's education has been considered important from various angles. The Education Commission Report (1964-66) that the education of girls should receive emphasis not only on basis of social justice but it also accelerates social transformation and then, free and compulsory education for all chidren upto the age of 14 and development of suitable programmes to ensue the completion of the set courses of study—as a proclamation of the Education Commissions and National Policy of Education are supportive of the imperative necessity of development in this area. The education policy further emphasised the need for special efforts to expand women's education at the college and university levels to have larger number of them available for positions of directional and organisational responsibilities.

The increase in the men to women ratios at the level of higher education, as documented by the Education Commission (1964-66), from 13-21 per cent in a period of 10 years from 1955-56 to 1965-66 was proposed to be increased to 33 per cent during the next 10 years to meet the needs for educated women in different fields. To provide a boost-up to this plan, scholarships, other kinds of financial assistance, suitable but economic hostel facilities more specifically to rural students and linking of higher education with specific avenues of employment were some of the measures further recommended by the Education Commission.

Famous NPE, i.e., National Policy on Education (1986) also emphasiseα upon a basic change in the status of women, education being the main agent for it. It included women's studies as a part of the various courses, educational institutions initiating active programmes to further women's advancement. A brief historical survey prior to the appointment of commissions on Education and National Policy of Education also shows a slow, but significant increase in the number of women going in for education.

The span of years from 1882 to post-independence era showed 33 times increase and 20 years from thence, 5.4 times growth in the number of girls under instruction. The actual figures are as below :

1882	127,066
1901–1902	356,413
1921–1922	1,224,128
1946–1947	4,156,742
1956–1957	8,767,912
1965–1966	22,494,000

This way, overall increase thus during the above 84 years was nearly 180 times. Female literacy in the recent times has also shown a clearly upward trend. From 18.69 in 1971, the percentage rate of female literacy went up to 24.82 in 1981 and the comparative figure during the next ten years, i.e., upto 1991 is 32.6 per cent. Another noteworthy trend has been the increase in the percentage of women going in for higher—technical and professional education.

The lowest percentage in comparison to boys of 14.86 per cent in polytechnics increases to as high as 32.59 per cent in Medicine, and 33.55 in Ph.D/D.Sc/D.Phil.

Educated Women Taking to Work

Consequent upon their educational accomplishments is the greater number of women having chosen to go for work. Their work participation in 1971 was 12.06 and 13.99 respectively in the years 1971 and 1981 against the total main workers female population. The comparative figures for 1981 and 1991, sex-wise are as under:

Table 11.1
Proportion of Total Main Works by Sex

	1981	*1991*
Total	33.45	34.12
Man	51.62	50.54
Women	14	16.43

Increase in the number of women going to work has added to the national productivity raised the family income and improved living standards. Living in terms of the needed resources has been facilitated and the added advantage of educated parents around has enriched the overall family atmosphere in certain ways. At the same time, it has also enjoyed multiple roles on the educated, working women.

Source: 1. Report of the National Committee on Women's Education 1959 and Report of the Education Commission 1966.
2. Selected Educational Statistics, 1987–88, New Delhi: NCERT.

Working Women's Roles

It is redundant pointing to the centuries old roles of women, but reiteration of them is essential to point out to the fact of enhanced responsibilities and increased amount of work they are needed to take upon themselves. Again a matter of free choice for them. But which husband does not wish the wife to work and add to the family resources? Kapur (1982) observed that 86 per cent of the husbands did not mind their wives to work. And then the demand for a 'working girl' while fixing up matrimony for young boys is the in-thing these days. *Kaam Karne Wali Bahu Chahiye* is the strong desire of the mother-in-law to be.

One of the significant roles of women is that of the house-maker. Married or single, looking after the household chores and catering to the necessities of the parents and other relations—visiting or permanently residing with the family becomes the duty—'expected to be pleasant' at that of the working woman.

Expectations of Family Members

In case, the women is married, the next step ahead, i.e., 'mothering', though an exciting and enjoyable experience presents a hoard of responsibilities. Child care and child-rearing becomes the foremost job of the young mother-working or non-working. Women no doubt are the most suited to this task. With their gentle, but firm nature personality building up of the child is safe in the hands of women.

Research studies in this area corroborate the special role of women as far as child care is concerned. One study by Lamb *et.al* (1984) showed specialisation of parents' behaviours with their young ones—the mothers being more caregiving and fathers more playful. The former were also seen to do more of talking (naturally) and having quiet interactions with the children. In the role reversal try out necessitated by the mothers', going to work, the caregiving fathers did not prove the mother style of interacting. Mother is more competent to handle the role of child-rearing for another reason. A study on working women (1978) showed that the 'married working women' had better emotional adjustment than the unmarried working women.

Emotional adjustment of mothers can be greatly contributory to the emotional growth and physical development of the child. In addition to the feminine roles of working women, they are also expected to take on more of masculine roles, they have to perform outdoor responsibilities. A study by Ohri (1988) found that (a) that working women were more masculine and androgynous than non-working women (b) the distribution of working women was largely in masculine and androgynous groups whereas non-working women found themselves either in feminine or undifferentiated categories. Educated working women thus uniquely combine in themselves the domestic and outdoor personality characteristics and the talk of equality with men in this respect is redundant since their contribution to national advancement and social reconstruction is much more than it is realised to be.

Paradoxes and Contributions

After undergoing through the above, a pertinent question that crops here is—are the multiple roles of women, as breeder, feeder and producer free of all hazards and difficulties? The reply surely is not in the affirmative. These roles pose innumerable dilemmas some of which have been highlighted in the present paper. Corresponding to the mothering role as mentioned earlier, it is often felt that the children of working mothers do not get as much attention and care as is needed. Sending them to creches or Balwaris is not a very trustworthy though it does enable women to go out for work. Hiring part/fulltime help for the purpose may not be possible for numerous reasons. This may become a potent source of stress in the absence of any positive, constructive solution.

Another area wherein work participation is unequal in India is more particularly within the family. The fatigued overstained female starts resenting her multiple roles and may therefore ventilate her irritability on children, other members within the family and may be, the husband himself.

Thus, role cycling is a source of stress for the female and in the case of the males it is an irksome job to be taking on the household responsibilities. The issue of identity becomes another source of discord. Besides their usual feminine and masculine identities, the question of status, the amount of participation in household activities, tension lines linked to women's self-concepts as good and wives and mothers and other people's criticism on them, masculine authority not remaining supreme and women's quality of assertiveness in the competitive world of work if percolating in the family interactions add up to the family disturbances.

Attending to Family Elders

One more area where work participation is unequal in India becomes a source of tension within the kin dilemma is still another source of strain in the dual career families. Being preoccupied and committed to careers, now both the spouses find it somewhat hard to accommodate to look after akin even as near and dear as the mother of the male spouse. The conventional style of life shortly the sensitive feelings and obligations of the husband though being adopted by the working wives in the present times does not come to be as naturally and as easily as it was in the past.

Problems of Socialisation

Issue of socialisation of friendships also form network of dilemmas in the dual-career couples. Working partners naturally find it more practical and easier to form friendships on a couple basis. In this condition, wife has as what a determining role as the husband, rather more of it since the overload of work falls most on her. So, the level of friendships and the amount of interactions are decided more by her which if not handled smoothly may become another source of tension. Each status in life has essentially rolecycle attached to it. Meshing or enmeshing their different rolecycles after marriage—i.e., of a participative partner, then taking on parenthood as one of the necessary of marriage and further the female partner assuming the role of care-taker of the child and combining it with domestic organisation with men needed to share the responsibilities curtailing of their social and recreational activities—all these eventually do become sources of stress. Delay in producing children, family planning in the strictness sense of the term of curtailing the demands of the career to suit their personal needs at home are some of the devices adopted to resolve the difficulties, but with how much of acceptance and satisfaction is the question.

Transfer of Either Spouses

A peculiar type of role-cycling comes from one of the partners having to shift in his/her place of work for purposes or promotion of some other cause like the marriage partners working at different places already. The chances of getting suitable and preferred placements at one and the same place, at times are blocked and thus, their role-cycling in such a case demands another kind of adjustment. Sacrifices here are required to be made either on the career front or staying away from family.

Miscellaneous

Again, career aspirations, need for fulfilment, wife's need for self-realisation wherein she would want to be more independent, correlative and comparatively from duties of domestic care; specially in our culture can become another source of tension.

The Way Out/Recommendations

Now, the issue that comes up next is—can these dilemmas be resolved? The answer has to be found in some of the practical psychological resolutions that are additive to adjustment and handling. As for the mothering/parenting issue, researches to-date support the contention that no directly negative affect on children can be traceable to mother's employment.

Sharing the mother's affection with a warm surrogate in a stable environment will help to a great extent. Study by Papalia and Olds (1978) and Margaret Mead (1982) point cut the fact that there are no bases for socially divided sex roles in natural differences between sexes.

Although women have been the primary care-takers in most of the societies, it has never been proved that only they have to be. The studies of Hetherington (1979) and Strother (1984) of children with mothers-at-work, called as Latch-key children revealed that the girls of these mothers were more independent and active and outgoing. Boys were also found independent, but they scored lower on examination of intelligence. Hurlock's (1985) observation that the effect of mother's working is related to the age of the child at which she starts working is another important finding.

And lastly results of Guttfried and Guttfried's (1988) study that mother's employment is a multivariate parameter, it is not a significant predictor of growth of child; others like SES, children's environment and number of siblings are more important further point to the absence of any negative effects of mother's work on children's growth and development.

(a) Sharing of responsibilities. At the domestic front precautions like shared responsibility, more of consideration for the female spouse in respect of her burden of work, her aspirations, her need for fulfilment in areas other than that of being a nice and fit wife and a mother need to be developed. The husband and the other members of the family need not sympathesise with her. What is required is empathy with her state of being.

(b) Mutually decided work style. Together working out a concern wherein concern for each other's needs and limited capacities, curtailing of one's own needs to the extent possible can be another way out. The senior members of the family in the situation of extended nuclear or joint families need to develop more of understanding of the dual-career couple situation. Attitudinal change on their part is as much required as in the case of husbands.

To conclude, in order to help increase awareness and appreciation of career women's roles and difficulties, mass media can take up special programmes to keep focussing public attention on the issues related to women at work. Accessibility availing of the counselling facilities at the community counselling centres or units can be another mean of resolving family tensions. It is not being recommended that specialised help is absolutely essential for tensions and strains that the working couples might be facing. But for those who need it, organisations like AIWC, Saheli, Sanjivni and Amity—a voluntary organisation consisting of a dedicated and involved group of marital counsellors could be got in touch with. For more severe cases of marital tensions, some action programmes are wanted to be taken up more vigorously. Projects on Family Advocacy Programmes (Munsen, 1980) patterned on the lines of social care work need to be initiated. Modules for these programmes can be evolved on the lines of social care work. These include Intervention, Educational Methods, Demonstration Projects, client groups, Coalition groups and the most used methods of today—demonstrations and oppositions. All said and done, friends, this paper should not be taken as a projection of women's woes. Let us not make drudgery/the work norm of the home situation since life offers many fulfilments and many compensations. Women work for intrinsic satisfaction, not only for economic objectives. Women with education feel unfulfilled by their domestic roles. Let the community and society help them to fulfil themselves in various ways. If the employment of women is the target of society in true sense of the word.

References

Census of India, Series-28, Chandigarh: Director of Census Operations, 1991.

Education and National Development, Report of the Education Commission 1964–66, New Delhi: NCERT, 1966.

Hate, Chanderkala A., *Changing Status of Women in Post-Independence India,* Bombay: Allied Publishers, 1969.

Hurlock, E.B., *Child Development* (7th Printing), New York: McGraw Hill, 1985.

Jayashree, *India and Indian Women as seen by Women of the World,* Aligarh: Granthayan, 1980.

Kanhere, Usha S., *Women and Socialisation,* Mittal Publishers, 1987.

Kapur, P., in Prakash Rao and Nandini Rao, *Marriage, Family and Women in India,* New Delhi: Heritage, 1982.

Kuzima, Kay, *Working Mothers,* Los Angeles: Stratford Press, 1981.

Papalia, Diane E. and Wendoks Sally Olds, Child Development, New York: McGraw Hill.

Rapaport Rhona and Robert N. Rapaport, Dual-Career Families Re-examined, London: Martin Robertson, 1976.

Selected Educational Statistics 1987-88, Ministry of Human Resource Development (Department of Education), New Delhi: 1989.

12

Muslim Women in Transition

Literature survey on Muslims in India gives the impression that Muslims are generally considered to be a backward community. It is supported by two major explanations *viz.,* a theory of discrimination primarily in matters of education and employment; and a greater conservatism and lack of initiative to use both within the community and outside.

In both the cases, the hypotheses emphasized the significance of the religious factor. The so-called backwardness of the Muslim women is particularly attributed to the religious orthodoxy of Muslims.

Religious Orthodoxy

It is a common belief that religious orthodoxy has influenced greatly the rural areas and the lower strata of urban society and that this orthodoxy is increasing in the rural areas because of the urban influence, particularly the spread of education[1]. This would imply that the status of women will further deteriorate as religious practices become more intense and exercise greater control over behavioural patterns.

Although Islam as a religion has treated women respectfully and through various religious injunctions offers them a much better status than is the case in other communities but in reality the situation is entirely different mainly because of misinterpretation of religious injunctions. Examples cited were *purdah,* polygamy and the unilateral right to divorce given to men. Early marriage, a higher fertility rate, illiteracy among women and their total seclusion.

Religious orthodoxy could be defined as holding currently accepted opinions which were not liberal minded or original but were generally accepted as right or true and in harmony with what were authoritatively established through religious texts. In the case of Islam, it means a belief in, and a consistent practice of, all those practices, etc., established as a normal and important part of daily life either by the *Koran* or other authoritative sources such as the *Hadith*.

For assessing the level of religious orthodoxy, obviously we should consider the level of awareness about religious matters, as also the extent to which the injunctions established by the religious sources were accepted as part of the normal every day life. The religious education and training received can be taken as an indicator of the awareness. Similarly, in the case of Muslims, regular offering of *namaz*. 'Fasting' during the month of *Ramazan* and recital of the *Koran* can also be taken as indicators of the degree of observance of religious practices, accompanied by certain other practices such as offering sacrifices, giving alms (*Zakat*) and holding religious functions (*Milad Sharif*, etc.).

To measure the intensity of observance of religious practices, three indicators i.e. *namaz, fasting* and *recital* of *Koran* were considered. Depending on the frequent performance of these activities i.e. regularly, sometimes and never, scores. 3, 2, 1 respectively wage allotted. Based on total scores achieved, respondents wage divided into these categories.

TABLE 12.1

Category	*Score*
High	Upto 9
Medium	Upto 7
Low	Upto 5

For measuring the intensity of observance of religious practices by family, three indicators were considered, making sacrifices *(qurbani)*, giving alms *(zakat)* and organizing participation in *milad, majlis* or other religious gatherings. Weights allocation, scoring and categorizations were conducted in the above manner.

Religious Education and Training of Respondents

The study revealed that the majority of rural respondents (55 per cent) had not received any religious education while in the urban areas, the trend of receiving religious education was consistent with the general education as 69 per cent respondents received religious education. The nature of religious education received by the respondents consisted of either the method of offering *namaz* or general information about Islam. It was also observed that the percentage of respondents receiving general information about *Islam* was greater among the middle and higher-socio economic strata.

However, the majority of respondents, both in the rural and urban areas expressed a desire to impart religious addiction to both small and female children. Religious practices—the study disclosed that in the case of the majority of respondents (67 per cent) the observance of religious practices was of moderate intensity. They occasionally offered *namaz,* fasted or recited the Holy *Koran.* Eighteen per cent respondents had low intensity of religious practices. In the higher socio-economic strata, a large percentage had a higher intensity of religious practices. The same trend was also prevalent in the case of religious practices of the male heads, where 61 per cent had a moderate observance but the percentage of low observance (24 per cent) was slightly higher than the females.

Whereas the daughters' lower observance (17 per cent) was equal with their mothers' (18 per cent) religious practices, the percentage of sons having lower observance (30 per cent) was higher than their fathers' (24 per cent)

In the case of urban areas, moderate observance was predominant in the case of all the family members. However, the percentage of observance among the urban females was significantly higher (39 per cent) in the case of the respondents and 31 per cent in the case of the daughters as compared to their rural counterparts. The sons' percentage of lower observance (27 per cent) was comparable with their rural counterparts.

In the case of religious practices of the family such as *qurbani, zakat,* holding of *milad* and other religious functions, the majority of rural households (53 per cent) had a low degree of observance and 37 per cent had a moderate observance as compared to 37 per cent low observance and 30 per cent moderate observance as compared to 37 per cent low observance and 30 per cent moderate observance in the urban areas. The higher socio-economic strata had a higher degree of religious observance.

There is no change in the degree of observance of religious practices within two generations in the case of females, but among the males it appears to cease both in the rural and urban areas.

Despite the usual belief of more religious orthodoxy among the rural population, the urban population appeared to be more orthodox, particularly in the case of females. The higher socio-economic strata appears to have a slightly higher degree of religious observance.

A marginally higher observance in the case of Muslim urban women of Delhi may not make us believe that the same would be true in the case of Muslim women in general. The religious observance would also depend upon the social millieu, particularly the reference group of a particular section of the population. In Delhi perhaps the higher socio-economic strata consists of the business class where religious observance may be higher as compared to households having higher educational achievements, and professional occupations.

In the urban areas, the illiterates had a low intensity of religious observance as compared to those respondents having received religious education or educated ones.

Purdah

Purdah system is responsible to a great extent for the backwardness of Muslim women. Sufficient attention is seldom paid to the actual nature of *Purdah* observance and the socio-economic background of the females and general perspective, therefore, has been too stereotyped and vague.

Purdah is not just an Islamic institution in the Indian subcontinent. Hindu women also observe *purdah* though the *purdah* of Hindus is not the same phenomenon as amongst Muslims. It is part of the Indian culture to maintain some degree of separation between the sexes, mainly for the purpose of imposing taboos on sexual relationships beyond socially approved arrangements.[2] The differences in the socio-economic background and social context affect the precise character of that separation. Cora Vrudedesteuers (1969) for instance, in her study of Muslim women in and around Delhi differentiated between strict, partial, intermittent and absent *purdah.*

Among some sections of Muslim women particularly in Northern India, the practice of wearing a *burqa* represents *purdah* prevalent whereas in other parts, particularly in Southern India the *'burqa'* is neglected and the women may cover their heads with a piece of cloth or with their saree when they meet strangers or go out of their homes.

Sociologically, what is important is the nature of *purdah* observance among Muslim women and its consequence for them. For example, did it stop their education and employment, restrict their movement outside the home or produce in curtailment of their social participation? Is it affecting their overall growth and development either to the extent of totally confining them to the four walls of their homes or is it imposing certain restrictions on their behavioural pattern only?

The respondents were asked about *purdah*-observance and its extent. The term *purdah* observance had different meaning for each respondent. It could vary from behavioural restrictions to total confinement. The wearing of *Burqa* was not seen in the rural areas although the majority observed complete *purdah* whereas in the old Delhi area from where the urban data was collected, '*Burqa*' clad women were quite frequently seen in the markets and other places, as also women without a *Burqa.*

Two categories of *purdah* observance were defined: complete observance and partial observance. Complete observance meant *purdah* observance in all situations and partial *purdah* meant *purdah* in some situations only.

In rural and urban areas, the majority of both men and women supported *purdah* observance but in rural areas the percentage of men favouring it was slightly higher. In the urban areas the percentage of men supporting it was slightly lower. The educational level of males had no association with disapproval of *purdah.* Data in respect of age-wise attitude of respondents revealed no significant variations.

Purdah Observance and Daughters

Ninety-five per cent urban and 71 per cent rural respondents observed *purdah.* 30 per cent rural respondents as compared to 5 per cent urban, observed no *purdah.* The data in respect of rural respondents indicated a significantly higher percentage of non-observance in the lower socio-economic strata. The percentage of non-observance in the lowest socio-economic strata being 40 per cent as compared to 17 per cent in the highest socio-economic strata. The higher non-observance of *purdah* in rural areas was due to the greater concentration of poverty and lack of religious education.

In urban areas, a slightly lower percentage of daughters observing *purdah* (78 per cent as compared to 95 per cent in the case of respondents) reflected a gradual change. Education which had a positive association with higher socio-economic status of the respondents also played an important role in the non observance *purdah* as the majority of the graduate respondents observed no *purdah.* In the case of daughters, the non-observance was up to 50 per cent where the respondents had achieved the 10th class level of education.

Non-observance of *purdah* among the younger generation, indicates a change in the attitude of Muslim women. Low *purdah* observance among the younger generation of women in the higher socio-economic strata, reflects a change in the higher socio-economic strata, where *purdah* was more rigidly followed since it was considered a status symbol. The women in the lower socio-economic strata were unable to observe *purdah* as they had lower social economic status and or a different ethos where observing *purdah* was not as a status symbol. The importance of education and the fact, that if *'purdah'* lost its importance as a status symbol, its practice would decline even in lower middle and middle classes, are indicated.

Purdah Related Problems

The majority of respondents (92 per cent rural and 81 per cent urban) faced no difficulty on account of *purdah.* The majority felt that their daughters and daughter-in-laws also faced no difficulty. *Purdah* did not prevent women from receiving formal education since only 8.5 per cent rural and 8 per cent urban respondents had held *purdah* responsible for their illiteracy and only 5.5 per cent rural and 29 per cent urban respondents had identified *purdah* as the reason for female children not attending schools. Similarly, only a very small percentage (12 per cent rural and 21 per cent urban) viewed the participation of women in politics as a violation of *purdah.*

The respondents generally felt that *purdah* observance in practice posed no problem for women since the *'purdah observance'* today did not mean absolute retirement of women from all outdoor activities. Purdah observance is now considered as a cultural trait of preserving the 'female dignity' by way of observing certain dress restrictions and providing a guideline of interactions with male after a certain age. It is therefore considerable to save note of the changes in the concept of *purdah* from a religious code to a cultural worm. This change in the concept of *purdah* describes the lesser anxiety on the part of the Muslim society to confine the females to their homes. The sight of *purdah* clad women moving freely in markets, schools and in other public places lends further credence to our theory of a conceptual change in *purdah* practice.

The majority of respondents even in rural areas felt that their daughters could receive education upto the age of 15 years only. It meant that *purdah* restriction of whatever nature operated only around the age of 15 years, or so, or if imposed, was only of a partial form. Therefore, *purdah*, even in earlier times was not more responsible for Muslim women's educational backwardness, as assumed by certain scholars. The higher non-observance in the case of daughters from higher socio-economic strata indicates that young girls are abandoning purdah altogether because they are adopting cultural norms prevalent in the wider society and not adhering to their own.

The majority of both rural and urban respondents (80 and 75 per cent respectively) and 85 per cent rural and 65 per cent urban 'Male Heads' supported *purdah* observance, thus signifying that these cultural norms were still being followed by the older generation. Similar attitude possibly would also be found among people of similar age-group in all religious sects, who still believed in traditional norms of Indian society and dislike growing westernization' among the younger generation. This being the attitude of the parents, the giving up of *purdah* by the younger generation supports conceptual change in *purdah* practice, as it exhibits the flexibility of the older generation in allowing the younger generation to avoid purdah. *'Purdha'* is now 'desirable' and 'not necessary' as it was two decades ago. Thus Muslims in India are change by the changes taking place in wider social milleiu. The degree to which they have changed; in comparision to other religious communities in India would only be established through an objective relative study which particularly takes into consideration their socio-economic background. If the change is slow in respect of the Muslim community as a whole, the often assumed hypotheses of greater religious orthodoxy and *purdah* practice do not emerge as major factors. The insights provided by the study should be enough to discard any theory of a stagnant and decaying Muslim society in India.

Education of Girls

The majority of people both in rural and urban area supported girl's education. The insignificant percentage of women having a negative attitude indicated that in all socio-economic strata, a favourable attitude towards educating girls is to be found even among illiterate women. Age-wise no significant variations were found in attitude of respondents towards education of girls.

Marriage Significance and Related Practices

Universality of marriage, with its inherent roles of wife and mother, determines the life pattern of women in many ways, providing no opportunity for choosing alternative roles for themselves. Indicative of the importance of marriage is the stigma attached to the non-marriage of eligible women. The social disapproval is greater if the non-marriage results from a conscious decision of the women indicated the importance of marriage, The age at which women marry in India also indicates the importance of marriage, the mean marriageable age of females has risen from abour 13 years (1901) to about 17 years (1971) less than 2 per cent of rural women remain unmarried by the age of 30 (Jeffery, 1979). The age at which marriage takes place, can have enormous consequences which affect the future of the women. An early marriage may terminate education earlier, as well as posing psychological and emotional stresses which the woman is too young to bear.

Cultural and religious practices related to marriage can affect the women's position and status sigificantly both within the family and in the society. The practice of dowry has caused more harm than any other single factor in degenerating woman's status in India. The nature of divorce laws can vitally affect women's status in society as also the structure of the marital unit. Polygamy is allowed within the Muslim Personal Code in India, although as Boserup (1970) points out, polygamy is very rare and polygamous marriages are generally only found among the most wealthy.[3]

Age at Marriage

Thirty-nine per cent rural respondents had attitude it towards early marriage of girls and 37 opposed it. Nearly 41 per cent of men had a favourable and a similar percentage had a negative attitude towards early marriage. A sizable number of both women and men preferred to remain indecisive, the same being the case in urban areas. In urban areas, the majority of both women and men opposed early marriage and significantly, a greater number of women as compared to men did not favour early marriage of girls. The percentage of rural women not favouring early marriage seemed higher in the upper socio-economic strata. The rural women with an educational level of 10-12 class had a negative attitude, otherwise educational level had not affected the attitude of rural women. In the urban areas, the percentage of educated women showing a negative attitude was significantly higher. Age had no significant relation with the attitude of women respondents (both rural and urban) towards early marriage of girls.

The median age at marriage (MAAM) amongst both Muslim males and females was equal with the MAAM for all religions. In the case of U.P. however, the urban Muslims had a slightly lower median age at marriage both in the case of males and females as compared to all India figures. Early marriage of girls in U.P. was a common feature in all religious groups.[4] In the rural areas, the MAAM amongst the muslims was higher both for males and females as compared to that of all religions including that of Hindus. The same was also true for the rural areas of U.P. Thus, Muslim women were better off in this respect than their counterparts in the majority community.

Fifty-two per cent rural and 55 per cent urban respondents were married after the age of 16 but before 20, while 39 per cent rural and 34 per cent urbans were married before the age of 16 years. 9 per cent of the urban respondents as compared to 4 per cent rural respondents married after the age of 20 years. Thus the MAAM worked out to be 17–25 years in the urban areas as compared to 16.55 years in the rural areas. Thus there is further improvement in this respect as the MAAM seems to be on the increase among the females, both in rural and urban areas.

In the rural areas, the custom of performing the *'Nikah'* (the only marriage ceremony for the Muslim) at an early age, with consumation of the marriage *(Rukhsati/Gauna)* taking place later, is still prevalent. This is also a common practice among the Hindus, particularly in the rural areas. This practice was rare in the urban areas as only 9 per cent urban respondents as compared to 44 per cent rural respondents said that marriage was consumated after a gap of few years from the date of the *Nikah.* No significant difference appeared among the different classes in respect of the marriageable age. The percentage of respondents marrying after the age of 16 was highest amongst the middle class in the rural areas. In the urban areas age was not significantly different in the various socio mamaqeable economic classes. Not even a single case of marriage before the age of 10 years was to be found amongst the higher and higher middle classes, though its incidence was negligible among the other classes in urban areas. The respondents regarding the ideal age of their daughters at marriage had the awareness of the problems posed by early marriage.

The majority of respondents (74 per cent rural and 91 per cent urban) would prefer their daughters getting married after the age of 16. The percentage of respondents preferring a higher age showed no significant difference in different socio-economic classes. However, educational level had positive association with preference for a higher age of marriage, both in rural and urban areas. In rural areas, 39 per cent respondents were married before the age of 15; whereas, only 25 per cent preferred marrying their daughters before that age and in urban areas 34 per cent respondents married before the age of 15 but only 8 per cent preferred marrying their daughters at that age. A greater change happened in urban areas as only 9 per cent respondents married after the age of 20 years, but 33 per cent preferred to do so in case of their daughters. The ideal marriageable age for boys was higher than the ideal age at marriage of girls both in rural and urban areas.

Consulting the Girl Before Marriage

The data in respect of consulting of girl at the time of marriage revealed that the majority of respondents (92 per cent rural and 85 per cent urban) were not consulted before their marriage. The marriage was arranged by the consent of both parents. A significant change is noticeable here since nearly 35 per cent rural respondents and 59 per cent urban respondents preferred consulting the girls prior to their marriage. The percentage of respondents preferring to consult girls was higher among the higher socio-economic classes, and preference for consultation had a positive association with the educational level of the respondents in the urban areas.

The majority of rural women (55 per cent) and men (46.5 per cent) had a negative attitude towards consulting girls prior to marriage where as majority of the urban women (55 per cent) and men (70.5 per cent) preferred consulting girls. Again, age-wise no significant variations were found in attitude of women respondents towards girl's consent in marriage.

Caste/Community Preference in Marriage

In the matter of marriage, caste played an important role in the selection of a marriage partner, especially in the rural areas. A significant majority of rural respondents (95 per cent) and comparatively fewer (55 per cent) urban respondents preferred marriage within the caste. The majority of men and women, both rural and urban, had a favourable attitude towards widow remarriage which indicates that in this respect, Muslim women are certainly better off than women in other communities, particularly in the rural areas. Widow marriage is approved by both rural and urban respondents without any significant variations on account of their age. The majority of women, both rural and urban, had a negative attitude towars inter-caste marriage was higher among the lower socio-economic strata. Educated women had a favourable attitude towards inter-caste marriage both in urban and rural areas.

This again brings out the rural-urban divide in the social practices since caste seems to be losing its hold in the urban areas. It is equally significant that an even a lower percentage of respondents preferring marriage within the caste was to be found among the higher socio-economic strata where other considerations such as the socio-economic status may be more relevant than the caste in the case of marriage of both males and females. This indicates that the caste system still exists even among urban Muslims though it exercises greater control over rural Muslims as it does among their Hindu counter-parts. Both rural and urban respondents do not seem to differ in their attitude towards inter-caste marriages on account of age. A sizable number of respondents (44 per cent and 42 per cent rural) stated that a girl's marriage posed economic problems for the family. This indicated poverty and the amount of expenditure normally incurred at the time of marriage.

Though the number of girls remaining unmarried was not high, the reasons given for non-marriage were significantly different in the rural and urban areas. The rural respondents found the main reason for girls remaining unmarried was economic, whereas the majority of urban respondents found the main reason non-availability of a suitable boy. They give more importance to the suitability of the bridegroom in terms of educational level, occupation personal attributes, etc., rather than caste and this explains why more urban respondents would not mind arranging an inter-caste marriage.

The urban respondents felt that the reasons for non-marriage of girls among non-Muslims were different from their own, whereas the rural respondents were either unaware of the reasons or felt hesitant to comment on the matter. It is significant that only 55 per cent rural and 41 per cent urban respondents felt that non-marriage of girls was a social stigma which indicates that an independent existence of a female outside her husband's home is more socially acceptable today.

Arranged Marriage

Arranged marriages were preferred by the majority of men and women, both rural and urban. The rural people had a stronger attitude in this regard. Analysed age-wise, except for a marginally lower percentage of urban women in the younger age group (below 30 years) who approved arranged marriages, no other significant variations were observed in both rural and urban samples.

Polygamy, Men's Right to Divorce and Problems Related to Divorce

The majority of both rural and urban respondents were expected to be in favour of abolishing polygamy. However, the percentage of respondents not in favour of abolishing polygamy was higher (31 per cent) in rural areas as compared to 21 per cent in the urban areas. Although the majority favoured a change, a sizable minority offered any change in the status quo. Incase of men's unilateral right to divorce, the percentage of women against the change (32 per cent) was higher in the urban areas as compared to 28 per cent in the rural areas. The majority of respondents thought never to seek a divorce, the reason being a combination of economic dependence, the problem of children and the social stigma.

In actual practice, very few cases of divorce or polygamy were found but again the reasons for polygamy showed a marked difference in rural and urban areas. In the rural areas, the main reason for polygamy was the desire for a child or a male child, whereas in the urban areas, the main reason was a love affair.

To check polygamy, the majority thought that the best way was to mobilize public opinion and to increase the social stigma attached to polygamy. The percentage of respondents (36 per cent) suggesting a change in the personal law was higher in the case of rural areas as compared to urban (8 per cent).

Incidently, education seemed to have a positive association with attitudes relating to a change in personal law, intercaste marriage, marriage cattle and in consulting girls before marriage, in the case of both rural and urban respondents. However, it could not be statistically tested because of the small number of educated respondents. Education seems to have no association with attitudes related to arranged marriages, divorce, polygamy or the man's right to divorce. The fact that a sizable number of males did not approve of the unilateral right of divorce was indicative of change and a decline in religious dogmatism.

A higher percentage of men, both rural and urban, supported divorce as compared to women. No significant difference existed in the attitude of urban men in the different socio-economic strata though in rural areas, the highest percentage of men favouring divorce was to be found in the highest socio-economic strata. A higher percentage of illiterate women favoured divorce in the urban areas. Urban respondents (females) more or less had a mixed attitude towards divorce irrespective of their age group. However, the attitude of rural women differed on account of their age, younger (upto 40 years).

The majority of women, both rural and urban opposed men's right to divorce as provided in the Personal Law of Muslims. The majority of men, both rural and urban, favoured this right. The percentage of urban men favouring it was slightly higher in the highest socio-economic strata, whereas in case of women, no significant difference was to be found in the different socio economic strata, though a higher percentage of educated urban women opposed it. The percentage of rural women opposing it was slightly higher than urban women, despite low educational levels. Agewise distribution of attitude of women towards men's unilateral right to divorce was marginally than the higher percentage of rural respondents in older age group, i.e. above 45 approved; while in the case of urban respondents a marginally higher percentage in above 40 years group disapproved of divorce.

Dowry Practice

The dowry practice in India has probably adversely affected the status of women more than anything else. The recent escalation in dowry deaths reflects its consequent miseries. The birth of a female child therefore, is generally regarded as a tragedy, even by the parents.

Muslim women in the areas under study were comparatively better off since though the dowry was given, it created no tensions and miseries as it happened among the Hindus because it is voluntarily gift by the parents and is not demanded by the bridegroom's family. The study revealed that in the majority of cases (99 per cent rural and 96 per cent urban) the dowry was voluntarily given. The majority of the respondents (76 per cent rural and 81 per cent urban) reported to have faced no problems either financial or inter-personal on account of dowry. A sizable number of rural respondents (31 per cent) favour dowry practice, the same attitude being exhibited by rural heads (31 per cent). The urban respondents and the male heads in comparison, in the majority of cases. Education appeared to have an effect on the attitude of the respondents either in the rural or urban areas as no significant differences existed in the responses education-wise. The urban respondents had rejected dowry possibly due to recent highlighting of the problems concerning the dowry system in the urban areas, particularly by the mass media.

***Mehr* Practice**

Among the Muslims a practice of 'Mehr' also prevails whereby the husband promises to give some cash (dower) to the bride after the marriage. Dower is generally divided into two kinds, prompt and deferred. Although it is payable, and is sometimes paid at the time the marriage contract is entered into. In India generally remains unpaid, and so like an on-demand obligation, it remains due at all times—the wife's right to the same not being extinguished by lapse of time. The wife's (or her guardian's) object in leaving the dower unreaslied seems to exist permanently a valid guarantee for her good treatment by her husband. The custom of fixing heavy dowers in India, generally beyond husband's means is based upon the intention of checking the husband from ill-treating his wife and above all, from his marrying another woman or wrongfully or needlessly divorcing the former.In case of divorce, the women can demand the full payment of the dower. In the case of the death of the husband, the payment of the dower has the first claim on the estate after funeral expenses; the law regarding it as a full-debt.

Some lawyers cansider dower an effect of the marriage contract, imposed on the husband by the law as a mark of respect for the wife; while others consider it an exchange for the usufruct of the wife, and its payment is necessary, as the permanency of the matrimonial tie depends upon the provision to support the wife. Thus, if it were not mentioned in the marriage contract, it would be still incumbent on the husband, as the law will presume it by virtue of the contract itself, and award it when demanded by the wife. In such a case, the amount of *dower* will equal to the dowers of the women of her rank and of the ladies of her father's family. The amount of dower is unlimited. It may be a very large amount, depending upon the position and circumstances of the bridegroom, but its minimum is never less than 10 '*dirhams*', so where it is fixed at a lesser amount, the law will augment it up to 10 *dirhams,* if called upon to do so.

In the case of the majority of rural families (59 per cent) the amount of Mehr was fixed according to Shariat laws—which is very nominal. Only in 14 per cent cases the amount of Mehr was more, i.e., Rs. 2001–5000. In the case of urban families, only 23 per cent fixed amount according to Shariat laws; in the case of 29 per cent the amount was 2000–5000 and in 17 per cent, the amount was more than Rs. 5000.

Thus, in the rural areas, the people are little worried to fix a higher amount of *Mehr*, either to prevent divorce or to provide for a reasonable amount of money in the event of divorce. This could be attributed to the lack of awareness or a lower incidence of divorce in the rural areas. The higher amount of *Mehr* in the urban areas reflects the people's awareness to use it as a means of preventing divorce, and to provide some degree of security to women in the event of divorce. Unlike the rural areas in the urban areas, the amount of *Mehr* is taken as a status symbol.

Inheritance, Marriage and Divorce in the Personal Law

The study indicated that 57 per cent urban respondents reported to be partly aware and 21 per cent fully aware about the provisions of marriage and divorce in the personal law as compared to 40 per cent partially aware and 13 per cent fully aware in the case of rural respondents. 23 per cent urban respondents as compared to 47 per cent rural respondents reported total unawareness about the provisions. Higher educational levels in the urban areas accompanied by greater religious training of urban respondents were responsible for greater awareness among the urban respondents. However, the majority of even the urban respondents was only partially aware showing that the religious training does not teach adequately about the personal law.

The majority of urban respondents (50 per cent) having some degree of awareness felt the provisions not serving the interest of the women whereas 34 per cent felt the other way. In comparison, 53 per cent rural respondents found the provisions favourable for women whereas 29 per cent felt otherwise. A sizable percentage of women identifying the provisions as favourable was indicative of the ignorance of the respondents regarding the provisions' implications for them.

The study indicated that very few women had any knowledge about the provisions regarding female inheritance in the personal law. Those having some knowledge of the women's share in the property were asked to specify the percentage of wife's/daughter's share in the property but the answers given were almost wrong. Knowledge about these matters was not provided through religious training and generally the women were totally in dark about their rights. In the majority of the cases the women reported had not received any share from their parental property.

Employment of Girls

The study revealed that whereas rural women (54 per cent) opposed girls employment, rural men (59.5 per cent) approved employment of women. On the other hand, urban women (54 per cent) approved employment of women but men (50 per cent) are disapproved of. However, a sizable number of rural women (40 per cent) and (44 per cent) urban men approved employment of women. The younger respondents (below 25 years) were more in favour of girls employment as compared to older respondents (above 55 years) in general. Negative attitude towards women's employment was higher among urban men as compared to rural men, where comparatively higher educational levels, the economic compulsions of city life as also a greater acceptance of women's role outside the home in general, should have favoured employment of women. The percentage of rural men disapprove *purdah* was lower than their urban counterparts—more urban men therefore wanted to allow their women to give up *purdah.* This ambivalence could be supported by the concept of women's employment. The rural men may hold a concept of women's employment whereby either she is employed in the family occupation like agriculture or caste occupation or else she is self-employed whereas in the urban areas the employment of women generally means employment outside the home. The strain that employment of women created in urban areas in terms of dislocation of the existing role relationship may have led to majority of men showing negative attitude towards women's employment. A slightly higher percentage of rural women (24 per cent) felt that their husbands would permit them to work outside home as compared to urban women (21 per cent)

Women's Participation in Social/Cultural Activities

The majority of both rural women and men opposed women's participation in social/cultural activities. A sizable percentage of urban women (50 per cent) had a positive but the urban men (46 per cent) had a negative attitude. Perhaps this is the indication of the worry of Muslims in general not to permit greater freedom to women, mainly because of the cultural norms of maintaining a greater segregation between the two sexes. A higher percentage of urban respondent in the younger age group (upto 40 years) favoured girls participation in social/cultural activities, while rural respondents showed no significant variations on account of age. This reflects a greater change in the urban areas particularly among young females.

Women's Participation in Politics

As far as women's participation in politics is concerned, the equal trend was observed about their participation in social activities. Except in the case of urban women where 47 per cent are approved of it but rural men and women and urban men are disapproved of it, perhaps due to the identification of certain roles as purely men's, such as holding of positions of power and administration of society in general. However, the approvals of urban women indicated an attitudinal change in Muslim women. Age did not appear to affect the attitude of women respondents towards their participation in politics.

The study revealed that the majority of women and men, both rural and urban, had an attitudinal level which made it difficult to either rate them as traditional or modern. It indicated a positive change in the attitude in some areas whereas in other areas the traditional ideas still persist. Except for a small percentage of rural women (18 per cent) who were classified as moderately traditional the rest were border lines cases, or moderately modern. When analysed age wise, a higher percentage of urban respondents in middle ages, i.e., 36—45 years obtained a neutral rating. As against this the percentage of those falling in the moderately modern group was higher in younger age group i.e. up to 30 years as compared to other age groups. In the case of rural respondents no significant variations were observed except that a slightly higher percentage of respondents in the age groups 31—40 years had moderately traditional attitudes.

The data in respect of attitudes towards considering men as superior to women indicated that the majority of both men and women, both rural and urban agreed to it. Only a small percentage of urban women disagreed with it. Thus even urban women did not claim an equal status with men, and would believe in the usual allocation of female and male roles based on the concept of male superiority. Age-wise both the respondents (urban and rural) do not differ significantly in this context.

Perception of Muslim Women on Marriage and Related Issues

The differences in the socio-cultural millieu of rural and the urban Muslims, the difference in their economic and educational levels and their response to several life situations, as brought out by the study, confirms Mujib's (1967) thesis that Muslims in India are not a homogeneous community. Despite having a common religion, their attitude and practices do not match a universal pattern which one assumes while using the term 'Muslim Community'.

The issue of the status of Muslim women hence raises many difficulties. Since, although Muslim women may have the 'Muslim' in common, their socio-economic context is characterised by similar variations as those found in other communities. Though, it is difficult to define the term 'status' precisely. Yet if it comes to the opportunities for self-development, the distribution of certain roles, the level of their participation in decision-making at home and outside, the prevalent social norms and social attitudes in respect of women, and more so their own perception their condition and their adjustment with it, then the insights provided by the study reveal that the status of Muslim women is to a great extent determined by their socio-economic millieu. Some specific practices, e.g., arranged marriages and *purdah* observance, etc., are generally not affected by their socio-economic status. The insights provided by the study disprove the notions of a stagnant Muslim society or even stagnant or deteriorating conditions of Muslim women.

The hypothesis propounded by Roy (1979) that the Islamic culture is still vitally conservative and maintains an unchanged, or at best a slightly changed fundamental value orientation, may well be true, but it is not the 'Islamic Culture' which determines the status of women, particularly their educational level and employment opportunities, and that the urban educated elite take as 'indicator of women's status.

The general criteria, in fact, used to judge the higher level of backwardness among Muslims as a whole, had been to look at figures of higher level educational enrolment, and to look for statistics of employment of Muslims at the top sections of the society. Similarly, in the case of women, more or less same approach is being adopted, accompanied by a comparison with their male counterparts, and with other women in general. Given the Indian demographic situation, and the socio-economic composition of the population in general and Muslims in particular, such a framework would always make one to the same conclusion that the participation of the minorities is ceasing on both these counts. But this does not prove the absence of any change within the Muslims or among the Muslim women. These indicators also do not provide any insight into the conditions of Muslims in general, a large majority of whom, like any other community, for historical reasons, have never reached high educational levels or consequently achieved well-paid white-collar jobs in the Indian context.

The dimension of backwardness of women based on such criteria also raises serious suspitions. In fact 'modernization' or 'progress' and 'development' are all value-laden terms and hence relative in nature. Therefore, we should look at the facts pertaining to Muslim women and possible reasons for their adopting certain life styles, from a wider perspective, based on an understanding of their existing social millieu.

Economic Profile

The rural Muslims were comparatively poorer than their urban counterparts, the general trend prevailing in India as also in most of the Third World countries. The reasons were greater concentration of developmental efforts in the urban areas, and the consequent concentration of facilities for human growth and development. A comparison of Muslims with the general statistics of people below the poverty line, revealed the greater disparity between the urban Muslims and their counterparts in other communities was as compared to that of rural Muslim and their counterparts in other communities. This could perhaps be supported by the occupational variations observed among the rural and urban Muslims. The rural Muslims were predominantly professimal cultivators or landless labourers.

The urban Muslims on the other hand, were predominantly businessmen or servicemen. Therefore, the urban Muslims' economic condition largely depended on their capability to compete with others in both areas. But it cannot be said whether it was their incapability or the existing circumstances denying them a fair opportunity of doing so. The socio-economic composition of the urban Muslim population may also be a factor. The urban communities in general may have a comparatively larger percentage of population in the upper two classes, i.e., Higher and Higher Middle. In the case of urban Muslims, only a small percentage belongs to the Higher and Higher Middle class.

Economic Status of Respondents

The study indicated that the majority of women were economically dependent as having no independent income. But, in the urban areas, a sizable percentage of women (25 per cent) were employed, and in the rural areas, the percentage of workers was comparatively small (11 per cent) but in both cases majority were part-time workers. In the urban areas, the majority of women workers were doing unskilled works or helping in the family business while 2.38 per cent were employed in white-collar jobs. The majority of rural women were engaged in unskilled work, caste occupation or agriculture related works.

In the rural areas, all women employees belonged to the lower socio-economic classes indicating that women in the well-off families not taking up employment. On the other hand, in the urban areas, most of the full-time employed women belonged to the upper socio-economic classes, whereas the majority of part-time employed women belonged to lower socio-economic classes. This indicated that only women from higher socio-economic classes in urban areas with access to higher and professional education, were for full-time employment whereas the women (both rural and urban) in the lower socio-economic classes did part-time unskilled work.

Educational Profile

As regards education, there was a general belief that Muslims were behind other communities, and Muslim women showing no improvement regarding educational achievements. The illiteracy rate among the urban Muslims was comparatively higher than other communities in the case of both males and females as a study revealed. Since the urban data was collected from Delhi for comparison illiteracy rates of Union Territories were achieved on the basis of the 1981 census data.

In respect of rural Muslims, the percentage of illiteracy among both males and females had marginal variations from the average illiteracy rates of males and females from rural areas of U.P. A comparative analysis at other levels of education could not be conducted due to lack of data in respect of educational level, statewise, on the basis of 1981 census. A close association appeared between socio-economic status and educational achievements in the case of both males and females. The higher socio-economic strata had higher educational achievements. Similarly, urban Muslims, both males and females, had performed much better as regards educational achievements than their rural counterparts, a trend again consistent with the general pattern in respect of other communities in India.

A substantial decline in illiteracy among the younger generation both males and females was apparent. Though, urban illiteracy rates are lower than those among rural children in the case of both male and female. The educational progress existed among the Muslims and particularly so among the Muslim women, though many would argue on the basis of a smaller percentage of females achieving tertiary level, that Muslim women were still way behind.

This invites an understanding of the socio-economic millieu and the consequent role expectations of Muslim women, for following the rationale behind their leaving school at the higher secondary level. Firstly, the majority of both the rural and urban Muslim population belonged to the lower socio-economic strata, secondly, only a small percentage of Muslims, even in the urban areas, belonged to a service class occupational group, and thirdly, due to the cultural constraints in India, the majority of women were still confined within homes, entrusted with the responsibilities of the upbringing of children and managing other domestic chores. Under these circumstances the post-secondary education may be considered as irrelevant.

In some respects, higher educational achievements for girls actually caused more harm than good, since it produced difficulties for their marriage prospects for highly qualified educationally than their prospective husbands, a practice yet unacceptable either in the rural or urban areas. Secondly, the custom of early marriage, still extensively prevalent in India, particularly in rural areas, further posed problems for girls if they remained unmarried beyond the age of twenty years.

The need for an alternative system of education to enable the women to function more effectively and thereby claim a better status was urgently required. The greater female ability to manage their real life situations effectively would generate more self-confidence on the one hand and on the other, would produce demystification of the existing stereotypes of female inability in certain fields, requiring independent decision-making.

Therefore, the worry of the elite class for imposing its own values on the people had been greatly responsible for calling the general masses as backward, since they refused and rightly so, to adopt the same values in their lives. It was, indeed, neither possible nor desirable to propagate higher education for Muslim women indiscriminately or for that matter for both males and females in general given the present socio-economic realities in India. The problem of illiteracy, which was already registering a decline even among females, was again not so much because of the religious orthodoxy of Muslims and their desire to keep their women secluded due to economic and social factors as it was largely determined by them. The lack of interest of children and parents was more socially determined, rather than a consequence of religious belief only. The larger concentration of illiteracy among the lower strata of the society, and the spatial differences in literacy rates of socio-economic influence.

Social Profile

In receiving religious education, the rural/urban locale and the socio-economic status of the respondents played an important role. The urban women, particularly in the higher socio-economic strata were receiving religious education to a greater extent than the rural women. However, the religious education only consisted of how to offer Namaz and the reading of the Holy Book, and not imparting knowledge of Islamic laws, imparted informally at home or in the neighbourhood. Thus, urban women's observance of religious practices was higher than their rural counterparts. Similarly, women's observance of religious practices was comparatively higher than males, although the majority of both rural and urban men and women were only observing religious practices moderately, registering a further decline in the case of younger males. The people in the lower socio-economic strata received less religious education and their level of observance of religious practices was low.

Marriage Practices

Early marriage was still practised but the median age at marrige both among Muslim males and females was not only comparable with other communities but in the case of females it was higher. The attitude of both rural and urban women with regard to the ideal age at marriage of both girls and boys and particularly so among the women with educational level of 10th class or above had changed. The majority of women, both rural and urban, would marry their daughters after the age of 16 years and nearly 45 per cent women in the rural areas and 34 per cent in the urban areas were married before the age of 16 years.

There was also a gradual change in respect of consulting girls prior to their marriages. Earlier the majority of respondents were not consulted at the time of their marriages. However, marriages are still preferred by the majority of people.

The dowry was given voluntarily and the amount of dowry was not discussed at the time of marriage. The majority of women reported facing no dowry problems, though marriage of girls did pose economic problems for a substantial number of families.

Polygamy and Divorce

The incidence of polygamy and divorce was negligible and the women strongly advocated abolition of polygamy by mobilizing public opinion. The majority of women opposed divorce mainly because of problems of children and economic dependence and they viewed it as socially undesirable. The majority of women both in the rural and urban areas advocated the change of the right to unilateral divorce given to men, again indicated a change in the female attitude.

An overview of the social practices among Muslim women indicated noticeable change in their attitudes and practices and it was more pronounced in some cases in the urban areas and particularly so among the women having education upto 10th class or above. The attitudes and practices of rural women also were changing and in many respects they appear to resemble those of women in other communities. The socio-economic millieu and their education level was positively associated with some of these practices, though in some fields the same social norms were held by women and men irrespective of their rural or urban and class positions, e.g., desirability of *purdah* observance, religious education and arranged marriages.

These cultural links shaped the identity of Muslims in India hence, there was a desire to preserve these. These social norms did not prevent women from using developmental opportunities e.g., education, thus signified that not the cultural ethos alone poses problem for Muslim women. The theory of religious orthodoxy and social stagnation appeared to be playing no vital role in preventing women from using developmental opportunities.

Social Participation

The women did participate in decision-making processes although the level of real and desired participation was different in the urban and rural areas. The rural ladies had a lower level of participation although a high percentage of women did participate in deciding matrimonial and educational matters related to marriage education and larger choices of their children. Urban women, on the other hand had a higher level of participation, and in many matters they divided independently. This indicated importance and authority accorded to ladies in the family set up. A very substantial number of households had a tradition of joint decision-making and the majority of respondents' ideal choice was also the same. It indicated the level of understanding and mutual respect for each other between the two sexes. The fact that a sizable percentage of rural and urban women even participated in discussing their husband's business topics further indicated female participation and involvement in the decision-making processes at home.

The majority of women participated in the elections as voters. Again the urban women showed greater independence while casting their votes, whereas the majority of rural women casted their votes as advised by their husbands. In the rural areas under study, there were hardly any welfare programmes for female participation and even in the urban areas the women were not aware of any local welfare programmes beneficial for them.

Thus urban women had a higher indoor and outdoor participation level, whereas rural women were comparatively less active. Non-availability of programmes nearby or lack of existing programmes was apparent cause of lesser female participation in welfare programmes.

Health

Though cases of females suffering from any long term disease were insignificant yet the number of living children and the incidence of infant mortality, and lack of public health services, particularly in the rural areas caused serious health problems to women. Since the majority of rural and urban women preferred the allopathic medical system, it indicated acceptance of modern system of medicine rather than belief in traditional forms of medicine.

Social Attitudes

The majority of women, both rural and urban, on the basis of their total scores, hold a neutral position in respect of various female matters. It could be interpreted as a state of indecisiveness whereby they were reluctant to assume a certain position. This uncertainty, indicated that while they were hesitating in adopting modern ideas, at the same time they were not arrogant about their traditional beliefs. The urban women appeared to display a greater degree of change in attitude as a sizable per cent fell into the class of moderately modern, as compared to 14 per cent rural women. A very small percentage of both rural and urban ladies got the rating of moderately conservative. It was a very positive reflection of attitudinal change among the women. The urban women appeared to be slightly more desirable to accept new ideas as compared to urban men. This was important, since the general belief was that generally the women were more unwilling to accept new ideas as compared to urban men, particularly so among the Muslims. This showed the thinking process of women being influenced by the changes taking place in society and it denied the assumption that Muslim women were 'frogs in a well'.

On the contrary, the rural data did showed a different trend where the men were more inclined to adopt new ideas as compared to women. The attitudinal position of Muslim women thus was resembled to the general trend in respect of Indian women where urban women were more likely to have an attitude of seeking changes in matrimonial and divorce practices, female education etc. The percentage of women in other communities in India accepting changes might vary from that of Muslim women as also the degree of change but nevertheless it indicated a change in the attitude of Muslim women.

An analysis of attitudes on particular issues disclosed that on some issues, e.g., *purdah*, arranged marriages, widow remarriage and beliefs in the superiority of men, a general consensus appeared both among men and women in rural and urban areas, in viewing these as desirable practices. The socio-economic background and educational level seemed to have no noticeable effect in determining these attitudes. These attitudes appeared to be originating from the cultural conditioning, both Islamic and Indian in nature. The Indian tradition also emphasizes segregation of sexes thereby forbidding interaction between the opposite sexes, creating some form of *purdah* observance by females. Similarly, arrnaged marriages and belief in male superiority was very much a part of Indian cultural tradition. In respect of widow remarriage, the Muslim women had a more modern attitudes than that of women in other communities. particularly among the Hindus. The Hindu marriage were seen as a sacrament and hence the bond continued even after the husband died. Therefore, Hindu women may find it extremely difficult to digest the idea of a second marriage.

The fact that the majority of both men and women, rural and urban approved girls' education, denied any theory of social dogmatism on part of the Muslims, particularly Muslim women.

Perspective of Change

The majority of respondents, irrespective of their urban/rural local during the past decade had not perceived any appreciable change in their social, family or personal life. At least some sections of respondents have experienced positive change in their economic status particularly the urban respondents in the upper socio-economic strata.

The perception of problems differed in the rural and urban areas. Though different respondents used varying terms to narrate their problems, yet the focus was on the general routine problems and particularly economic crisis. The majority of women from the upper socio-economic strata having no problem supported this impression. Male dominance, lack of mobility, ill-treatment by in-laws, etc., had not been discribed as the main problems by either the rural or urban respondents. Perhaps the main problem for the majority of women was poverty since a large number of women particularly from the lower socio-economic strata wanted some larged gainful employment at home to increase their income. In the case of rural women, understandably, a sizable section of them wanted health facilities. Therefore the issues perceived by the ordinary women were significantly different from those perceived by urban educated women.

Increase Indicators of Female Status

The relationships within the family of the respondents were fairly harmonious and the women generally took their meals after feeding the males first. Similarly, the birth of the girl evoked no feeling of depression or displeasure in the household although a male child was still preferred by the majority of people both rural and urban. Non-marriage of girls no longer evoked social disapproval, a change in the attitude towards women. A good percentage of urban women went out reflected with their husbands whereas rural women generally did not.

However, the majority of women, both rural and urban, found their condition worse as compared to men, due to economic dependence. Yet the majority of both rural and urban women were satisfied with their life. Women faced hardships having no economic and other resources and access to facilities like health. Despite these hardships a tendency to express satisfaction with their life was reflective of their capacity to adjust with their prevailing situation and a fatalistic attitude.

The subject of the 'Status of Muslims Women' is vast, and of bewildering complexity, as Srinivas (1976) stated in the context of Indian women. It had many facets, and generalization was pretty nearly imposible because considerable variations existed between rural and urban areas and between classes. As Lowie (Primitive Society: 1920) emphasized, there was considerable difficulty in establishing casuality when the events under consideration are various and the relationship between them extremely complicated.

There was definite evidences to show that the Muslim women were undergoing change, though the rate and extent thereof varied between the rural and urban areas, and in different socio-economic classes. Religious orthodoxy appeared not increasing, particularly in the rural areas, or the religious orthodoxy or more specifically, *purdah* observance could not be taken as a major factor for the backwardness of Muslim women. Indices such as female literacy, marriage of girls, female participation in decision-making and economic activity, indicated that the rural women were way behind their urban counterparts.

A comparison of Muslim women with the women in other communities indicated that the status of Muslim women was more comparable opposite to the assertions generally made about the greater backwardness of Muslim women in India, though a comparison of achievement of higher educational levels was difficult. Ironically, this had been considered as an important indicator to assess the backwardness of Muslim women. Particularly in case of rural women, the status of Muslim women greatly resembled with that of women in other communities. However, as the study indicated a sizable percentage of both rural and urban respondents 'felt' the women of other communities more educated.

The female work participation rate in India on the basis of 1971 census was 11.85, 6.61 per cent for urban females and 18.09 rural. Ashok Mitra and others (1980) questioned these figures. According to them the female participation rate was 19.60 per cent on the basis of 1971 census data. The rural FWPR was computed as 21.73 per cent as compared to 11.01 per cent in the urban areas. The same study gives FWPR in U.P. as 10.75 per cent. The rural FWRR in case of U.P. was 11.60 as compared to 5.25 per cent urban. This indicated that the FWPR were much higher in the rural area as compared to urban areas. The data provided by the present study revealed that in case of Muslim women the FWPR both in the rural and urban areas were much lower as compared to the general FWPR. Secondly there was significant difference between rural F.W.P.R. (4.0) and urban F.W.P.R. (3.0).[5] The notable difference was that majority of full-time workers in the urban areas belonged to upper socio-economic strata whereas the majority of full-time workers in rural area belonged to lower socio-economic strata.

Working long days, performing uncountable domestic duties including the processing of agricultural produce lacking remuneration imposes a substantial burden on poor rural women. Only a small percentage of the total women workers (20 per cent) was employed in non-agricultural jobs. Out of this percentage only a fraction of female workers was employed in white collar occupations like teaching, medicine etc., since it required higher levels of educational achievements. Hence in general the majority of country's female workers (88 per cent)[6] worked in the unorganized sector, uncovered by labour legislations. The employers were not bound to pay minimum wages nor were employees entitled to security of tenure, gratuity, pension and paid leaves etc.:

1. Mitra et. al. suggested that for the overall socio-economic development, more women be employed for earning their livelihood.
2. They be employed outside of agriculture sector and drudge work of low status and low pay.
3. They be employed outside of home, away from traditional occupations of low skill and productivity.
4. They be given a required level of skill, education and training not only for their employment, but as necessary requirement for their independence, freedom and being a fully developed (social cultural being).

The implementation of the first three suggestions to a great extent was associated with the implementation of the fourth one, coupled with a radical change of the society ensuring a more equitable distribution of fruits of development, particularly raising the share of the weaker sections. FWPR signifies the hardships of women, and hence the women not subjected to these hardships could be considered better off, than their counterpart who had to undergo this drudgery. Women on account of socio-cultural factors could not come out of their homes and hence still preferred employment within their homes or nearby.

A study of labour force in relation to economic development in respect of Pakistan and Bangladesh[7] (Ghazi, 1975) argues that low urban female activity rates were a reflection of how little the traditional division of functions between women as home-makers and men as bread winners (referred to as traditionalism) had been altered. The study indicated that the low female labour force participation in the two countries was not the result of dominance of of Islamization, instead lack of adequate education, vocational training and suitable jobs contributed to lower urban activity rates.

The socio-economic composition of the Muslim community and the cultural constraints, partly Indian and partly Islamic in nature greatly determined the achievement levels of female education and their subsequent employment outside their homes and their marriageable age etc. Considering these behavioural practices against the existing socio-economic realities in India, it was completely difficult to term them as irrational and hence backward. The whole issue of assessing women's backwardness, requires some reconsideration and a conceptual framework which can transcend the overt realities. As a married couple got older, as a young wife matured into a mother and mother-in-law, the relationship between the husband and wife become increasingly egalitarian ... but this was concealed more or less effectively by symbols of wifely difference, and expressions of devotion to the Lord Master". He emphasized the female participation in the decision-making, though still remaining in background.[8]

The existing distribution of labour between the sexes and its implications on various social practices had been brought out by many studies. It had been stated that higher education and subsequent employment of women had only marginally brought any change in the traditional roles of women, thereby creating greater tensions for them individually and for the entire family on the whole. On the other hand, the lack of access to facilities like health can hardly be attributed to a lower status accorded to women. The study reveal that the rural women had no access to health facilities due to poverty and lack of facilities in the area.

To conclude:

1. The socio-economic background had a positive association with female educational level.
2. Urban women had better access to educational and health facilities and disaplayed great of change in their social attitude and practices.
3. Religious orthodoxy was not increasing nor it caused women's lack of access to education and heatlh.

The following measures might be helpful in framing a suitable policy of women welfre:

1. An alternative approach be adopted to women's education particularly for women in the lower socio-economic strata in the urban areas and rural women in general.
2. Condensed courses be started for educating young girls with particular emphasis on skill building started in both urban and rural areas.
3. Voluntary efforts from within the community encouraged to supplement governmental efforts to achieve these objectives.

References

1. *Syed,* 1998.
2. See the report of the Committee on the status of Women in India (1974), for *purdah* observance practices among different religious communities in India.
3. See also Towards Equality—Report of the Committee on the Status of Women in India, Department of Social Welfare, Government of India, New Delhi, 1974.
4. (Women in India—A Statistical Profile, Department of Social Welfare, Government of India, 1978, p. 60).
5. Karlekar: 1982.
6. Mitra, *et. al.* 1980.
7. Ghazi, 1975.
8. Srinivas, 1976.

13

Women in Punjab and Haryana

Status of Punjab and Haryana are known to be highly prosperous. Per capita income of Punjab has been highest in whole India. Even infrastructural development in these two states is much more as compared to other northern states and the rest of India. Despite all this, status and position of women in Punjab and Haryana is no better than rest of India. Female foeticide is practiced the most in Punjab. Why else, female sex ratio is the lowest of whole country in Punjab.

In 1966, Punjab was divided into two states of Punjab and Haryana on the basis of language. Since the present state of Haryana was carved out of Punjab, both the states have great similarity in their social and cultural values and their economy is mainly based on agriculture. As per the 1981 census, Punjab comprised 16.79 million persons out of whom 8.94 million (53.24 per cent) were males and 7.85 million (46.75 per cent) females, while Haryana consisted of 12.92 million persons, of whom 6.91 million (53.48 per cent) were males and 60.1 million (46.51 per cent) females.

In both states of Punjab and Haryana agriculture is the main occupation of the people. The dominant religion in Punjab is Sikhism while in Haryana Hinduism comes first and Sikhism comes afterwards. Historically, both states in the past had always attracted foreign invaders. Alexander the Great conquered Punjab in the fourth country B.C. After him, the Greeks, Sakas, Kushans and Huns attacked Punjab. The Mughals also came through Punjab and after them came the Britishers who conquered Punjab in 1850. After almost a hundred years of struggle Punjab won freedom alongwith India in 1947.

Thus throughout history the first aggressive onslaught and fury of the invaders was borne by the people of Punjab. As a consequence of numerous and repeated invasions, the women of this territory were most confined to the inner parts of their homes. This gave rise to child marriage, the *Purdah* system and a variety of other evil practices prejudical to women.

Societal and Domestic Perspective

Education of Women

Let's start with education of women. The position of women's education was rather hair raising in the past. The custom of early marriage and the conversation of the people were the main reasons for the slow growth of education among women. Again, there was a dearth of women teachers and separate schools for girls. Still, before India's independence various socio-religious organisations like the Arya Samaj, the Dev Samaj, the Singh Sabha and the Chief Khalsa Diwan and the Muslim Anjumans performed a significant role in the spread of women's education.

The British government also took interest in the education of women. The report on the advancement of women in the Punjab for the year 1938-39 remarked that 'the limiting factor has usually been a matter of finance and not the apathy of the people' (Proceedings of the Dept. of Education, Punjab 1938-39). After India's independence rapid changes have been taking place in improving women's education. There has been a significant growth in the number and percentage of institutions as well as women scholars in both the states. As per the 1981 census, the female literacy rate in Punjab and Haryana is 34.14 and 22.23 per cent respectively as against 24.88 per cent for the country as a whole.

Table 13.1
Region and Sex-wise Literacy Rates in Punjab and Haryana in 1981

Region →	*Punjab*		*Haryana*		*India*	
Sex →	*M*	*F*	*M*	*F*	*M*	*F*
Total	46.59	34.14	47.18	22.23	46.72	24.81
Rural	40.91	28.35	42.87	15.34	40.62	17.99
Urban	61.12	49.57	64.89	47.23	65.58	47.65

Source : Census of India, Series I Paper 3 of 1981.

Figures above show that the female literacy rates in Punjab are fairly above the national level whereas in Haryana they are lower in the total as well as in rural-urban areas. Another important fact is that the gap between male and female literacy is relatively much wider in Haryana, especially in rural areas.

It further shows that the gap between rural and urban female literacy is also much wider indicating thereby that, first of all, female literacy in general in Haryana is less than half of the male literacy and then, rural female literacy is much lower than male literacy in the state. Apart from the rural-urban variations, the level of female literacy also differs with the level of socio-economic development of the district; for example, in Punjab, female literacy rates are fairly high in Majha and Doaba (Amritsar, Julllunder, Kapurthala, Hoshiarpur, Ropar, Ludhiana, etc.) but quite low in Malwa (Sangrur, Bhatinda, Faridkot and Ferozepur) as these districts are comparatively less developed.

Similar variations exist in Haryana and female literacy rates are much lower in comparatively less advanced districts of Jind, Bhiwani, Hissar and Sirsa. Literacy rates also varied between the Sikhs and the Hindus. The Singh Sabha and Akali Movement laid great stress on female literacy and opened various schools for women.

Darling (1934) states that 'it is typical of the Sikh that he is almost as eager for the education of his daughter as his son, for the dual reason that she may be able to read the Granth Sahib and be an economical wife.' Kapur (1986) also states that the 'Singh Sabha emphasis on female education among Sikhs ensured an even higher number of females literate among the Sikhs than among the other communities in Punjab.' A more realistic character of the progress of female education is the female enrolment in schools. In Punjab the total women's enrolment is 43.6 per cent of the total enrolment whereas in Haryana it is 39 per cent.

On the whole in both the states the percentage increase in women's enrolment, relatively speaking, is much higher in the primary stage indicating thereby a higher dropout rate at higher age groups. Although on the whole in both the states there has been a phenomenal increase in women's education, still Haryana remains behind Punjab as one of the major fourteen states. Punjab occupies the third place whereas Haryana occupies the eighth position in terms of female literacy in the state.

Work Role of Women

One significant variable that is closely related to the status of women is their work role, particularly their employment outside the home. The census data indicate that female labour force participation rates are the lowest in the country in both these states. Punjab in fact has the lowest proportion of female workers and Haryana has the second lowest. Various reasons have been attributed to it. Throughout the past, this part of India was the scene of frequent attack from the west by the Aryans, the Greeks, the Huns and the Mughals, etc. The recurrent war was here necessitated a closed society for the women in which they were to remain in *Chardwari* (the four walls of the house) and *Purdah*. Chandna (1967) also points out that in Punjab women belonging to the upper castes do not take part in agricultural activities at all, because of cultural taboos.

The cultural history of the region does not allow much freedom and mobility to females also discourages their participation in outdoor activities. D'Souza (1975) argues that in Punjab women usually work only when there are economic compulsions; when it becomes inevitable due to some other reason, men allow their women to enter the labour force and they like to withdraw them as soon as their status has improved. We came across significant variations within each state in the proportion of female workers to total female population. In Punjab the proportion of female workers is comparatively low in the Malwa area (Sangrur Bhatinda and Faridkot). These are comparatively less advanced areas and the proportion of scheduled caste population is also low in them. In Haryana the areas lying south of the Ghaggar river (Bhiwani, Sonepat, Rohtak, Hissar and Jind) have quite moderate to relatively high female participation in work. Even before Punjab's reorganisation these areas had much higher (30 per cent) proportion of females in the working force. As said by Chandna (1967) the cultural background of the people of this part of Haryana approves of female participation and the economic hardship forces females to join with males in the economic field. The predominantly agrarian society, the social backwardness of the people and poor literacy standards, are some of the factors associated with high female participation in work in this region of Haryana. An analysis of the data on occupational structure for India as a whole reveals that the bulk of the female labour force is concentrated in rural parts and absorbed in agriculture-related activities. But the situation is just the reverse in Punjab (Table 13.2) where the proportion of female workers is more in urban areas. In Haryana too, it was so till 1971 but from 1981 the proportion of rural women workers has increased.

Table 13.2
Percentage of Women Wokers in Agriculture, Household Industry and Other Workers in 1971 and 1981

State	*Cultivators*		*Agricultural labour*		*Household industry*		*Other workers*	
	1971	*1981*	*1971*	*1981*	*1971*	*1981*	*1971*	*1981*
Punjab	5.58	10.42	10.92	26.95	7.21	6.53	76.29	56.00
Haryana	36.96	49.30	25.96	22.20	3.97	2.85	33.11	25.00

Next important aspect of the occupational structure of these states is that in Punjab 37 per cent of females are involved in agriculture-related activities and 56 per cent are other workers and this means that more women in the state are found in manufacturing processes and other services than the two main agricultural operations of cultivators and agricultural labourers. However, in Haryana nearly 50 per cent of the women are cultivators and another 22 per cent are agricultural workers. In Haryana the proportion of female workers engaged in agriculture-related activities is even more than that of men. This is why it is said that in comparison to a Sikh Jat farmer who considers it below his dignity to allow females to work outdoors a Hindu Jat farmer has no such inhibitions. Women in Haryana are actively involved in agriculture and these women even plough the fields. However, the 1981 census has revealed a significant increase in female workers in both the states. In Punjab, the green revolution has resulted in rapid growth in agricultural productivity, which in turn has created a new demand for labour supply. This is evident from the fact that Punjab has attracted a large number of migrant workers from the other states (Sethi 1984).

There has also been an improvement in the cropping pattern in Punjab during the last decade because of which rice and vegetables have become important new crops. The growth of these crops is concerned with the requirement of female labour (Garewal 1980). In Haryana too the increase in women's activity rate may be partly due to agricultural and industrial development and partly due to speedy development of industrial centres at Faridabad, Sonepat and Bahadurgarh.

State of Marriage and Domestic Afffairs

Practice of keeping one wife, i.e., Monogamy is the most widely practised form of marriage in Punjab and Haryana but in the past a second wife was sometimes taken if the first wife was barren or gave birth only to female children (Reed 1908). Polygamous unions are however not altogether hidden from people. Several writers have reported the existence of polyandry among Jat Sikhs and other low castes where two or three brothers sometimes share same wife (Westermarck 1926, Singh 1976). The incidence of dowry is fairly common and high in both the states although there are some intra-regional variations. For instance, in Punjab the incidence of dowry is seen to be much more in Majha and Malwa than in Doaba. In Majha it is more because of the prosperous farm economy of the region while in Malwa it remains a legacy of the erstwhile feudal system. Doaba is a region of small land holdings and a substantial portion of displaced persons. Although divorce did not exist as a commonly institution in the past, a person was at liberty to sever all connections with his wife if she did not give birth to a male child or was unchaste. Widow remarriage was also usually not allowed. The relation between husband and wife was a sacrament indissoluble save by death. But widow remarriage was common among the Jats and other agricultural castes, artisans and menial sections (Census 1911).

Both the states have a patriarchal set-up and follow patrilineal mode of descent. The male is the perpetuator of the line and the family name. The common mode of family organisation among land-owning people is the joint family though this way of life has been undergoing considerable change due to urbanisation, modernisation and social mobility. As said by Karve (1968) in the family there are two sets of women. In the first set are women who are brought to the house as brides, wives and daughters-in-law and to the second belong women was are born in the family, i.e., sister or daughter. Various codes of behaviour for daughter and daughter-in-law are prescribed. A daughter-in-law is expected to adjust herself to her in-laws' household and she is generally placed under several restrictions particularly in rural areas, and she has little say in decision making and is subordinate to her mother-in-law. She has to show deferential manners to all elders in the household. Her status in the family is partly because of her husband's contribution to the family economy and the amount of dowry she brings and partly on the number of sons she produces.

On the other hand a daughter has great freedom at her father's house and uses it even when she comes back. Leaf (1972) in his study of a Sikh village says that when a girl approaches the marriageable age, the sense of future parting becomes dominent and the girl is treated with the greatest solicitude. She is given lighter work and better clothes, not only to make herself happy, but also to make her more desirable as a wife through showing her appearance and her family in a good light. Like other Indian states, here also, in the family there is a strong desire for male children. The birth of a male child is considered jubilantly, whereas the birth of a female is a matter of bad luck.

That is why why Darling (1934) says: 'Feed son and bullock well : both are bread winners.' The social status of women who gives birth to more female children declines in society. From the very beginning girls are reared in a different manner. The practice of observing still exists in rural areas especially in the presence of the father-in-law and the elder brother of the husband. In villages it is mainly confined to the higher castes and the gentry or to those who would pass as such. It is in fact, a veil which is drawn across the face.

The rigour of full Purdah according to Darling (1934) derives from the terrors of past invasions but the veil owes its origin to the rules and restrictions of the joint family order. A woman must veil herself in the presence of an elder, superior or stranger. They also forbid all communication between a daughter-in-law and a father-in-law and sometimes even between a wife and her husband's elder brother. The Purdah is much more widely prevalent in the state of Haryana than in Punjab. The report of the National Committee on the Status of Women (1974) pointed out that the highest percentage (72.61 per cent) of women in Haryana observed Purdah in front of the father-in-law whereas this percentage was 44.6 per cent in Punjab.

System of Inheritance

As is widely known, in Punjab, the Mitakshara school of law is prevalent. In addition to being governed by the Hindu Personal Law, people are also governed by customary law. From the passing of the Hindu Marriage Act of 1955, the Hindu Succession Act of 1956, Hindu Minority and Guardianship Act of 1956, also apply too Punjab. With the start of the Hindu Succession Act 1956, the customary practice of inheritance has undergone a change. In accordance with the provisions of this act the property of the deceased is divided equally among sons and daughters, widow and mother. But it has not been accepted by the people and therefore in actuality the Act is found to be not implemented at all. Even the Punjab Legislative Assembly made an attempt to exclude the daughters from the right of inheriting the family land.

In 1960, a corresponding bill was placed before the Punjab Assembly. It was accepted by the Cabinet in 1968, but fell through in the Punjab Assembly the coming year (Mies 1980). Sibia's (1985) study reveals that women are rarely given a share in the father's property. The level of awareness regarding the Act was found to be very high in both the states of Punjab but at the opinion level there was very little approval of it. The main argument of men against the Act was that giving a share to a daughter in the father's property would generate many problems. It would lead to fragmentation and subdivision of the family land. It would also lead to the sale of ancestral property because of the exogamous nature of marriage and, since in Punjab there existed a right to pre-emption on the disposal of ancestral property it would give rise to many problems. Moreover, it was said that the daughters did get a share of the family property at the time of marriage in the form of dowry and that's why, had no right to a share in the family land.

Women in Politics

In these two states, the political status of women can be judged from their political awareness, voting behaviour and freedom enjoyed by them in shaping or sharing on power front. In both these states, as far as Assembly seats are concerned, women's participation is very low. In Punjab since 1965 the percentage of women in the Assembly has not been more than 2 to 3 except in 1977 (5 per cent) and in 1985 (6 per cent). In Haryana the maximum percentage was in 1968 when women had 9 per cent seats in the Assembly whereas in 1982 they had 6 per cent seats. Women's position in different political parties including the ruling party is also not very impressive. Also, there are no women trade union leaders. The findings of the National Committee on the Status of Women (1974) reported that in Punjab women voters in urban areas had outstripped the men but not in Haryana. A study conducted in Haryana (Mittal) shows that there is no linkage between the level of literacy in the district and the level of female participation in politics.

Family Welfare and Health

Physical status of women is one of the major concerns of society. The health status of women and children, particularly of mothers, is the concern of the government in both these states and the state health service are practiced at the district level. Women in these states have benefited from the general decline in mortality. Their sex ratio has been improving, maternal mortality and female infant mortality rate has declined and there is an increase in their life expectation.

In Punjab, in 1901 the sex ratio was 120 whereas in 1981 it became 114 per 100 females while in Haryana it was 116 in 1901 and it came down to 114 in 1981. In the same manner, female infant mortality in Punjab and Haryana was found to be 110 and 113 respectively in 1981 as against 135 for the country as a whole. Female life expectancy was 56.8 years for Punjab and 55.6 years for the state of Haryana in 1981 and the corresponding figure for India was 49 years. In spite of these improvements, female infant mortality is still higher than male infant mortality, and life expectancy is less than that of males.

Indicators of Fertility

It is shocking that two important indicators of fertility, namely child-woman ratio and total fertility, show declining trends. The table below shows the total fertility and child-woman ratio in both the states (see Table 13.3).

Table 13.3
In Both the States, Total Fertility and Child-Women Ratio in 1971 and 1981

Geographical Area	*Total Fertility*		*CWR*	
	1971	*1981*	*1971*	*1981*
Punjab	6.32	5.28	6.11	5.12
Haryana	6.68	6.21	7.81	6.20
India	5.78	4.99	6.55	5.46

Source: Family Planning Year Book 1983–84.

While the data show a declining trend in fertility still it is higher than the national level. The birth rate was 30.3 and 36.5 for Punjab and Haryana respectively in 1981 and the corresponding rates for the country was 33.9. All these figures show that fertility is declining in both the states and the decline is more in Punjab than Haryana. The fertility level in a given region relies upon the number of women in the reproductive age group and the acceptance of family planning. The data indicate that in1981 the proportion of females in the reproductive age group, i.e., between 15-44 years for Punjab and Haryana was 80.64 and 69.39 per cent respectively while the corresponding percentage for the country as a whole was 83.90. A close look at the acceptance of family planning discloses that the percentage of couples effectively protected by all methods is fairly high in Punjab and Haryana: it is 42.9 and 40.2 per cent respectively in Punjab and Haryana as against 29.2 per cent at the total country level. In fact Punjab and Haryana hold the second (Maharashtra being first) and third position in this respect.

This way, on the whole health services have improved and fertility has been declining in both the states, the decline being comparatively higher in Punjab. The greater downfall in Punjab may be attributed to higher age at the marriage, higher literacy rates, lower proportion of women in the reproductive age and greater acceptance of family planning. To conclude, hopefully, some positive developments are taking place.

References

Chandana, R.C., 1967. 'Female Working Force of Rural Punjab,' *Manpower Journal,* Vol. 2, No. 4.

Darling, M., 1934. *Wisdom and Waste in Punjab Villages* (Humphrey, Milford: Oxford University Press).

D'Souza, V.S., 1975. 'Family Status and Female Work Participation,' in Alfred de Souza (ed.) *Women in Contemporary India* (New Delhi: Manpower).

Garewal, D.S., 1980. *Agricultural Labour in Rural India,* Punjab University (unpublished dissertation).

Government of India, 1983-84. *Family Welfare Programme in India, Year Book.*

Griffin, L.H. 1909. *Chiefs and Families of Note in Punjab* (Lahore: Minerva).

ICSSR, 1974. *Status of Women in India, the Report of the National Committee on the Status of Women.*

Kapor, R., 1986, *Sikh Separatism—the Politics of Faith.* (London: Allen and Unwin).

Karve, Irawati, 1968. *Kinship Organisation in India* (Bombay: Asia).

Leaf, M.J., 1972. *Information and Behaviour in a Sikh Village: Social Organisation Reconsidered* (New Delhi: Oxford University Press).

Mies, Maria, 1980. *Indian Women and Patriarchy* (New Delhi: Concept).

Minkler, M., 1970. 'Fertility and Labour Force Participation,' in *Journal of Family Welfare,* Vol. XVII, No. 1.

Randhawa, M.S., 1960. *Out of Ashes* (New Delhi: Oxford University Press).

Rees, J.D., 1908. *The Real India.*

Saini, B.S., 1977. *The Social and Economic History of the Punjab 1901-1939* (Delhi: Ess Ess).

Sethi, R.M., 1984. 'Changing Pattern of Female Labour in Agriculture: the Case of Punjab,' in *Social Action,* Vol. 34, October-December.

Sibia, Kiran, 1985. *Hindu Personal Laws Pertaining to a Study of Their Perception by Rural Women,* Punjab University (unpublished M.Phil dissertation).

Singh, Harbans, 1983. 'Status of Women in Sikhism,' in Yash Kohli (ed.), *The Women of Punjab* (Bombay: Chic).

Singh, K.P., 1980. 'Economic Development and Female Labour Force Participation : The case of Punjab,' *Social Action,* Vol. 30, April-June.

Singh, K.P., 1976. 'Polyandry among the Jat Sikhs of Punjab,' paper presented at the *Thirteenth All India Sociological Conference.*

Singh, Yogindra, 1973, *Modernisation of Indian Traditions.* (Faridabad: Thomson Press).

Westermarck, E., 1926. *The History of Human Marriage,* Vol. III, (London : Macmillan).

Wyon, J.B. and J.E. Gordon, 1971. *The Khanna Study* (New York: Harvard University Press).

Virk, K.S., 1983. 'Sandu's Punjab,' in Marcus Franda (ed.), *Punjabis, War and Women.*

Chattopadhyaya, Kamaladevi, 1929. *The Status of Women in Modern India,* ed. by George Evivns and Choksi Mothan, D.B. Taraporewala Sons and Company, Bombay.

Census of India, 1911, Vol. VII, Bombay, Part I Report, p. 101.

Census of India, 1961. Incidence of Polygynous Marriages in India (mimeo), Reported in 'Towards Equality', p. 66.

Divekar, V.D. (1982), 'Western India's Economy' in *Cambridge Economic History of India,* pp. 332-333.

Dobbin. Christina, 1972. *Urban Leadership in Western India* (London: Oxford University Press) pp. 53-77, 249-253.

Dutt, Ramesh, *Economic History of British India,* pp. 262-263.

Enthoven, R.E. 1986. *The Cotton Fabrics of the Bombay Presidency.*

Everett, Matson Jana, 1978. *Women and Social Change in India,* p. 61.

Government of India (GOI) (1974), *Towards Equality Report of the Committee on the Status of Women in India,* p. 62.

Government of India, Ministry of Education, 1985. *Challenge of Education—Policy Perspective,* p. 1.

Heimsath, Charles H., 1964. *Indian Nationalism and Hindu Social Reform.* Princeton University Press, p. 337.

Imperial Gazetteer of India, 1909. Provincial Series, Bombay Presidency, Vol. I (Calcutta: Superintendent of Government Printing).

Joshi, N.M., 1936. *Urban Handicrafts of the Bombay Deccan,* Gokhale Institute, pp. 48-49.

Karkal, Malini, 1985. 'How the Other Half Dies in Bombay?' *Economic and Political Weekly,* Vol. 20, No. 34, August 24, p. 1424.

Karkal, Malini, 1986. 'Discimination—Women in Employment' in *Social Intervention for Social Justice,* R.K. Hebner (ed.) Golden Jubilee Publication of Tata Institute of Social Sciences, Bombay.

Karkal, Malini and Irudaya Rajans, 1985. 'Age at Marriage in India: Has it shown an increase?' paper presented at the Seminar on Demographic and Socio-economic Aspects of Nuptiality in India, jointly organised by the Population Research Centre, JSS Institute of Economic Research, Dharwad and Population Centre, Bangalore from 1-3 February 1985 at Dharwad, Karnataka.

Kumar, Ravindra, 1983. *Essays in Social History of Modern India* (Delhi : Oxford University Press), pp. 6-7.

Morris, Morris D., 1966. 'The Recruitment of an Industrial Labour Force in India, with British and American Comparisons' in *Comparative Studies in Society and History,* Vol. II, No. 3, p. 321.

Montgomery, R. Martin, 1837. *History of the Possessions of the Honourable East India Company* (London : Whittaker) Vol. I. pp. 354-355.

Rogers, B., 1980. *The Domestication of Women in Developing Societies* London: Tavistock) p. 125.

Sen, S.N., 1979. *History of Modern India 1765-1950* (New Delhi: Wiley Eastern), p. 101.

Sovani, N.V., 1965. 'British Impact on India' in Metraux Guy S. and Crouzet Francois (ed.) *Studies in Cultural History of India,* UNESCO, pp. 296-297, 324-325.

14

The Better Half of Madhya Pradesh

They say, it needs two to make a row and it needs and a man and a woman to make a family. But still, one gets inferior and the other man superior treatment in a family. Despite the fact that above neither man nor woman can have a complete life. Together they can perform what is ordained of them by nature. It should follow that they are equal and also complementary to each other with their differing attributes. Woman is by nature dedicate whereas man is physically strong. The physical strength is often misinterpreted as 'superiority' giving woman subordinate status. Woman's delicate nature has also been misconstrued as submissiveness and taken advantage of. As a consequence woman were denied freedom to make their own choices even in personal matters.

Interestingly, it was man who noted the discrepancy in status and advocated a change. Plato, the Greek philosopher, for example, pleaded for the free admission of women to all duties and rights of man indicated the loss to the State as a result of their restricted sphere of activity (Stern 1959: 443).

The nineteenth century saw the greatest advocate for women's cause in John Stuart Mill, the famous political economist and philosopher of his time. But the fervour did not catch up, for the majority of men believed like Aristotle that men are by nature superior and thus fit to rule and women should be ruled. Status is a very complex phenomenon to study. There can be self-perceived status, group-perceived status objective status (Mukherjee 1975). A person who is quite high up in one type of status can be very low in another reflecting status inconsistency. The problem has to be unambiguously clear if a viable solution is to be found. The

Table 14.1

Educational Levels	*Sex Ratio*			*Femininity Proportion*		
	1959-60	*1970-71*	*1982-83*	*1959-60*	*1970-71*	*1982-83*
1. Enrolment in						
Primary school	405	253	195	19.4	28.3	33.9
Middle school	483	327	284	17.1	23.4	26.0
High school and above	599	342	226	14.3	22.6	30.7
	1961	*1971*	*1981*	*1961*	*1971*	*1981*
2. Level of Education						
Illiterate	82	80	80	54.9	55.5	55.6
Literate without formal education	387	270	252	20.5	27.0	28.4
Primary and middle school	507	344	271	16.5	22.5	26.9
Matriculation and above	684	446	330	12.8	18.3	23.3
3. Literate by age-group (in years)						
5-14	288	221	196	25.8	31.2	33.7
15-24	393	290	242	20.3	25.7	29.2
25-34	527	392	309	16.0	20.3	24.5
35 and above	781	608	493	11.4	14.1	16.9
Total	421	318	215	19.2	23.9	27.0

Sources: Government of India, *Education in the States—1959-60;* Government of India, Ministry of Education and Social Welfare, *Selected Educational Statistics—1982-83,* 1983; Government of India, Ministry of Education and Culture, *A Handbook of Educational and Allied Statistics,* 1980; Computed from *Census of India 1961, 1971, 1981,* Madhya Pradesh, *Social and Cultural Tables.* 1961—Part II-C(i), 1971—Part II-C(ii), 1981—Part IV-A.

several ways by which the status of women has been defined have caused more confusion than clarity.

For example, woman's status has been defined as the level of their access to social and material resources within the family, society and community (Dixon 1978); as the authority and power she holds within the family/community and the prestige she commands from other members of the family and society (Mukherjee 1975); as a position in the social system distinguishable yet related to other positions (Committee on the Status of Women in India).

Some Variables About Women

Certain aspect of women's life in their geographical region needs to be highlighted like sex ratio, work participation and marital status, etc. and above all, their education with which we are starting in the table that follows:

Table 14.1 shows the education level in relation to sex ratio in the state. Obviously, less educated women are more dependent on their spouses and families. Their economic dependence can be decreased by women's own monetary income they would enjoy a better status. Employment being a major determinant of the level of monetary income, employment-related aspects namely, level of work participation and sex ratio of agricultural and non-agricultural workers will be discussed here. Wage differentials will also be looked into in brief.

Table 14.2 shows that there is a wide gap between male and female work participation rate. It is obvious that if women in Madhya Pradesh are to obtain equal status through employment, they have a long way to go.

Table 14.2

Level of Work Participation by Sex 1961–1981

Sex	*Work Participation Rate (Total Population)*			*Work Participation Rate (10 + Population)*		
	1961	*1971*	*1981*	*1961*	*1971*	*1981*
Male	60.21	53.74	53.52	86.31	78.23	74.06
Female	43.99	18.65	22.35	63.91	27.58	31.35

Source: Computed from "Census of India", 1961, 1971, 1981, Madhya Pradesh, General Economic Tables, 1961-Part II B (i); 1971-Prt B(i), 1981-Part III-A & B (i)

Table 14.3
Percentage Distribution of Workers and Non-Workers by Sex Age Groups, Level of Education, 1981

Age/Group (years)	*Sex*	*Level of Education*					
		Up to Middle School		*Matriculation and above but below graduation*		*Graduation and above*	
		Workers	*Non workers*	*Workers*	*Non workers*	*Workers*	*Non workers*
15-19	Male	17.09	82.91	10.62	89.38	10.36	89.64
	Female	2.92	97.08	1.47	98.53	2.96	97.04
20-24	Male	76.75	23.25	50.22	49.78	39.38	60.62
	Female	6.07	93.93	7.94	92.06	12.57	87.43
25-29	Male	93.78	6.22	88.14	11.86	80.62	19.38
	Female	7.42	92.58	13.89	86.11	24.47	75.53
30-34	Male	96.61	3.39	96.11	3.89	95.52	4.48
	Female	8.13	91.87	19.86	80.14	35.03	64.97
35 and above	Male	90.88	9.12	92.07	7.93	95.01	4.99
	Female	11.10	88.90	26.09	73.91	51.48	48.52

Sources : Computed from *Census of India 1981*, Madhya Pradesh, Part III-A and B (ii) General Economic Tables; Part IV-A *Social and Cultural Tables.*

Next Table, i.e., Table 14.3 presents percentage distribution of workers and non-workers for males and females by level of education and age-group. Male-female disparity in work participation rate is shown for each age group for all levels of education. Looking at female participation rates for the same age group by level of education, it is seen that from age group 20-24 onwards participation consistently goes up.

Clearly, level of employment is related to education. For each educational level also, female work participation increases with age, indicating that those with education are able to leave behind their inhibitions with advancing age and take up jobs. However, in the traditional society of Madhya Pradesh, higher level education does not always meet the social or individual demand. Hence it seems that among those who are not working (particularly those with higher education) a majority could be discouraged workers and unemployed women.

As it is known that employment is examined in the context of ability to provide monetary income and a better economic status, the type of employment assumes importance. Next Table, i.e., Table 14.4 shows that agriculture absorbs the largest number of labour, both male and female, but the concentration of women workers in agriculture is overwhelming. Combining this with the fact that sex discrimination exists in wage rate (see below) the presumption that the employment of women by itself would raise their status perceptibly appears to be wide off the mark.

Table 14.4
Percentage Distribution of Male and Female Workers by Agricultural and Non-agricultural Sectors, 1961-71

Sectors	*Males*			*Females*		
	1961	*1971*	*1981*	*1961*	*1971*	*1981*
Agricultural	73.44	76.03	71.61	87.75	89.79	87.89
Non-agricultural	26.56	23.97	28.39	12.25	10.21	12.11

Sources: Government of India, *Education in the States—1959–60;* Government of India, Ministry of Education and Social Welfare, *Selected Educational Statistics—1982-83,* 1983; Government of India, Ministry of Education and Culture, *A Handbook of Educational and Allied Statistics,* 1980; Computed from *Census of India 1961, 1971, 1981,* Madhya Pradesh, *Social and Cultural Tables.* 1961—Part II-C(i), 1971—Part II-C(ii), 1981—Part IV-A.

Even more revealing are the data on non-agricultural workers (Table 14.5). About two-thirds of the female workers in the non-agricultural sector are in the category which includes labourers. Further, the occupations of the majority of non-agricultural female workers are of low status, monotonous, time-consuming and tedious. Earnings in these occupations are low. Any substantial upliftment of status cannot be hoped through such employment.

Table 14.5
Percentage Distribution of Non-agricultural Female Workers by Occupation, Sex Ratio and Femininity Proportion, 1981

Occupational division	*Occupational family*	*Per cent of women workers*	*Ratio*	*Femininity proportion*
1	*2*	*3*	*4*	*5*
I Professional Technical and Related	All	11.04	528	15.92
	Nurses	1.76	5	95.18
	Midwives and Health visitors	0.15	70	58.69
	Middle school teachers	1.42	416	19.37
	High school teachers	0.98	362	21.62
	Primary school teachers	3.32	465	17.60
	Pre-primary school teachers	0.32	43	70.08
	Others	3.09	—	—
II Administrative executive and managerial	All	0.48	4167	2.34
Clerical	All	2.41	2418	3.97
	Clerks—general	1.15	1290	7.19
	Others	1.26	—	—
III In Sales	All	7.46	958	9.45
	Retail trade	4.68	1022	8.91
	Street vendors	2.16	373	—
	Others	0.62	—	—
IV In Service	All	8.88	576	14.78
	Ayah, nurse maids	0.15	28	78.42
	Domestic servants	3.40	61	62.10
	Sweepers, cleaners and related workers	3.05	170	7.43
	Others	2.28	—	—

V Farmers Fishermen, Hunters, Loggers etc.	All	5.42	755	11.70
	Cultivators	1.17	226	30.63
	Others	4.25	—	—
VI In Production are related; transport equipment operation, labour	All	60.96	458	17.91
	Quarry workers	0.97	271	26.92
	Weavers and related workers	1.31	740	11.90
	Grain millers and related workers	1.65	307	24.54
	Bidi makers	18.59	106	48.49
	Tailors and dress makers	1.45	1078	8.49
	Potters and related clay workers	4.82	222	31.07
	Basketry weavers and brush makers	5.12	139	41.93
	Construction workers	2.78	268	27.14
	Labourers	12.55	268	27.15
	Others	11.72	—	—
VII Unclassified	All	3.35	519	16.15

Source : Collected from *Census of India 1981,* Madhya Pradesh, Part III-A & B(v), General Economic Tables.

Like other states of India, wage discrimination based on sex prevails in Madhya Pradesh also. For example, in districts like Nimar, Raipur, Ujjain, Mand, etc., a male sower earns Rs. 5/- a day as against Rs. 4/- a day for women sower (Government of India 1982). The same kind of differences are observed for agricultural labourer, reaper, harvester, etc.

Marriage and Family

As we all know marital status is often used as an index of women's status. The contention seems to be that marital status, particularly the proportion never married at the younger ages, is significant indicator of possible access to options other than marriage and the relative acceptability of remaining single for both sexes and age group (United Nations 1984: 30).

Table 14.6 shows that in all age groups a considerably higher proportion of males are never married. But in a society where marriage is universal, the very small proportion of never married women would include, besides those who are not willing to get married, those who cannot get married at the 'right' age due to financial problems and therefore will have to accept it as fate and those who are mentally or physically disabled. To put it other way, the explanation given by the United Nations that it is indicative of alternatives available and acceptable of single status as normal, may not be applicable. Further, the larger proportion of unmarried males is to be expected in a society having more men than women. In Madhya Pradesh, the proportion of widows is several times more than that of widowers. Again if this is considered alongwith the fact that a larger proportion of unmarried men are there in society, one wonders whether it could be due to social pressures against widow remarriage. If this presumption is true it reveals a low status for women.

Table 14.6
Mean Age at Marriage and Marital Status Distribution by Sex 1961-81

	1961		*1971*		*1981*	
	Male	*Female*	*Male*	*Female*	*Male*	*Female*
Mean age at marriage (in years)	18.4	13.9	19.3	15.0	20.6	16.5
Marital Status distribution of 10 + population (per cent)						
Never Married	24.98	10.66	28.37	15.46	33.28	21.00
Just Married	68.38	72.54	66.33	70.97	62.26	67.35
Widowed	5.62	15.99	4.68	13.03	3.77	10.89
Divorced/separated	1.02	0.81	0.49	0.45	0.65	0.72
Percent never marrried in age group						
10-19	71.90	40.21	78.05	53.40	85.93	66.13
20-49	9.07	0.77	9.09	1.10	11.05	1.92
50 +	2.78	0.28	2.21	0.14	1.83	0.15

Source : Government of India Statistics, State government reports.

Thus, by using education, employment, marriage and mortality variables the objective status of women in Madhya Pradesh has been examined. All the indices point out that women are at a disadvantage against men. The share of women is very low at all levels of education except the zero level, the illiterates.

Their work participation rate is low and an overwhelming proportion of women workers are in agriculture. The non-agricultural work of women is also such that it cannot improve their status. Girls are married at a very early age and widow marriage seems to be less acceptable than widower marriages. Women, who are biologically superior to men, have high death rate and lower expectation of life at birth. There are still 'dowry deaths', suicides, physical ill treatment of women by husbands or the latter's immediate relatives, etc. in a set up where laws and regulations are aplenty for the protection of women's rights. It appears that laws are made only to be violated. A new threat is the medical technology which makes it feasible to know the sex of the foetus and these tests 'are increasingly used to discern the sex of the unborn foetus, with a view to abort female children' (Gnanadason 1986: 1631). One is not sure to what extent this technological threat has reached the masses of Madhya Pradesh.

To conclude, the solution to all this lies in a change of *attitude*—a realisation that man and woman together form a whole. If this can be realised, the rest will automatically follow. Marx's words seem apt even after a century: 'The social progress (of a society) can be measured with precision by the social status of the female sex' the better half are men.

1 Janabai

Janabai gives her age as 45. Though she appears much older, her tiny frame is erect and strong. Each of her arms bears two dozen green bangles and is covered with tattoos in decorative geometrical patterns. She refers to these as the only thing she will carry with her into death.

A neo-Buddhist, she was born in a village in Satara District, Maharashtra. She first came to Bombay as a child with her family but returned to the village when the family decided that their land offered a more secure income than urban employment. She never took part in actual tilling of the land, but spent her time in the home. She was one of eleven children, but only three survived – Janabai and two older brothers. She never went to school. She says she would have liked to, but in those days girls were not sent to school.

Her marriage was arranged when she was about 12 years old. Her husband, a farmer of the same religion, paid a bride-price of Rs. 60. They remained in the village, Janabai giving birth to two sons. They left the village about twenty five years ago because of an incident in which her husband, returning from the fields one day, stepped on a snake, which bit his chappal. He wound the snake around his umbrella and threw it into a nearby tree. The legend goes that a snake, once harmed, remembers the injury and seeks revenge. A month later they were disturbed in the house by the "noises of a cock". The neighbours said the snake had come to take the revenge, and Janabai advised her husband to leave the village to escape the snake. They decided to come to Bombay, and settled in the slum, where the husband's mother and brother were living. After one year, they moved into the room where they are now living.

They did not have to pay any 'pugree' for their room, which is about 8 feet by 10 feet, with an enclosed verandah of about 4 feet by 6 feet. The interior room, which is used as a kitchen-cum-washing area, is dark and sparsely furnished with one small barred window close to the ceiling. The verandah, slightly more cheerful as it receives the daylight from a large front window, contains a small bed, a sewing machine which belongs to the community at large, several photographs, including large ones of Nehru and [illegible] Janabai's eldest son's [illegible]

15

Female Slum-Dwellers of Mumbai

Present chapter is an extract of a research study conducted on women in a slum of Mumbai. It contains some leading case studies highlighting their social economic life and their outlook towards various aspects of life and community as well as their misconceptions/prejudices apart from adult women, young minor girls house also been included for case study. The slum to which these women belong is mostly inhabited by Maharashtrians; 53 per cent are Hindus, 16 per cent Muslims, 8 per cent Christians and 23 per cent neo-Buddhists. (The neo-Buddhists in Maharashtra belong to the Mahar caste. The members of this caste are untouchables, who followed Dr. B.R. Ambedkar in a mass conversion to the Buddhist religion.) They represent different ages and communities.

There are approximately 750 women to every 1,000 men in this slum. The majority of these women are in the age group 35-55. Literacy is almost nil for the women over 35, whereas in the 5-14 age group, 47.2 per cent are literate. In the 15-24 age group, 39.5 per cent and in the 25-35 age group, 29.5 per cent are literate. Only 12.3 per cent of the female population is employed. Of the age group 15-54, only 18 per cent are employed.

Table 15.1
Working Slum Women and their Income

Work type	*Percentage distribution of the working women*	*Average income in rupees*
Semi-skilled	20	80
Unskilled	30	62
Domestic	27.5	27
Petty Shopkeeping	15	28
Miscellaneous	7.5	25

(A) Janabai

Janabai gives her age as 45. Though she appears much older, her tiny frame is erect and strong. Each of her arms bears two dozen green bangles and is covered with tattoos in decorative geometrical patterns. She refers to these as the only thing she will carry with her into death.

A neo-Buddhist, she was born in a village in Satara District, Maharashtra. She first came to Bombay as a child with her family but returned to the village when the family decided that their land offered a more secure income than urban employment. She never took part in actual tilling of the land, but spent her time in the home. She was one of eleven children, but only three survived—Janabai and two older brothers. She never went to school. She says she would have liked to, but in those days girls were not sent to school.

Her marriage was arranged when she was about 12 years old. Her husband, a farmer of the same religion, paid a bride-price of Rs. 60. They remained in the village, Janabai giving birth to two sons. They left the village about twenty five years ago because of an incident in which her husband, returning from the fields one day, stepped on a snake, which bit his chappal. He wound the snake around his umbrella and threw it into a nearby tree. The legend goes that a snake, once harmed, remembers the injury and seeks revenge. A month later they were disturbed in the house by the 'noises of a cock'. The neighbours said the snake had come to take the revenge, and Janabai advised her husband to leave the village to escape the snake. They decided to come to Bombay, and settled in the slum, where the husband's mother and brother were living. After one year, they moved into the room where they are now living.

They did not have to pay any 'pugree' for their room, which is about 8 feet by 10 feet, with an enclosed verandah of about 4 feet by 6 feet. The interior room, which is used as a kitchen-cum-washing area, is dark and sparsely furnished with one small barred window close to the ceiling. The verandah, slightly more cheerful as it receives the daylight from a large front window, contains a small bed, a sewing machine which belongs to the community at large, several photographs, including large ones of Nehru and John Kennedy, and Janabai's eldest son's Wireman

Apprentice certificate. They paid Rs. 600 to have water and electricity installed inside the house.

Janabai's children are almost all grown up now. It addition to the two sons born in the village, she has three sons and three daughters. One son died in infancy. The three daughters are all married and live separately. All three were sent to school. Janabai's eldest son, who is the only child to have completed the S.S.C. is also married and has one child. He and his family live with Janabai and her husband, as do the four unmarried sons. The youngest son, aged 14, is still in school; the other three have all left school, but have not found jobs. One son suffers from epilepsy and is under treatment.

The eldest son and Janabai's husband provide the family income. She says both work for a transport company which deducts Rs. 200 monthly from their salaries and supplies the family with provisions. Janabai manages the rest of the income, pays the rent (Rs. 10 per month), and runs the household. Most of her time is occupied with cooking, cleaning, washing, and looking after the ten hens she keeps for eggs and breeding. Although she sold vegetables in the market at one time, she now feels tied to the house as her daughter-in-law 'cannot cope' with the work on her own. This daughter-in-law, who was married to Janabai's eldest son at the age of eighteen, comes from Janabai's village and studied there upto seventh standard. Now she rarely goes out and seems to be entirely in the background in the household. Neighbours say she is often beaten by her husband. He has a mistress in a nearby tenement and thus neglects his wife even further.

Janabai is worried about her husband's health. He has been short-tempered and hard of hearing lately. She thinks something is wrong with his head. He has been talking shock treatment at a local hospital, which seems to help, but the family must bear the expense. They fear retrenchment if they apply for medical assistance from the employer; the company does not know of this illness.

Janabai's social life consists of a visit to her married daughter in Colaba once a month, and the occasional community function. She does not see films, but listens to the radio for news and music. She returns to her village once every 4 or 5 years. Although she feels it is necessary for women to work outside the home to meet the rising cost of living, the problem of caring for the children remains unsolved.

One of Janabai's sons is supposed to be the re-incarnation of her husband's father, as he was born at the same time that the old man died. They must, therefore, treat him with special respect. If she should beat him, her arms ache until she begs his forgiveness. He will be married soon, and Janabai is looking forward to the arrival of her new daughter-in-law to free her from the household. She wants to return to selling vegetables in the market place.

(B) Shevanti

Shevanti is twenty-two. A Hindu of the Dakshini caste, she is attractive and animated and has an air of self-assurance about her, voicing her opinion with conviction. Originally employed as a domestic servant, she found this type of work distasteful and left it. While looking for another job, she did various kinds of handiwork—embroidered handkerchiefs, woven table-mats, and so forth, to get an income. After more than a year of unemployment, she found her present job in a ready-made garments factory. She earns Rs. 100 per month.

Shevanti was born in a village in Satara District, Maharashtra. Her mother, with the mother's brother, was a joint owner of some land. Because of friction between them, Shevanti's family came to Bombay. Shevanti was five years old at that time. She says her father was in the military and the family stayed in army housing at Colaba for some time. Later, they moved to Sion, and recently to the slum where they purchased a room for Rs. 1,100. The room is about 10 feet by 10 feet and is sub-divided to provide a separate area, which is rented out to another family. Shevanti's newly married brother, sister-in-law and sister also live with Shevanti and her parents. A long shelf holds tins of grain and foodstuffs, and in one corner there is a makeshift table with some books on it. The family paid Rs. 13 for an electric connection. They have no water tap, however, and must pay 25 p for every *ghada* of water brought from outside. They use a public latrine.

Shevanti never went to school, but has taught herself to read and write Marathi. She also speaks fluent Hindi, unlike most of the women in the area. She regrets not having had any formal education because it restricts her employment opportunities.

When Shevanti was twelve, a marriage was arranged for her with a Hindu boy of the same caste. He was a matriculate and lived in Bombay. According to tradition, Shevanti returned to her parents' home after five days with the husband. Her brother intervened at this point to encourage her not to return to her husband, who was, she said, shiftless and a good-for-nothing. The parents were persuaded that the marriage had been a mistake and a divorce was obtained after a year. Today, Shevanti is accepted as any unmarried girl; not many people know of the marriage. However, the neighbours criticise her for the remaining single. Shevanti defends her position by saying that she supports herself is not a financial burden on anyone. She is not concerned about getting married, but says she would consider marriage if she knew a suitable man.

Shevanti works from 7 a.m. to 6.30 p.m., six days a week. Her mother, younger sister and sister-in-law manage the household work, but Shevanti makes many of the decisions. She spends half her salary on provisions and sets half aside for other expenses. Her brother also work in a nearby factory. Her father has now retired. At present her mother has a temporary job in Kuwait as a domestic servant. Shevanti says she is well paid.

Shevanti spends her free time visiting friends and doing handiwork. She is eager to join a local badminton club, but this would mean getting home as late as at 10 o'clock in the night. The neighbours would talk about her, she says. She rarely sees films because she does not like them. She reads Marathi newspapers and borrows magazines from a local library. She enjoys listening to the radio, especially to Marathi dramas, but rarely gets her choice of programmes. Poverty is responsible for the parents' inability to provide for their children, she says. She thinks that the parents must be educated to be able to make correct decisions for their children.

Shevanti says that women must work outside the home, not only because it is necessary to provide extra income, but also to avoid being dependent on anyone else. She is proud to be self-supporting, and thinks that the only way to combat the rising cost of living is for each individual to seek employment.

Shevanti's chief ambition is to organise embroidery classes to teach other women 'a marketable skill'.

(C) Lucy

Lucy is a twenty-seven-year old widow, a Roman Catholic who lives with her four children and a man in a room in the slum. The room is 8 feet by 10 feet with a tin roof. The walls have turned black from the kerosene fumes from the primus stove. In one corner of the room, there is a wall about two feet high which encloses an area of 2 feet by 2 feet. This is the mori which is used for bathing and cleaning utensils. A clothes line hangs between two walls. On this are hung the washed clothes. There is an iron bed in one corner. A broken down wooden cupboard stands against the wall. The only light that comes into the room is from a small barred window high up on the back wall. Lucy does not have electricity, since she cannot afford to pay for the electrical connection. She obtained a water tap inside the room after paying a fee.

Lucy's whole life has been spent in this room. Her mother left their village near Nasik after separating from Lucy's father and came with her son to the slum. Lucy was born in this room, which her mother bought for Rs. 150. The mother supported the two children by doing domestic work. Lucy attended a municipal school in the area. When she was in the fifth standard, her brother, who was working in the Railways, was killed in a train accident. Lucy had to leave school and she became a domestic servant.

Her deceased brother's wife and son lived with Lucy and her mother. The wife took a job in a local hospital and left the child in Lucy's care. She also made advances to a neighbouring bachelor, but he rejected these since she was a widow. The sister-in-law retaliated by spreading a rumour that he was having an affair with Lucy. To scotch this rumour, he married Lucy, who was then sixteen. She did not like the idea, but accepted it as the only way out of a difficult situation. The sister-in-law later remarried, but left her son to be raised by Lucy. He is now 18 and tills some family land in their village. He does not send money to Lucy.

Lucy's husband, also a Roman Catholic, was employed as a peon in the Railways. He died two years ago at the age of thirty-five of meningitis, a disease common in the slum. Lucy's four children range in age from six years to one month, and for a while she sold vegetables in the market to help support her children. However, she found it difficult to manage this job as well as care for the children; she gave up the job.

Now that the children are slightly older, Lucy is desperately looking for a job—any job, she says. The Provident Fund she received after her husband's death was spent on the funeral and repayment of old debts. She now receives a pension of Rs. 64 per month. This is supplemented by Rs. 25 per month from Lucy's church. She has enclosed the small verandah in front of her room and rents it out for extra income.

A Muslim man from U.P. lives with Lucy. He earns two to four rupees daily, selling fruits. Lucy says that this is not a reliable source of income. She puts in the capital and he does the selling. He seems attached to Lucy and her children, but Lucy feels it is not right for her, as a widow, to have any personal happiness. Lucy cooks only one meal a day. She says she cannot afford more than this and makes *chapatis* and occasionally a dal or a vegetable. Usually, the *chapatis* are eaten with tea. She and her children look under-fed and wear badly tattered clothes. Her daughters, aged 6 and 8, help her cook and clean the utensils.

Lucy spends her whole day in the house. She has gone out of Bombay only twice in her life—once to Virar with her husband, and once to Nasik to visit her father. She has not been out socially since her husband's death. She likes films, but cannot afford to see them. Sitting on the nearest suburban railway platform or at nearby church seems to be her only recreational activities.

Lucy's neighbours treat her as a social outcast. Most mothers are reluctant to send their daughters to her house. They comment on her going out alone, and frown upon her relationship with the man she lives with. Recently, her daughter fell into a pot of boiling rice and ghee. The neighbours accused Lucy of trying to get rid of her children because her husband was dead. Lucy reports this sadly and shrugs her frail shoulders. She mentions frequent incidents of wife-beating in the slum and suggests that, rather than take such treatment, women should support themselves and their children on their own. She thinks that employment for women is inevitable for economic reasons, but says that they must be relieved of a part of their household work.

Educating her children seems to be Lucy's role aspiration for the future. She laments her own lack of education, which hampers her employment prospects, and does not want her children to suffer the same fate. However, her meagre income makes this a difficult task. Her eldest daughter, who had to discontinue school after her accident, has still not gone back to school.

(D) Kalyani

Kalyani lives in a room 5 feet by 8 feet with her husband and three children, aged 10 years, 2 years and 4 months. This room serves as the kitchen, bedroom and sitting room. A corner of the room provides a *mori* for washing and bathing. Two pregnancies in quick succession and an accidental knee-injury during her last pregnancy have left Kalyani in a very poor state of health. Her whole day is spent in cooking, cleaning, and looking after the children. Their cramped living conditions and her poor health make this work particularly burdensome to Kalyani. Her husband, who works as a welder in a factory, is away from home from 6 a.m. to 11 p.m., six days a week. His long working hours involve considerable overtime. He cannot find time to take Kalyani to the hospital for a follow-up treatment of her knee injury. He was advised to have a vasectomy after her latest delivery because she was so weak. However, he cannot take leave from his job, as he is not yet confirmed. They came to Bombay about two years ago, from Calcutta. They left their home town because her husband lost his job there. He now earns Rs. 300 a month—about Rs. 100 per month more than previously.

Kalyani studied upto the Intermediate Science, and was working in a Family Planning Centre before her marriage. She says her marriage, arranged by her parents, put a stop both to her education and her employment because of objections from her mother-in-law and her husband. Her husband used to drink excessively and generally behaved badly, Kalyani says. They have been married now for 11 years, and Kalyani claims that there has been some gradual improvement in her husband's behaviour.

Her husband gives a different version of their marriage. He says that she was married before and that it was her first husband who drank heavily and used to beat her. He says that he was living with Kalyani and her first husband as a paying guest. The husband accused him of having an affair with Kalyani and threw her out of the house. He then took her in and married her. He claims her oldest son is not his, but of the first husband.

Kalyani's poor health and two very young children greatly restrict her social life. She cannot walk very much because of her painful knee. At home, her husband does not like her to join him and his friends in their conversations. She likes to read, but finds no time away from the children. She also mentions wife-beating as a widespread problem in the slum. Complaints from the mother-in-law are generally responsible for these beatings, according to Kalyani. The men also drink heavily and then vent their frustrations on their wives. The beatings are often severe, resulting in broken bones and mutilated faces. Kalyani has herself spoken to some men in the area about this, but they say that they must act when their mothers complain. It is not uncommon, she says, for the women to be actually turned out of the house. In such cases, the neighbours usually exert pressure on the family to make them settle their quarrels.

Kalyani favours women's employment. Most family quarrels are over money, she says, and extra income would help considerably. She sees household problems and social attitudes as the main obstacles to the woman who wants to work outside the home.

(E) Christine

Christine is a lonely young girl of 13 who is engaged to be married to her first cousin. This marriage was arranged at Christine's birth. Her family is Roman Catholic, and their church does not permit a girl's marriage until she is 16. So the family is exerting pressure on the church to permit the marriage, and they are likely to succeed.

Christine studies in the 7th standard in a municipal school. She likes school and wants to continue her education. She is reluctant to get married at this stage, but seems resigned to it if the family succeeds in persuading the church.

Christine lives with the nine other members of her family in a room about 8 feet by 10 feet. They have lived in this room since her parents came to Bombay from a village near Ahmednagar, 25 years ago. There is a sewing machine lying idle in a corner of the room, which Christine's father bought in the hope that it would provide a living to one of his four unemployed sons. The father is the sole earner and works as a fitter in Burmah Shell. Christine's fiance was educated by Christine's family and has lived with them most of the time. He too is employed in Burmah Shell. Christine's 'Cousin', a middle-aged woman with a slightly disfigured face, manages the household and the income. Although she is not legally married to Christine's father, she is in fact like a second wife and has replaced Christine's mother as female head of the household. She is defending family interests, the 'Cousin' says, in insisting on an early marriage for Christine, and adds that, after all, they are allowing Christine to continue her education. She mentions, with some pride, that they expect to spend Rs. 7,000 on the wedding.

Christine is the only young girl in the house, and she enjoys a few luxuries which other girls of her age in the slum can never hope for. She gets a small allowance and is taken on outings and occasionally to films. But she is not allowed out on excursions without either her mother or the Cousin. Christine sees her impending marriage as a threat to the life she now leads. Her smiling face becomes grave when the conversation turns to her marriage. She thinks women should be educated and work outside the home. She glances hesitantly at her Cousin and says she herself would like to work some day in a factory.

It is generally believed that slum dwellers maintain close contact with their villages. This assumption is belied by the interviews presented here. In fact, it can be seen that all the respondents have lost contact with their villages and show no desire to return to them. Most of the women have grown to adulthood in the slums. This would indicate that the social environment of the slum is not simply one of village life transported to the city. It is, rather, an organic part of urbanisation. The entry of slum women into jobs that take them out of their homes is a product of this situation. Because of constantly rising prices, these women look to employment as a supplement to the family income. However, they face many difficulties in getting jobs—lack of education, a heavy load of domestic responsibilities, absence of child-care facilities. The middle-class resistance to working women is noticeably absent here. However, employment is not so readily available to slum women as to middle—class women.

In addition to the problem of finding employment, slum women must face the daily difficulties of their environment. Their living quarters are cramped. There is an acute water shortage. The scarcity of sanitary facilities leads to misuse of the little available open space. Although the men in the slums have managed to create some recreational facilities for themselves, for example sport clubs, the women have no access to these and no alternative facilities. Their social activities are confined to the home. These women are also subjected to frequent beatings by their husbands. In many cases, the woman is found to be living with a second or third husband having been abandoned by her previous mates. The husband may leave at any time, taking with him the family's livelihood. In many cases, the husband will return to the first wife when the children are grown and supporting the family. It is apparent that such marital situations make life even more insecure for the women."

16

Keralite Nuns and Nurses

This chapter is an edited version of part of a study conducted on various aspects of life of Keralite women. Here, in the present chapter, we are bringing to light some information, some facts about nurses of Kerala working outside their state and the nuns of Kerala. One can well assume that the women of Kerala are conscious of being independent and of "having a job". One finds them employed in all walks of life, from the most mundane to the greatly responsible; there are judges, engineers and doctors and there are the others in spectacular professions like the circus artists from Tellicherry. The class of "professional" Kerala women under research here are the ones who are in the middle of the scale: the nurses and nuns. These women, while not exactly occupied in mundane jobs, do not live and spectacular lives either, nor are they in any decision-making positions.

Most girls from middle class families, particularly with a Christian background, flock to these professions because they offer security. These females are not inhibited by the fact that jobs are not always available within their own environmental bounds. They are quite willing to leave their homes, endure the restrictions of hostel life and manage with minimum luxuries. As a result of this, nurses and nuns from Kerala can be found anywhere in the country. What then is the push which pushes them careering to all corners of the earth? This was the major question I bore in mind while talking to nurses and nuns coming from different kinds of backgrounds. We must admit that we started off with some pre-conceived notions which were soon proved. "Being a non-Keralite myself, I tended to think that the Marumakkathayam (matriarchal) Nair society had fostered the idea of independence early among Kerala women. Subsequent talks with both men and women who had lived under the old *tarwad* (joint family) system indicated that this was not really true. Under that old system, while the women were socially and economically quite independent of their husbands, they were very much under the control of the "Karanavan" or chief of the household who was often an uncle or brother. Therefore, Keralites in general feel that the emancipation of Nair women is a more recent phenomenon."

One great influence on the social life of Kerala was the advent of Christianity, which is supposed to have come down to this part of the country as early as 52 A.D. with St. Thomas the Apostle. It has taken strong root in state culture. The church's message of service, alongwith the efforts of various missionaries to induce girls to work in their charitable organisations seems to have germinated the idea of girls leaving their homes for the sake of work. It is natural, therefore, that jobs involving "service" are the ones which have traditionally attracted girls from Christian environment. The social pressure in more latest times, which have forced so many Kerala girls to seek employment, are those which are to be found everywhere in the country, but which have taken on a kind of concentrated force here due to some of the problems peculiar to the state.

A dense population (548 people to a square mile) and a rather high percentage of literacy (60.16) are two of the most basic reasons. A dowry system prevalent especially among the Christians is another incentive for girls to work . . . they want to collect enough money to attract good husbands. Many men seem to prefer wives with jobs and in fact the dowry is generally reduced with the wage earning capacity of the girl.

Nurses

Without astonishment even to a casual observer, it is remarkable how many Keralite nurses one can find in any hospital anywhere in the country. In Kerala itself one hardly ever comes across a non-Keralite nurse. Over 80 per cent of the nurses seem to come from Christian families.

"After speaking to several nurses, I found that hardly any of them came because they wished to care for the sick. They came mostly because it was a job which did not require a college degree, yet gave almost guaranteed employment. Only among the older cadre did I find women who had defied their families and joined this rather "lowly" profession.

An author says Smt. Chandramathi, the Senior Nursing Superintendent, a small, brisk lady is one of those pioneers who became a nurse in spite of opposition from her rather traditional Hindu family. She has been abroad twice, once under a Rockefeller Fellowship and once on a study tour sponsored by W.H.O. While talking of Kerala nurses and their migratory habits, she related a quite interesting experience which she had made. While in Canada, she had to go to Musgrave Harbour, a remote township, 63 miles away from the nearest big town, Gander. The moment she went around the hospital thinking she had really reached the end of the earth, the sisters there told her that three Indian girls were working as nurses at Fogo Island which was connected only by ferry to Musgrave Harbour. Astonished and thrilled that there should be such adventurous Indian girls, she rang them up at Fogo Island . . . and found they were all Malayalees!

While talking of nursing in Kerala, Smt. Chandramathi said that since it was started by Swiss Missionaries, originally the emphasis was more on service and less on service rules. This, she felt, had left its stigma and even today service conditions were rather below par. This probably accounted for the number of girls who migrated in search of higher pay.

(a) Teresa Gomes, whose father was a shopkeeper, went to Bombay to become a nurse, and returned a few years ago to get married. She now works as a nurse in the Medical College Hospital. After leaving school, she said, she badly required a job and one of the nuns in the convent in which she studied helped her to get into this profession. But, says Teresa, she would not have minded becoming a teacher or enter any other profession. Teresa's husband is a clerk in a printing press and she now has two children.

(b) Shanthakumari, a 34-year old nurse, has worked in Bombay for seven years. She loved the life there and she stayed with her relatives. She too returned to get married. Shanthakumari's mother is a nurse. (This I found quite typical. Many of the girls said, they had become nurses because they had relatives in the profession who wanted them to join.) "Also

I wanted to travel and see some places," she said. This too seemed to be quite a common motivation.

(c) Next young girl whom I spoke to, was a student in the college of nursing. She came from a fairly well-to-do Christian family and had worked several years in Delhi before returning to Kerala to study. She said that while the conditions outside much better, she had found life there very lonely. "Girls going from here do not realise how lonely and difficult it can be," she said.

(d) Manorama was a very enthusiastic young Auxiliary-Nurse Mid-wife who is eager not only "to stay in this job until I die," but also to better her prospects (so she is studying at the college of nursing) and to work for a while outside Kerala. Manorama is the daughter of a teacher from a village in Quilon district. Her father wanted her to work, but as a teacher. She even did some Hindi examinations to pass as a Hindi teacher, but in the meanwhile she managed to get this job without her father's knowledge and so she became a nurse. She is probably the only girl I met who even after nine years as a nurse expressed great sense of dedication and true love for her profession. She has also persuaded one of her sisters to become a nurse.

(e) About the kind of girls who come to the profession and the problems of training them, Miss Peters, the Director of the College of Nursing, had a lot to say. Miss Peters, who became an army nurse during the war comes from a well-to-do Christian family. She has travelled much (which was her original motivation to join the Army) and accomplished her M.Sc. in Nursing under a Rockefeller Fellowship. Miss Peters is rather disillusioned with the nursing profession. Although it is actually a largely skilled job, calling for technical training, she said it was often treated as a kind of mindless profession. The kind of girls it attracted, therefore, were not the type who would give it the thought and concentration it required. She also felt that in Indian society which still places great emphasis on segregation of sexes. Nursing was looked down upon because girls had to look after men and often perform intimate chores for them. She felt the difiiculty could be eased if male nurses were encouraged.

(f) One more person who is faced not only with training but also organisational problems, is Devakiamma, the matron of the Medical College Hospital. This lady who comes from an orthodox Hindu family became a nurse after some tragic family situations. She has now to cope with organising the hospital schedule with never enough nurses to go around. If patients complained that nurses have no time for them, she said it was no shock because they were so overworked.

A Review

In Kerala the nursing movement began rather informally in 1906, when some nursing nuns from Switzerland were asked to come and help in the general hospital there. The half a dozen sisters who came were given a cool, highly spacious bungalow in the heart of the hospital complex. Gradually, they began taking in a few girls to help and it was only in 1934 that it became a formal recognised profession.

At present, all the nursing nuns in the hospital are Indians. One old Swiss nun who came with one of the first batches, now lives there in semi-retirement. She spoke of the girls who first came to work as nurses . . . they were so excited and hard-working, she said. They came from good families and their upbringing was apparent in the way they devoted themselves to their work. Strangely enough, maximum of them were Hindus, she said. Now, although no longer actively associated with the hospital, she had observed that the sense of dedication was missing. She felt since there was such a demand for nurses, one could no longer decide on the type of girls one wished to train.

Nuns

Let's now talk about the nuns. There are over 12,700 nuns in Kerala, highest of whom are Malayalees. Becoming a nun, offers a life-long security. So, even though the girls have to pay a "dowry" while joining the convent they are quite willing to do it, since they will be taken care of for the rest of their lives. Apart from this, of course, there is the strong religious feeling which makes every Catholic family anxious to send at least one daughter as the "bride of Christ".

"Among the nuns I interviewed, many spoke of the 'entire family rejoicing" when they went home on holidays. However, they also spoke of their anxiety to get away from the turmoils of family life and back into the insulated atmosphere of the convents."

Amongst the nuns, was a lively young woman who is the headmistress of a convent school for girls. She said that she for one loved convent life and found herself so fully occupied she hardly had time to think of her own home. However, there were nuns who found they could not adjust themselves and had to leave. When a nun leaves the convent, she is given back her dowry. Sometimes in extreme cases, where the girl is not able to pay her bit, the convent pays her expenses and takes her in. It was little more difficult talking to the nuns. They did not want to talk about themselves, nor did they required any "publicity". They did not really like to talk of their personal lives.

At last, as they were persuaded to speak, they talked of the spirit of dedication and "the call" and so on. Ultimately, when asked why they personally chose such a life, they could not only say that they felt determined towards being nuns and their families and priests had given them all the encouragement.

"Most of the nuns I spoke to came from middle class families . . . that is, they had not become nuns because they direly needed food and shelter, but because this kind of life gave the peace and security they lacked in their own homes. All of them had joined the convent at an early age (16 or 17 years) and none of them seemed to repent this decision. When asked how they were able at such tender ages to make up their minds to dedicate the rest of their lives, they spoke of the village priest who had helped them decide or of the example set by other brothers, sisters, uncles or aunts, who had become nuns and priests."

Since figures say that only about 16 per cent of the population of Kerala lives in urban areas, one finds very few city-bred girls employed in these professions. The typical parental home of a nurse or nun could be seen in any of the villages which stretch endlessly from one end of the state to the other. Many of the girls' fathers are farmers or teachers or shopkeepers. They generally come from large families which they help to support. In spite of all the independence the girls (especially nurses) achieve by earning their own livings far away from home, they remain at heart simple rural girls who are obedient to their parents' wishes, and who ultimately return home to marry partners found for them by their parents.

"I would like to go out of the state to earn a better pay, but my parents are not sending me," is a common complaint. In the case of nuns, it is just a question of switching over from being obedient to their parents or elders to being obedient to their mother superiors. To girls who have never enjoyed the luxury of total independence such a switch-over is fairly easy. The remarkable thing about it all is that these girls inspite of all their travelling, despite their Western clothes, and habits, have remained essentially Keralite.

To conclude, both nuns and nurses of Kerala lead life of wantlessness, simplicity and sacrifice. But this is always not out of choice. Who does not want to enjoy luxuries of life, if provided but compulsions, at time win. We should not first glorify their sacrifice rather make efforts to put them at ease so that they too can lead and enjoy their lives as happy human beings.

17

Conclusion

Status and position of women in Indian society has been subject to constant change from time to time and place to place. While in Vedic days, they enjoyed a status of equality with men especially, the upper class and upper middle class women, Mughal period witnessed a great decline in their position due to various social evils like infanticide, *Sati Pratha,* ill-treatment of widows, sanction on widow remarriage, prostitution and Devdasi system, polygamy, child marriage and refusal of properly rights to women etc. These evils pertaining to women drew the attention of nineteenth century social reformers and numerous social reform movements including Brahmo Samaj, Prarthana Samaj and Arya Samaj etc. came to existence for the uplift of women.

The first nationalist level organisation, i.e., Indian National Congress kept its membership open to women since its very inception i.e., 1885. But their participation in freedom movement received impetus due to the efforts and charismatic personality of Mahatma Gandhi who realised the strength of women to do miracles if involved in the movement. The need for their participation in national struggle prove helpful in their emancipation and exposure also as they had to be pulled out of four walls of homes in order to take part in non-violent movements of Gandhi and his Satyagraha. It has been reported that Gandhi used to address women's meetings, grant interviews, discuss personal and national issues and correspond with them on individual and collective basis. This proved to be of great help in instilling confidence in women.

Constitution of Republican India granted women equal status with men and included a clause in Article 15 (4) of Fundamental rights which said that to bring women at par with men, state can make special provision for them. A number of enactments to provide them social, domestic and work security have been passed. Recently, 73rd and 74th Amendments have been made to the Constitution of India to strengthen participation of women in grassroot level politics. These Amendments make it mandatory for states to reserve 33 per cent seats for women in rural and urban self governance at all offices as representatives and elected heads. A bill for extension of this reservation in state and central legislatures is also in process.

But all this does not mean that there are no problems being faced by women in free India. Infact, there are more legal arrangements and and will power required to implement these provisions in completely lacking. Women have been able to receive partial benefits only from these provisions. If we go through civil statistics about sex ratio, level of education, mortality rate, health and nutrition levels of women, we see that situation is not much better that what it was immediately after independence. Not even a single five year plan has met targets set for women's betterment. Wife battering domestic violence and even rapes are very common incidents even today. A latest trend of victimisation of women which has been acknowledged now is violence at work place. To counter this, Supreme Court has directed to organised sectors to formulate sexual harrassment committees to redress grievances of women at work but due to a consistent pressure of a senior, who generally happens to be the victimiser, women cannot raise their voice.

Working women have to undergo difficulties at domestic front all the biggest problem is of child upbringing. Other household responsibilities also generally do not reduce. A working women is expected to perform her household chores in the evening after reaching home. An understanding husband and supportive in-laws family can be of great help in such a situation. Her assertiveness developed because of being working should not be condemned at home. Women in unorganised sector suffer from economic inequalities also because despite of equal remuneration for equal work law, women casual workers in agriculture and in factories etc. are always paid less than men for the same work. This needs to be sincerely monitored by the machinery.

In the field of planning families also, it is women only who have taken initiatives and have borne sufferings. It is clear from the Govt. statistics have most of the family planning methods are used by females spouse only. This is true almost every time of about sterilisation where hardly a husband offers himself. Is not it a great paradox that how many children have to be born, is always decided by the husband and when it comes to practising contraception going for sterilisation, it is women who is pushed forward?

Position of women at regional scenarios is noway better than the standard Indian situation. Be it women of Punjab, Haryana or Madhya Pradesh, or slum women of Mumbai or even working women nuns and/or nurses of Kerala, they all suffer from same kind of deficiency just by virtue of being a female. Therefore by attacking any one aspect, the problem cannot be striked. There is a need to adopt an approach for an all-over amelioration of women. But first of all, female foeticide of present day needs to be checked and special attention needs to be paid to health and nutrition of women and girl children since a number of women in India die due to malnutrition. Then we should strengthen educational arrangements and then other social-economic and political evil should be attacked. By collective efforts sincere attitude, the target of male-female equality can be achieved.

Bibliography

Books by M.K. Gandhi

Constructive Programme, Navjivan Publishing House, Ahmedabad, 1948.

Gandhi Shikshan (Gujarati), Part V, Stri Swatantraya, Nagindas Amulakhari, Bombay, 1923.

Mind of Mahatma Gandhi, Edited by R.K. Prabhu & C.U.R. Rao, Navjivan Publishing House, Ahmedabad, 1967.

My Experiments with Truth, Navjivan Publishing House, Ahmedabad, 1970.

The Role of Women, Gandhi Series, edited by Anand T. Hingorani, Bharatiya Vidya Bhavan, Bombay, 1964.

Satyagraha from Gandhi, edited by N.K. Bose, Navjivan Publishing House, Ahmedabad, 1948.

Self-restraint vs. Self-Indulgence, Navjivan Publishing House, Ahmedabad, 1947.

Speeches and Writings of Mahatma Gandhi with an Introduction by C.F.ÿAndrews and a biographical sketch, G.A.ÿNatesan & Co., Madras, 1922.

Striyan aur Unki Samasyaan (Hindi), Navjivan Publishing House, Ahmedabad, 1969.

To the Women, Gandhi Series, Edited by Anand T. Hingorani, Karachi, 1941.

To Ashram Sisters (Bapu's letters from 16-12-1926 to 30-12-1929), edited by Kaka Kalelkar, Navjivan Publishing House, Ahmedabad, 1952.

Tyagmurti and Other Essays (Gujarati), Navajivan Publishing House, Ahmedabad, 1938.

Woman's Role in Society, compiled by R.K. Prabhu, Navajivan Publishing House, Ahmedabad, 1959.

Women and Social Injustice, Navajivan Publishing House, Ahmedabad, 1950.

Other Books

Altekar, A.S., The Position of Women in Hindu Civilisation, The Culture Publishing House, Banaras Hindu University, 1938.

Andrews, C.F. Mahatma Gandhi's Ideas including Selections from His Writings, George Allen and Unwin Ltd., London, 1929.

Athavale, Parvatibai, My Story: The Autobiography of a Hindu Widow, Jr. Rev. Juslin & Abbott, C.P. Putnam's Sons, 1930.

Chattopadhyaya, Kamaladevi and others, The Awakening of Indian Women, Everyman's Press, Madras, 1939.

Chattopadhyaya, Kamaldevi, The Struggle for Freedom in Women of India, Ed. by Tara Ali Baig, the Publication Division, Government of India, 1958.

The Constitution of Indiε, Government of India, New Delhi.

Desai, N., Woman in Modern India, Vora & Co., Bombay, 1957.

Draft Fifth Five Year Plan, Planning Commission of India, New Delhi.

Duverger, Political Role of Women, UNESCO, 1955.

Gadgil, D.R., Women in the Working Force in India, Asia Publishing House, Bombay, 1968.

Ghose, J.C. (ed.), English Works of Raja Ram Mohan Roy, Oriental Press, Bhowanipore, 1885.

Hate, C., Changing Status of women, Allied Publishers Pvt. Ltd., Bombay, 1969.

Kalapi, Kalapi No Kekarava (Gujarati), To Widow Sister Baban, ed. J.D.ÿTripathi, Kalapi Smarak Fund, Baroda, 1946.

Kapadia, K.M., Marriage and Family in India, Oxford University Press, Bombay, 1955.

Mazumdar, B.B., Heroines of Tagore, Firma K.L. Mukhopadhyay, Calcutta, 1968.

Myrdal Gunnar, Asian Drama, Vol. II, the Penguine Press, London, 1968.

Naidu (Smt.) P.P., "Women's Welfare in Development Project" in Kurukshetra, Vol. V, Publications Division, Government of India, 1955.

Natesan, G.A., Gopal Krishna Gokhale's Speecites, G.A. Natesan & Co., Madras.

O'Mallym, Modern India and the West, London, 1941.

Ranade, Ramabai, Himself: The Autobiography of a Hindu Lady, Longman's Green & Co., New York, 1938.

Sen Gupta, Padmini, Women in India, Ministry of External Affairs, New Delhi, 1964.

Sen Gupta, Sankar, A Study of Women of Bengal, Indian Publications, Calcutta, 1970.

Shridevi, S., A century of Indian Womanhood, Rao & Raghavan, Mysore, 1965.

Tendulkar, D.G., Mahatma in Eight Volumes, Times of India Press, Bombay, 1952.

Tendulkar, D.G. and others, Gandhiji. His Life and Work, Karnatak Publishing House, Bombay, 1964.

Unnithan, T.K.N., Gandhi and Free India, Vora & Co. Bombay, 1956.

Periodicals

Harijan, March 1937, February and June, 1940, April 1946.
Navjivan, July 1928.
Pacific Affairs, Vol. XXV, No. 3, September 1952.
Reports of the National Committee on Women's Education, UNESCO, Paris, 1970.
Report of the Khadi and Village Industries' Commission, 1972-74, Bombay.
Span, January 1974.
The Times of India, May 1974.
Young India, August 1921, August and September 1926, February 1927, February 1929.

Index